This is the journal of

_____

Compiled by Carol Mersch &
Sherry L. Jackson

A

Year of

Promise

365-Days of Inspiration
To Guide Your Day & Guide Your Way

*For every subtle, strong temptation, for every cry of
need, for every low moan of disappointment, for
every locking of the jaws in the resolution of despair,
for every disheartened look out into the morrow, for
every yearningly ambitious heart there comes
tonight that unmistakable ringing promise of His
- ye shall have power.*

- S. D. Gordon, *Quiet Talks on Power*

iUniverse, Inc.
New York Bloomington

A Year of Promise
365 Days of Inspiration to Guide your Day & Guide your Way

iUniverse books may be ordered through booksellers or by contacting:

iUniverse
1663 Liberty Drive
Bloomington, IN 47403
www.iuniverse.com
1-800-Authors (1-800-288-4677)

Because of the dynamic nature of the Internet, any Web addresses or links contained in this book may have changed since publication and may no longer be valid.

ISBN: 978-1-4502-2592-2 (sc)
ISBN: 978-1-4502-2593-9 (ebk)

Printed in the United States of America

iUniverse rev. date: 7/21/2010

About this book

God is with us *now*.

In the midst of change and upheaval, we need to bear in mind a few simple truths. Every day, whatever that day may bring, is a day spent in His presence. Every day, in the activities that make up the texture of our lives, through the people we live and work with—He blesses us and upholds us, shares the bounty of His love, and transforms us by His grace.

A Year of Promise unfolds, page by page, the poignant and timeless inspiration of thirteen religious writers, drawn from the extraordinary wisdom of their years, that allows us to become more aware of God's presence and His work in our lives. As you walk with them through these pages, you will find respites along the way in which to refocus your thoughts.

The opening page, *My Good Life* is an opportunity to redefine the things you hope to realize in the year ahead—those things that pull you forward to achieve all you can become as a unique, irreplaceable creation of God

Throughout the 365-days of the year, each devotional will open your day with fresh inspiration and renewal and a space to journal the revelations and insights to carry you through to the next. February 29, leap year day, is inserted to provide a perennial devotional-journal, good for any year.

At the end of each month, *My Gratitude* offers a full page to reflect on the lessons learned in the preceding weeks and those things in your life— past, present, and future—that will help you bless all that your heart touches. With gratitude for today, you will swing wide the door of possibility for tomorrow.

At the close of the year, *My Self Promise* provides a place to identify those goals that serve to redefine you and move you forward in the coming year with the confidence to become all that you can be—and to know more fully that you, and only you, possess the unique God-given qualities to fulfill His special purpose for you.

Every day of your life is a day in the year of our Lord. And that makes this truly—*A Year of Promise.*

We begin . . .

Looking forward . . .

"And thine ears shall hear a word behind thee, saying, This is the way, walk ye in it." ISAIAH 30:21-KJV

To hear the word behind you, you must first step forward. This means moving forward, even when the way seems impossible, or filled with chance. As many people proved through countless stories in the Bible, faith is powerful. If your motives are right and you are following God's direction, you will have all the provisions you need for the road ahead.

- **Listen for God's voice.** He will point the way. The Christ, God's message of love, is present at every trial, twist, and turn to comfort and guide you right to where you need to be. Simply praying for His guidance isn't enough. You must listen for it.

- **Exercise moral courage.** It's about doing what's right. It may not be popular, but it's right. You forfeit popularity, but you gain Christianity.

- **Stop looking back.** You rob your future by continually looking in the rearview mirror. Like a Ferris wheel—you go around and around and get nowhere. You think if you keep looking back you'll find the answer that allows you to go forward. But you never do. It's just one more trip around.

- **Confirm His presence.** Stand porter at the door of thought, admitting only such images as you wish reflected in your life. Doubt and confusion have no place in God's kingdom. Pray to see the ongoing love, peace, and renewal of all that is necessary for you to live a full, unlimited, and abundant life.

- **Then take the step forward.** Step out into the New Year with the determination to be all that you can be—*and all that God has empowered you to be.*

-Carol Mersch

$\mathcal{M}$y Good Life . . .

Envisioning the future—my wish for what the coming year can bring

_____

_____

_____

_____

_____

_____

_____

_____

_____

_____

_____

_____

_____

_____

_____

_____

_____

_____

_____

_____

_____

_____

_____

_____

_____

_____

*"Thou crownest the year with thy goodness; and thy paths
drop fatness."* PSALM 65: 11 KJV

Wake Up!

"Now it is high time to awake out of sleep: for now is our salvation nearer than when we believed." ROMANS 13:11

What good is life without living? Taste it, live it—even at the risk of occasional failure and adversity! If you are going to stand at the plate, then take a swing at the ball! "Suppose I miss?" you say. Well, I say, "Suppose you miss out, and you haven't even taken a swing?" Have you any passion to triumph? Your desire to protect yourself from further disappointment has placed you in a comatose state. Wake up and play! You are not dead! There may be many things about you that are dead, but you are not dead!

> *"If you are going to stand at the plate, then take a swing at the ball!"*

I feel like God is speaking to someone who has quit. No one knows you have quit, but inside, you have thrown in the towel and said, "I give." You wanted to make a difference, but since you ran into some obstacle, some cross, you decided to adjust your expectations to your limitations and just keep smiling!

You are wrong! I am blowing a trumpet loudly into your rigor mortis-ridden ear! God has too much for you to do! Arise, breathe deeply of this moment. There will never be another moment in your life like this one! I can't spare you tears, fears, or traumas; each passion has its "cross of validation." In fact, it is the cross that validates the enormity of the passion. It is what you endure that expresses how deeply you desire.

T. D. Jakes, *365 Days to Healing, Blessings, and Freedom*

Take the Snake by the Tail

"Trust in the Lord with all thine heart; and lean not unto thine own understanding. In all they ways acknowledge him, and he shall direct thy paths." PROVERBS 3: 5,6-KJV

When Moses threw down his favorite old shepherd's rod, it became a serpent and he literally ran from it. (See Exodus 4:3-4.) Things got worse when God said, "Pick it up by the tail." Nearly everyone knows that is a foolish thing to do because that leaves the "business end" of the snake loose and free for action.

It didn't make much sense to throw down the rod, but it made no sense at all to pick up the snake by the tail! Moses had been in the desert a long time and he knew a poisonous adder when he saw one. But God told him to pick it up by the tail.

> *"It made no sense at all to pick up the snake by the tail!"*

During your training trip through the wilderness of relinquishment, you will probably think God is leading you the wrong way, or that He is saying something that doesn't make sense. God's commands aren't always accompanied by explanations. The point is that even when we cannot figure out what God is doing, we must trust Him.

When Moses reluctantly picked up the snake it became a rod again. From this place forward in the narrative, that rod is never again referred to as "the rod of Moses." It is referred to as "the rod of God." (See Exodus 4:1-20; 17:9.) Because Moses released it and the snake was taken out of it, it was God's rod. The one thing Moses thought he could trust in the most had to be relinquished to God. God may strip you of everything in order to let you see and understand your total dependence on Him. With that stripping, with that relinquishment, comes power.

Sometimes there are things we just want to hold onto that we have to release so God can remove the snake from it.

Tommy Tenney, *The Daily Chase*

Healing of the Mind

"Finally, brethren, whatsoever things are true, whatsoever things are noble, whatsoever things are just, ...think on these things." PHILIPPIANS 4:8

One of the great challenges of our walk with God is to resist the temptation to allow what happened in the past determine who we are today. We each must begin to understand and declare: "I am not what happened yesterday. I endured what happened. I survived what happened, but I am not what happened yesterday!"

> *"I am not what happened yesterday. I endured what happened. I survived what happened, but I am not what happened yesterday!"*

Many people are plagued all their lives by memories of failed marriages, broken promises, and personal calamities . . . These negative impressions, armed with memories and flashback "movies," strengthen themselves by rehearsing past failures and wounds over and over again. It is somehow like bad television reruns—we don't even enjoy watching them, yet we find ourselves transfixed to the screen. In the same sense, you must remind yourself that you don't have to watch the "movie" in your mind if you are not enjoying what is being played. That's right—hit the remote control. You do have control over your thoughts. The Bible teaches us that if we are going to be healed in our own mind, then we must occasionally reprogram ourselves to "think on better thoughts."

You must choose what you are going to meditate upon. Choose carefully, though, for you will ultimately become whatever it is you meditate upon. The enemy knows this, so when he wants to destroy your morality, he doesn't start with an act; he starts with a thought.

T. D. Jakes, *365 Days to Healing, Blessings, and Freedom*

Can You Find the Place?

"But you, when you pray, enter into your inner room, and when you have shut your door, pray to your Father which is in secret; and your Father which sees in secret shall reward you openly." MATTHEW 6:6-7

The place of solitude with the Lord is a chamber, not a conference room. The carpet does not indicate significant wear; one will not have to elbow his way through crowded corridors to get there. Expansion plans would be wonderful, if they were necessary. Presently there appears to be ample space.

Our Lord mentioned entering a closet to pray (see Mt. 6:6). Personally, I have never seen a closet that could accommodate a lot of people. He is not referring to a literal closet, but to a place where the two of you can meet. Not many can cite the exact address of this locale. They are able to point you in the general direction, but having never ventured there themselves, they are not familiar with the floor plan.

> *"They have not stumbled on this secret place accidentally; they have been on their knees and in the Book searching for clues."*

This is not an amusement park for juvenile Christians to participate in frivolity. It is not a banquet hall with exquisite entrees and exceptional ambiance. It is a holy convocation attended only by a few; it is not a camp meeting packed with thousands.

Those who enter have paid their dues and are there to conduct important business. They have not stumbled on this secret place accidentally; they have been on their knees and in the Book searching for clues... These people are pacesetters, not jet-setters; they are world changers, not miracle chasers. Mingling in crowds is not their forte, but quality time with Christ is their priority.

Those who choose this path walk a lonely road, many times being misunderstood. What others fail to understand is that by separating from complaining carnality, these people have stood in the cleft of the rock and beheld the glory of God.

Ability and Responsibility

"Fear not: for I have redeemed thee, I have called thee by thy name; thou art mine." ISAIAH 43:1-KJV

What lies behind you is history and what lies before you is future, but these are both tiny matters compared to what lies within you. You may not be able to change your past, and your future is yet unlived, but the present provides you with opportunities to maximize your life and the ability that lives within you.

> *"Don't just talk about your potential dreams, visions, and ideas. Step out now and determine to do them."*

You must take responsibility for your ability—no one else can do it for you.

Are you living a stillbirth life? Are you aborting your entire purpose for living? I encourage you to take responsibility right now for your ability. Determine to activate, release, and maximize your potential for the sake of the next generation. Leave your footprints in the sands of the history of your country. Live fully so you can die effectively. Let your life write the speech of your death and give your potential to the family of man for the glory of God. Remember "well done" is much better than "well said." Don't just talk about your potential dreams, visions, and ideas. Step out now and determine to do them. Dare to believe that what you have already accomplished is but a minute percentage of what you can do. Move beyond the familiar patterns and experiences of your life to the dreams and plans and imaginations that wait within you to be fulfilled.

Myles Munroe, *Releasing Your Potential*

You Are an Original!

"Now there are diversities of gifts, but the same Spirit. And there are differences of administrations, but the same Lord. And there are diversities of operations, but it is the same God which works all in all."
I CORINTHIANS 12:4-6

Everybody is different, yet he or she has to fit into the human race and human society to become a success. Many people do not find a fit that satisfies them or those around them. They fail to find the key issue, the bottom line of what it takes to fulfill what they desire and hunger to be and to do.

In many ways the earth is a junk pile upon which are heaped human beings who fail to find their place and who are unfulfilled and disillusioned. That does not have to be. We need only to begin to understand and believe that there is a higher Power, who is God and that He is interested in and concerned about us. When we look toward the invisible by turning ourselves toward the Supreme Being, we will find the impossible much easier than we thought. God desires each of use to awaken to His awareness.

> *"God gets no glory out of us all being just alike."*

I learned that God has a specific life and calling—a specific purpose—He wants each of us to know and follow in every area of our lives. He alone can show us how to walk through the pitfalls of life.

God gets no glory out of us all being just alike. Each of us is unique and irreplaceable. I learned that God has called each of us to be an original instead of being made out of man's mold! He knew us before we were born.

Things aren't always going to be even. There are rough spots ahead. They will often catch you by surprise. You may or may not know how to handle them at the moment. You may feel like quitting...Don't quit no matter how you feel. God will make a way where there seems to be no way. By listening you will find your place, and it will be the greatest fit possible.

Oral Roberts, *Still Doing the Impossible*

Live With Purpose

"Even for this same purpose have I raised you up, that I might show my power in you, and that my name might be declared throughout all the earth."
ROMANS 9:17

I want you to know that there's more to life than punching a time clock. There's more to life than spending five or six days a week at the office; or weekends spent working in the yard, doing housework, or watching television. There is a reason why you are here. God has something that you and only you can do. It is your purpose, and it will contribute to the construction of a better world.

Think about how unique you are. No one else has your fingerprints, your voice pattern, or your face. No one else has ever had your thoughts.

> *"There is a reason why you are here. God has something that you and only you can do."*

No one else could ever take your place. And I believe that if you don't fulfill the purpose God has in mind for you, He'll raise up someone else to do it—but it won't be done as well.

Take the Old Testament character of Jonah, for example. God told him to preach to the inhabitants of Nineveh and tell them that they were going to be destroyed if they didn't repent from their wicked ways. As I'm sure you know, Jonah didn't want anything to do with the rough characters in Nineveh, so he ran in the other direction.

What did God do about Jonah? He sent a storm to blow against the ship on which Jonah was sailing, ultimately causing him to be thrown overboard. He sent a big fish to swallow Jonah... Then He had that fish vomit Jonah onto dry land, still alive and kicking. Why did God go to all that trouble? Perhaps he knew that Jonah would be more effective than any other prophet of his day. Whatever the reason, the only thing we can really know is that there was a purpose for Jonah's life, just as there's a purpose for yours and mine.

Once you've discovered what your purpose is, purpose to do it well. Act as if your life has meaning—because it does.

Pat Williams, *American Scandal*

$\mathcal{A}$ Clogged Channel

"Give, and it shall be given unto you; good measure, pressed down, and shaken together, and running over, shall men give into your bosom."
LUKE 6:38

Out in Colorado they tell of a little town nestled down at the foot of some hills—a sleepy-hollow village. You remember the rainfall is very slight out there, and they depend much upon irrigation. But some enterprising citizens ran a pipe up the hills to a lake of clear, sweet water. As a result the town enjoyed a bountiful supply of water the year round without being dependent upon the doubtful rainfall. And the population increased and the place had quite a western boom.

One morning the housewives turned the water spigots, but no water came. There was some sputtering. There is apt to be noise when there is nothing else. The men climbed the hill. There was the lake full as ever. They examined around the pipes as well as possible, but could find no break. Try as they might, they could find no cause for the stoppage.

> *"—pull out the plug."*

And as days grew into weeks, people commenced moving away again, the grass grew in the streets, and the prosperous town was going back to its old sleepy condition when one day one of the town officials received a note. It was poorly written, with bad spelling and grammar: "Ef you'll jes pull the plug out of the pipe about eight inches from the top you'll get all the water you want." Up they started for the top of the hill, and examining the pipe, found the plug which some vicious tramp had inserted. Not a very big plug—just big enough to fill the pipe. Out came the plug; down came the water freely; by and by back came prosperity again.

Why is there such a lack of power in our lives? Something in us clogging up the channel and nothing can get through. How shall we have power, abundant, life-giving, sweetening our own lives, and changing those we touch? The answer is easy for me to give—it will be much harder for us all to do—pull out the plug.

S. D. Gordon, *Quiet Talks on Power*

January 9

Two-Way Conversation

"Now the purpose of the instruction is love out of a pure heart, and of a good conscience, and of faith sincere: from which some having swerved have turned aside unto empty babbling; desiring to be teachers of the law; understanding neither what they say, nor of what they affirm."
1 TIMOTHY 1:5-7

Have you ever tried to develop an intimate relationship with Jana Jabberbox? She's the gal who has lots to say and loves to hear herself say it. You try to say something when she takes a breath—which isn't often—but she keeps right on talking. She never listens. It's a one-way conversation, and you are left out. Even when someone is very special to you, you do not get too excited with a steady monologue. Listening is an important part of developing a closeness with someone else. If you want to get to know the Lord, you must seek Him not only with a whole, clean, and pure heart, but also with a listening heart.

> *"If you want to get to know the Lord, you must seek Him . . . with a listening heart."*

"Be anxious for nothing; but in everything by prayer and supplication with thanksgiving let your requests be made known unto God. And the peace of God, which surpasses all understanding, shall keep your hearts and minds through Christ Jesus." (Philippians 4:3-9 TSB)

As you spend time with God during your daily devotional time, learn to listen to Him as you read of His love and thoughts about you in the Bible. Think about what He is saying to you personally. Sit silently and write what impressions come to your listening heart. As you read and study His love letters, the Bible, you begin to see what He really thinks of you and what wonderful plans He has for you. As a result, your devotion grows and grows.

_____

_____

_____

_____

_____

_____

_____

Debbie Jones & Jackie Kendall, *Lady in Waiting—Meditations of The Heart*

*E*xtravagant Praise

"And he said unto them, "Why are you fearful, O you of little faith?" Then he arose, and rebuked the wind and the raging of the water; and said unto the sea, "Peace, be still." And the wind ceased, there was a great calm."
LUKE 8:24-25

Today we are inhibited by a lack of desire rather than a lack of time. Distractions that bid for our attention prevail over spending time with our Lord. Self-gratification conquers servanthood. An old cliché says that "we get through praying but don't pray through." When passion returns to our hearts, power will return to our gatherings. Passion is that magnetic force of energy that has the ability to push and pull. It is the power necessary to boost us from the launching pad and into orbit, in spite of being inept. It is the winch that pulls us from the pit of despair. Recorded in the pages of history are innumerable examples of those challenged by a lack of ability, yet who succeeded because of passion. Something inside them refused to surrender to limitations. When intellect, physical strength, or natural ability were not in abundance, they fell back on that burning desire to achieve.

> *"Passion is that magnetic force of energy that has the power necessary to boost us from the launching pad and into orbit."*

We labor long hours and take on extra jobs to purchase material possessions that fail to pacify the inner cry of the soul. We study the globe and plan our next vacation, only to return weary. There is a place, a Utopia, that does not require arduous flights over oceans. Cares of this world are not permitted beyond its walls. Whether the Dow Jones is making history with gains or plunging into unprecedented losses is of no concern here. Should Wall Street collapse, these walls will remain intact.

There is a haven whose tranquil shores offer shelter from life's angry waves. The Master's arms are ever open to embrace the storm-tossed sailor and rescue him from his sinking vessel.

Morton Bustard, *The Impassioned Soul*

Stop Looking Back

"And God shall wipe away all tears from their eyes; and there shall be no more death, neither sorrow, nor crying, neither shall there be any more pain: for the former things are passed away." REVELATION 21:4

My mind was more than ready to move on with my life. The problem was my heart didn't want to follow. My heart hung on stubbornly to past memories of people, places, and things, both good and bad. In the chambers of my heart were events and circumstances that I didn't want to let go of. There were injustices that I wanted righted before I would close the chapter on them. There were circumstances that couldn't be reversed, and I held onto my desire for them like a petulant child. I silently nagged God, asking Him, "Why can't things be different than they are?" He had long answered me, but I kept asking every time I refused to let go of my past.

> *"No one cares to hear about your yesterdays for very long, not even God."*

For a while, God let me hold on. He was willing to allow me to stay stuck in yesterday's goals, achievements, misfortunes, tears, and relationships. And I learned the hard way that no one cares to hear about your yesterdays for very long, not even God. Eventually, He becomes silent. He won't join you in your private pity parties anymore. He will not overstep your will to remain stuck. He will watch you chain yourself to painful, devastating memories and past accomplishments until you are tired of hearing yourself talk about them. He'll wait until you are sincerely ready to turn them loose and receive the new and exciting changes waiting just for you.

Dr. Wanda Turner, *Celebrating Change*

Just Ask

"And Jesus said unto him, "Receive your sight: go your way; your faith has made you whole." MARK 10:52

The God of Ages honors those who have eyes to see and ears to hear—who come with nothing but emptiness and neediness, holding on in trust and confident prayer.

Jesus asked: "What do you want me to do for you?" And blind Bartimaeus replied, "My teacher, let me see again." It seems a somewhat odd question · what do you want me to do? Jesus should know this already, aside from the fact that it was probably abundantly obvious what a blind man might want. So why does Jesus ask? For one reason and one reason only – we need to ask. We need to acknowledge our utter dependence and total reliance on a Higher Power. We need to own our brokenness and need—to concede the hard truth that we cannot save ourselves.

> *"We need to own our brokenness and need—to concede the hard truth that we cannot save ourselves."*

Bartimaeus makes a profoundly simple faith statement: I want to see. I want not only to see physically, but I want to see spiritually. I want to see God better, to see the needs of my neighbors better. To see my blind spots better. No words to get in the way of the cry from the heart of our utter human brokenness and our need of God.

Jesus told him: "Go, your faith has made you whole"—fascinating. It is not so much the magical divine power that heals him, it is his own faith and trust. The blind man who asks simply for mercy is given sight. Bartimaeus had confident faith—faith in God's unseen blessings—expectant faith—faith that knows there will be an ultimate reason revealed, that healing will come despite the pain of the present How utterly simple, the profound wisdom in this story: Blindness. Crying out. Persistence. Saving faith.

A life changed forever.

Penelope Black, Priest, Holy Trinity Anglican Church, North Saanich, BC Canada

Jesus Said, "I Think I Found One..."

"But he said unto them, 'I have food to eat that you know not of.'" JOHN 4:32

Do you know what God eats when He's hungry? Worship. Do you remember the woman at the well? When Jesus told her about His living water and said that His Father was seeking true worshipers, she gave the answer He was looking for. She said, "I want that water." In that moment Jesus might have mused, I think I found one. That is what I was waiting for.

When the disciples came back, they said, "Lord, we've got Your Burger King for You," or "Here's Your McDonalds Big Mac, Master." They were shocked when He said, "I have food to eat that you know not of." It was as if He were thinking, You wouldn't understand it, but I've been receiving worship from a rejected woman at the well. I've done My Father's will and found a worshiper. After that feast, I don't need anything you have for Me.

> *"Can you hit this note?"*

Jesus auditioned the woman at the well in search of that "high note" of transparency and purity. He gave her the opportunity to answer a question for which He already knew the answer: Can you hit this note? He wondered, as He searched under the "rock of the human will" for a worshiper. Then He told the woman, "Go get your husband." She could have hidden her sin or covered her broken life with the fig leaves of a lie, but for once in her life she thought, No, I know it's not very pretty, but I'm going to tell Him the truth. Then she said, "I have no husband."

This was the high note of transparency and purity He was looking for. Now He had something He could work with.

Don't Be Afraid to Try

"So that we may boldly say, 'The Lord is my helper, and I will not fear what man shall do unto me.'" HEBREWS 13:6

No one can climb beyond the limitations he has placed on himself. Success is never final—failure is never fatal. It is courage that counts courage and the willingness to move on. A great deal of talent is lost to the world for want of a little courage. Every day sends to the grave, obscure men, whom fear and timidity have prevented from making their first attempt to do something. Never tell a person that something can't be done, because God may have been waiting for centuries for someone ignorant enough to believe that the impossible could be possible.

> *"Success is never final— failure is never fatal"*

The poorest of men are men without a dream. Don't be so afraid of failure that you refuse to try. Demand something of yourself. Failure is only an incident. There's more than the failure-there's success deep behind that failure. Failure is the opportunity to more intelligently begin again. When you fail, that is a great chance to start again. Learn from it and move on. Don't be paralyzed by the failure.

One good thing about failure is that it is proof that you tried. The greatest mistake you can make is to be afraid of making one. People who do nothing in life are usually people who do nothing. People who don't make mistakes in life are usually people who didn't have a chance to make any because they never tried. Challenge your potential. Demand things of yourself that are beyond what you have already done. Expect more from yourself than the accomplishments that are easily within your reach. What you have is not all you are. The limit of your potential is God. It is better to attempt a thing and fail, than to never try and not know you could succeed.

Broken and Released

"For I say, through the grace given unto me, to every man that is among you, not to think of himself more highly than he ought to think," ROMANS 12:3

It is imperative that we understand the working of God. He will allow us to be confronted with circumstances that will make us or break us. We are not so much affected by what happens as we are by our attitude of what has happened.

Our perception of a situation determines the outcome. We can allow ourselves to be absorbed in self-pity, thinking we are expected to endure situations no other will encounter. Or we can say as Job did, "When He hath tried me, I shall come forth as gold" (Job 23:10b).

> *"He will allow us to be confronted with circumstances that will make us or break us."*

The devil will offer you anything as long as you will avoid your appointment with the Potter. You need to make the decision of whether you want to be: the potter's wheel or the potter's field. The latter is filled with those who thought it was possible to be blessed without being broken.

It is of absolute importance to be filled with the Holy Spirit. The battle we are engaged in is spiritual, not physical. Having a positive attitude in a negative society is beneficial; being filled with God's power is crucial...

When we smash the ornate alabaster containers and release the incense of sacrificial praise, we will be catapulted to spiritual heights unlike anything we have ever experienced... Then brokenness will give way to blessing.

Morton Bustard, *The Impassioned Soul*

Remaining Vertical With God

"...when he was insulted, insulted not in return; when he suffered, he threatened not; but committed himself to him that judges righteously:"
I PETER 2:23

Have you ever been wrongfully accused? Oh, the need to defend and justify becomes so great. "What will people think if they believe these things are true?" we reason. Imagine what Jesus thought as they hurled insults and threats upon Him. The God of the universe had visited planet Earth only to be slandered and accused of blasphemy.

Jesus could have done two things in response. He could have used His power to put the people in their place. He could have responded "horizontally." He could have fixed the problem right then. However, He chose to respond in a different way. He chose to "entrust Himself to Him who judges justly." It requires great faith to entrust ourselves to God in the midst of personal assault.

> *"Avoid the temptation of responding horizontally."*

However, if we can do this, we will discover a level of grace and wisdom that will be birthed from this experience that we never thought possible. We will discover a freedom in God we never knew before. Whenever we suffer for righteousness without seeking to protect our reputation and rights, we are placing our total faith in the one who can redeem us. This activates God's grace in our lives and enables us to experience god's presence like never before.

Ask God to give you the grace to stay vertical with Him. Avoid the temptation of responding horizontally each time some event comes into your life that you want to "fix." Entrust yourself to the one who judges justly. It may be a divine appointment for your growth to another level in grace.

_____

_____

_____

_____

_____

_____

_____

*F*ailure is Tough; Success is Tougher

"But without faith it is impossible to please him: for he that comes to God must believe that he is, and that he is a rewarder of them that diligently seek him." HEBREWS 11:6

Be careful when you want to buy everything you never had or ever wanted. Beware when you begin to think that you can't fail. Watch when your personal walk with God grows stale and your secret place with Him is abandoned. It is at that hour that you have brought yourself to the precipice of greatest peril.

> *"Beware when you begin to think that you can't fail."*

Solomon, the richest and most successful man ever to live, uses the term "meaningless" no fewer than 31 times as he laments abut his life in the Book of Ecclesiastes. For him the struggles of youth had brought great obedience and focus. But he allowed the success of maturity only to bring him great distraction and ruin. It is a powerful lesson to remain vigilant.

Satan is always one step behind you. He will urge you to touch the tithe, or to borrow it. To covet someone else's gifts. To sell your birthright for a quick reward. If you do these things, it is all over, as Esau learned (see Genesis 27:30-38; Hebrews 12:17).

I once asked God to define faith to me. His answer changed my life. He said, "Faith is when the Holy Spirit supernaturally empties you of doubt, and fills you with a knowing, so in that moment you cannot doubt!" You can step out in faith and reach your potential as God has called you. You can become so faith-conscious that a knowing will enter your spirit. In my experience, when the knowing is there, I cannot doubt. Miracles happen.

Oral Roberts, *Still Doing the Impossible*

The Test of Character

"Let your light so shine before men, that they may see your good works, and glorify your Father which is in heaven." MATTHEW 5:16

Many years ago a young soldier stationed in Florida was reading a book he'd picked up in a second-hand bookstore. He came across some handwritten notes—in a feminine hand—in the margin. He was intrigued and turned to the inside cover...sure enough, there was the name, address, and phone number of a woman who lived in New York.

He wrote her a letter and was overjoyed to hear back from her in a matter of days. That was the beginning of frequent correspondence...but before they could meet, the young man was sent overseas to fight in World War II.

> *"He immediately chose friendship over physical attraction."*

The soldier made it safely through the war and made plans to meet his friend at Grand Central Station in New York...she told him she would be wearing a red rose in her lapel. On the day of the meeting, he was waiting at the scheduled place when a beautiful young woman came walking toward him. His heart began to beat faster as he thought she was the most beautiful creature he had ever seen. He desperately wanted to see a rose on her lapel, but sadly for him, there was none.

Even so, the woman smiled a perfect smile as she walked past and asked, "Going my way, soldier?" He thought about following her—rose or no rose—but then he noticed another woman—one who was wearing a rose. She was what you might call matronly—plump, with gray hair pulled back into a bun. The soldier didn't hesitate for a moment. He immediately chose friendship over physical attraction, stepped forward, and introduced himself to the older woman.

The older woman smiled, shook her head, and said, "I don't know what this is all about, but that young lady asked me to wear this rose on my coat." She gestured toward the beautiful young woman who had smiled at him. "She said that if you introduced yourself to me, I should tell you that she'd be waiting for you in the restaurant across the street.

Pat Williams, *American Scandal*

*T*rouble Has a Purpose

"And he spoke this parable unto them, saying, "What man of you, having a hundred sheep, if he loses one of them, does not leave the ninety and nine in the wilderness, and go after that which is lost, until he finds it?" LUKE 15:4

We find ourselves faced with trouble when God is trying to move us from a place of disobedience to one of obedience. It's so easy to do what you feel like doing when you're not being punished for it. But God loves us too much to allow us to stay on a path that will surely lead to destruction. He would rather hurt you to put you back on the right path, so that you'll remember the pain the next time you think about straying.

> *"God loves us too much to allow us to stay on a path that will surely lead to destruction."*

Have you seen those wonderful paintings of Jesus as the Good Shepherd, carrying a little lamb on His shoulders? In actuality, you find shepherds carrying sheep in that manner when the sheep is prone to wander away from the flock. Jesus said that a good shepherd will leave 99 sheep to go find the one that is lost. And He loves us enough to find us and take steps to see that we don't get lost again. For the child of God, trouble is the merciful hand of a loving Father brought down to correct before it comforts. Hebrews exhorts us not to hate the chastening of God. It's proof that He loves us.

The purpose of trouble is simply to change our behavior. Its God's way of saying, "Stop that!" Trouble hurts. It's supposed to. How many of you give your child an ice cream cone when he acts up? The only right response to trouble is obedience. When you find yourself in trouble because of something you've done, or are even playing at doing, you need to obey, because disobedience puts you on a path away from God. And disobedience can only prepare you for another act of disobedience.

Obedience does just the opposite. It brings you closer to God and prepares you for another act of obedience.

Dr. Wanda Turner, *Celebrating Change*

ℛefiner's Fire

"That the genuineness of your faith, being much more precious than of gold that perishes, though it be refined with fire, might be found unto praise and honor and glory at the revelation of Jesus Christ" I PETER 1:7

Let me warn you: God places His prize possessions in the fire. The precious vessels that He draws the most brilliant glory from often are exposed to the melting pot of distress. The bad news is, even those who live godly lives will suffer persecution. The good news is, you might be in the fire, but God controls the thermostat! He knows how hot it needs to be to accomplish His purpose in your life. I don't know anyone I would rather trust with the thermostat than the God of all grace.

> *"The good news is, you might be in the fire, but God controls the thermostat!"*

Every test has degrees. Some people have experienced similar distresses, but to varying degrees. God knows the temperature that will burn away the impurities from His purpose. It is sad to have to admit this, but many times we release the ungodliness from our lives only as we experience the dread chastisement of a faithful God who is committed to bringing about change. How often He has had to fan the flames around me to produce the effects that He wanted in my life. In short, God is serious about producing the change in our lives that will glorify Him.

His hand has fanned the flames that were needed to teach patience, prayer, and many other invaluable lessons. We need His corrections. We don't enjoy them, but we need them. Without the correction of the Lord, we continue in our own way. What a joy to know that He cares enough to straighten out the jagged places in our lives. It is His fatherly corrections that confirm us as legitimate sons and not illegitimate ones. He affirms my position in Him by correcting and chastening me.

Do You Even Know He's in Town?

"Which, when it is sown in the earth, is less than all the seeds that be in the earth: but when it is sown, it grows up, and becomes greater than all herbs, and becomes a tree, and shoots out great branches; so that the birds of the air come and lodge in the branches thereof." MATTHEW 13:32

The priority of God's presence has been lost in the modern Church. We're like bakeries that are open, but have no bread. And furthermore, we're not interested in selling bread. We just like the chit-chat that goes on around cold ovens and empty shelves. In fact, I wonder, do we even know whether He's here or not, and if He is here, what He's doing? Or are we just too preoccupied with sweeping out imaginary crumbs from bakeries with no bread?

> *"The Messiah passed right by their door while they were inside praying for Him to come."*

On the day Jesus made what we call His triumphant entry into Jerusalem on the back of a little donkey, His path through the city probably led Him right past the entrance to the temple of Herod. I believe the reason the Pharisees were upset at the parade in John 12 is because it disturbed their religious services inside the temple.

I can hear them complaining, "What is all this going on? You're disturbing the high priest! Don't you know what we are doing? We are having a very important prayer service inside. Do you know what we're praying for? We're praying for the Messiah to come! And you have the audacity to have this noisy parade and disturb us?! Who is in charge of this unruly mob anyway?"

Uh, do you see the guy on the little donkey?

They missed the hour of their visitation. He was in town and they didn't know it. The Messiah passed right by their door while they were inside praying for Him to come. The problem was that He didn't come in the manner in which they expected Him to come. Had Jesus come on the back of a prancing white stallion, or in a royal chariot of gold with a phalanx of soldiers ahead of Him, the Pharisees and priests would have said, "That might be Him...."

We can be inside praying for Him to come while He passes by outside.

No Obstacle Is Too Big

"For, if God so clothe the grass of the field, which today is, and tomorrow is cast into the oven, shall he not much more clothe you, O you of little faith?"
COLOSSIANS 3:12,13

It's late at night as he paces the floor. Sleep has evaded him for several days. His mind is occupied with thoughts of his son. He did not hang a sign in the vacant bedroom window that read "Room for Rent" when the boy ran off. He tells the maid to go ahead and set the son's place at the table. He tells the farmhand to put that certain calf in the greenest part of the pasture.

When the prodigal finally comes home, Dad leaps off the front porch, runs to him, and kisses him. He is not about to sit casually by and watch the humbled son return. He places the ring on the son's finger and orders the best robe to be placed around his shoulders and shoes on his feet. (See Luke 15:4-24.)

> *"The Lord sees your plight and knows exactly what you are going through."*

No one has gone too far or sunk too deep for Him. Isaiah said, "Behold, the Lord's hand is not shortened, that it cannot save; neither His ear heavy, that it cannot hear" (Is. 59:1). Who does He have time for?

The Lord sees your plight and knows exactly what you are going through. Lightning may not be flashing, you may not be sitting in the company of an angel, but the Lord has a message for you. You may be reading it.

Determine in your heart that you are going to make it through whatever test or trial you are in right now. By God's grace you will overcome all obstacles and be victorious. He saw Moses on the backside of the desert; you are not out of His eyesight.

Morton Bustard, *The Impassioned Soul*

One Shepherd

"And other sheep I have, which are not of this fold: them also I must bring, and they shall hear my voice; and there shall be one flock, and one shepherd."
JOHN 10:16

A friend of mine told me a story about an experience he had in Israel. They were in the country visiting some of the famous biblical sites when they saw a group of sheepherders. A shepherd brought this flock of sheep into a round pen for the night. Then a few minutes later, another shepherd brought his flock into the pen. Then a few minutes later, yet

> *"Only his sheep followed his voice."*

another shepherd brought his sheep into the pen. Then there were three groups of sheep in the pen with no identifying marks among any of them. My friend wondered how in the world they would separate their sheep the next day.

The next morning, a shepherd came over to the pen and made a comment to his sheep. One by one, the sheep filed out to follow him. Only his sheep followed his voice. My friend said it was an amazing scene to see only that shepherd's sheep follow him and the others remains in the pen. What a picture of Jesus' words spoken centuries earlier.

Hearing and responding to Jesus' voice is the key to having a two-way relationship with God. It is the difference between having religion and relationship. Can you recognize God's voice in your life? Are you listening to the Shepherd's voice? Do you respond when He calls? Ask Jesus to help you increase your ability to hear. Give more time to spending quiet moments in His presence to hear His voice. He wants to be your Good Shepherd.

Change Is Not An Option

"And you will hear a voice behind thee, saying, this is the way, walk ye in it."
ISAIAH 30:21-KJV

Change is not an option. It's a necessity. It is change that processes a sinner to the righteousness of God. Paul said that if any man is in Christ Jesus, he is a new creature; old things are passed away and all things become new. Imagine that. Without change, there would not be one righteous among us. Without change, there would be no leader to follow, no healing for sickness, no wealth to replace poverty. Sadness would never find joy without change.

Without change everything would remain the same. We would be fallen; the wages of our sin would still be owed. Change is that difference that brings one into destiny. How can we get where we want to go if we aren't willing to change from where we are? How will we ever see the future if we are determined to live in the past?

> *"The greatest gifts of His presence are found in our greatest tribulation."*

Change is not always pleasant at first, but through the unpleasantness, through the wilderness, we see the faithfulness of Jehovah at its most brilliant. I think of the children of Israel in their wilderness. God gave them manna and quail to eat. He made water come from a rock to quench their thirst. He had already parted the Red Sea for them and defeated their enemies. They just needed to believe He would lead them to the land that He had promised them.

In many wildernesses, we are given the manna of God's Word to sustain us. In our rockiest places, our thirst is sated by a kind gesture from a friend. There are those who go to war in the spirit realm on our behalf and deliver messages to us from the throne. Be grateful for every wilderness you find yourself in. The glory of God is so close in those times. He leads, protects, pushes, feeds, and comforts us in the wilderness. The greatest gifts of His presence are found in our greatest tribulation. That is why we are to count it joy when we fall into them.

_____

_____

_____

_____

_____

_____

Dr. Wanda Turner, *Celebrating Change*

Duty=Courage+Compassion

"Greater love has no man than this, that a man lay down his life for his friends." JOHN 15:13

I think one of the reasons we've forgotten about duty is that we've come to see it in a bad light. We think of duty as slavish obedience produced by guilt. When we do use the word, it is usually in a negative way. For instance, we may shake our heads over the sad state of the man who is regular in his church attendance, not because he loves God but because he has a sense of duty to God. We feel sorry for the woman who stays in an unhappy marriage out of duty to her husband.

> *"When I use the word duty, I am talking about actions that are driven by compassion for others."*

When I use the word duty, I am talking about actions that are driven by compassion for others, love for God, and a determination to stand up for what's right. It was this type of duty that motivated the men and women of the New York City Fire Department to go into the World Trade Center following the terrorist attack of September 11, 2001. When they ran into those buildings, they knew they might be headed toward their own destruction, but they didn't hesitate.

No one would have blamed the firefighters if they had taken one look at those burning buildings and said, "I'm not going in there! No way!" But they didn't think twice about it. People were trapped on the upper floors, and those firemen gave their lives in an attempt to save them. In doing so, they showed the greatest possible love for their fellow human beings.

This kind of duty—rather than blind nationalism—is what motivates reasonable men to go to war in behalf of their country or to give their lives in an effort to liberate those who are oppressed by tyranny.

Pat Williams, *American Scandal*

It Is Expensive To Be Blessed

"For unto whomsoever much is given, of him shall be much required: and to whom men have committed much, of him they will ask the more." LUKE 12:48

Success cannot be defined in generalities; it can be defined only according to individual purpose and divine direction. You would be surprised at how many highly anointed people are tormented by a need to evaluate themselves in the light of another's calling. Your assignment is to dig for your own gold. Just cultivate what the Lord has given to you. It's simple: Find out what you have to work with, and then work it, work it, work it!

> *"Finud ot what you have to work with, and then work it, work it, work it!"*

I am always concerned that Christians not manipulate each other by trying to get people to worship their talents rather than God's purpose for their lives. How can any person know you well enough to discern whether you are successful, other than the God who created you?

There are no ifs, ands, or buts; the greater the blessing, the more the responsibility. It is expensive to be blessed. Everyone can't handle the success. Some may choose tranquility over notoriety. They don't like criticism and they abhor pressure. But if you are the kind of person who desperately needs to attain the hope of his calling, then go for it. Some people will never be satisfied with sitting on the bench cheering for others who paid the price to play the game. Locked within them is an inner ambitious intrigue not predicated on jealousy or intimidation. It is built upon an inner need to unlock a predestined purpose. For them, it does not matter. Inflationary times may escalate the price of their dreams, but whatever the price, they are compelled, drawn, and almost driven toward a hope.

*I*t Takes Divine Belligerence

"Then Jesus answered and said unto her, "O woman, great is your faith: be it unto you even as you will." And her daughter was made whole from that very hour." MATTHEW 15:28

We've become so "churchified" that we have our own form of "political correctness" and polite etiquette. Since we don't want to be too radical, we line all the chairs up in nice rows and expect our services to conform to equally straight and regimented lines as well. We need to get so desperately hungry for Him that we literally forget our manners!

Everybody whom I can think of in the New Testament record who "forgot their manners" received something from Him. I'm not talking about rudeness for the sake of rudeness; I'm talking about rudeness born out of desperation! What about the desperate woman with an incurable hemorrhaging problem who elbowed and shoved her way through the crowd until she touched the hem of the Lord's garment?7 What about the impertinent Canaanite woman who just kept begging Jesus to deliver her daughter from demonization in Matthew 15:22-28?

> *"We need to get so desperately hungry for Him that we literally forget our manners!"*

Even though Jesus insulted her when He said, "Let the children first be filled: for it is not right to take the children's bread, and to cast it unto the little dogs." (Mt. 15:26b), she persisted. And she was so rude, so abrupt, and so pushy (or was she simply so desperately hungry for bread) that she replied, "Yes, Lord: yet the little dogs under the table eat of the children's crumbs which fall from their masters' table." (Mt. 15:27).

To be honest, I'm hoping that God grips men and women in His Church and causes them to become so obsessed with the bread of His presence that they will not stop. Once that happens, they don't want just a "bless me" touch. They will want Him to show up in the place no matter how much it costs or how uncomfortable it may feel.

Tommy Tenney, *The God Chasers*

Weary Yet Willing

"Jesus answered and said unto her, 'Whosoever drinks of this water shall thirst again: but whosoever drinks of the water that I shall give him shall never thirst.'" JOHN 4: 13,14

Be careful when you need a hand up and you're asked for a handout. If you are suddenly placed in the position to serve, don't react in bitterness. Perhaps life has not been treating you fairly, and now, as if your duties are not enough, another one is shoved before you. How will you react?

God never creates a task too great for us to accomplish. You may be a single mom because of a delinquent dad who never could deal with responsibility. Perhaps you are left to finish the race alone since your beloved has gone on before you. Whatever the situation, be willing. If a need arises, be there and be willing.

> *"God never creates a task too great for us to accomplish."*

You may have gone through more marriages than an accountant has numbers. The chap you are living with at the moment takes what he wants but will not give you his name in return. His free spirit and fear of commitment will not permit him to enter into a marriage contract. These irresponsible, poor excuses of the male gender may have disillusioned you, but the Man sitting at your well is different. If you will give Him what He asks, He will give you what you need.

Morton Bustard, *The Impassioned Soul*

Join the Club ...

"Take heed to yourselves: If your brother trespasses against you, rebuke him; and if he repents, forgive him." LUKE 17:3

Are you looking for hope? Are you desperately seeking the missing link that will release you? Perhaps you realize you have been held in bondage, and now you are thinking, I have also held other people in bondage. Now the armies of the enemy are encamped around me. How can I disperse them?

> *"...forgive and release those people or circumstances that have hurt you."*

The Holy Spirit is waiting to release you, if you will forgive. Don't let the excuses of your flesh or your mind distract you from what is most important right now.

I've been wronged. Who hasn't?

Life's dealt me a bad hand. So what? Join the club.

I was lied to. You're not the first one. You won't be the last one. Your Master was lied to. Are you any better than He is?

Those who were supposed to have been my friends forsook me. Join the club. Jesus is president. They all forsook Him and fled.

If you need help, ask God to help you forgive and release those people or circumstances that have hurt you. Ask Him to forgive you for every sin and failure in your life. He is faithful to forgive.

It all begins with the same first step: Experience the power of divine forgiveness.

Tommy Tenney, *The Daily Chase*

*I*t Takes Trust

"Both riches and honour come of thee, and thou reignest over all; and in thine hand is power and might; and in thine hand it is to make great and to give strength unto all." 1 CHRONICLES 29: 12-KJV

The basis of any relationship must be trust. Trusting God with your successes isn't really a challenge. The real test of trust is to be able to share your secrets, your inner failures and fears. A mutual enhancement comes into a relationship where there is intimacy based on honesty.

Jesus told the woman at the well, a woman whose flaws and failures He had supernaturally revealed, "...true worshipers shall worship the Father in spirit and in truth: for the Father seeks such to worship him. God is a Spirit: and they that worship him must worship him in spirit and in truth." (John 4:23-24).

> *"The real test of trust is to be able to share your secrets, your inner failures and fears."*

We have nothing to fear, for our honesty with the Father doesn't reveal anything to Him that He doesn't already know! . . .He doesn't have to wait for you to make a mistake. He knows of your failure before you fail. His knowledge is all-inclusive, spanning the gaps between times and incidents. He knows our thoughts even as we unconsciously gather them together to make sense in our own mind!

The Lord knoweth the thoughts of man, that they are vanity. Psalm 94:11 (KJV).

Once we know this, all our attempts at silence and secrecy seem juvenile and ridiculous. He is "the all-seeing One," and He knows perfectly and completely what is in man. When we pray, and more importantly, when we commune with God, we must have the kind of confidence and assurance that neither requires nor allows deceit. Although my Father abhors my sin, He loves me. His love is incomprehensible, primarily because there is nothing with which we can compare it! What we must do is accept the riches of His grace and stand in the shade of His loving arms.

$\mathcal{P}$rotect Your Spirit Personality

"For the word of God is quick, and powerful, and sharper than any two edged sword, piercing even to the dividing asunder of soul and spirit, and of the joints and marrow, and is a discerner of the thoughts and intents of the heart." HEBREWS 4:12

Prayer is a spirit force. It has to do wholly with spirit beings and forces. Now a spirit being can go as quickly as I can think. If I was to go to London it will take at least a week's time to get my body through the intervening space. But I can think myself into London more quickly than I can say the words, and be walking down the Strand.

> *"Prayer has these qualities of spirit beings of not being limited by space or by material obstacles."*

Further, spirit beings are not limited by material obstructions such as the walls of this building.... But the spirit beings who are here listening to us, and deeply concerned with our discussion, did not bother with the doors. They came in through the walls, or the roof, if they were above us, or through the floor here, if they happened to be below this level. Prayer has these qualities of spirit beings of not being limited by space or by material obstacles.

Prayer is really projecting my spirit...to the spot concerned, and doing business there with other spirit beings....And it gives great simplicity to my faith...to remember that every time such prayer is breathed out, my sprit personality is being projected...and in effect, I am pleading the power of Jesus' victory over the evil one there..and on behalf of those faithful ones standing there for God.

S. D. Gordon, *Quiet Talks on Prayer*

*M*y Gratitude

Loving what I have—what I am grateful for:

_____

_____

_____

_____

_____

_____

_____

_____

_____

_____

_____

_____

_____

_____

_____

_____

_____

_____

_____

_____

_____

_____

_____

_____

_____

_____

"Enter into his gates with thanksgiving, and into his courts with praise: be thankful unto him, and bless his name." PSALMS 100:4 (KJV)

*T*he Battlefield in Prayer

"And this is the confidence that we have in him, that, if we ask anything according to his will, he hears us: and if we know that he hears us, whatsoever we ask, we know that we have the petitions that we desired of him." 1 JOHN 5:14-15

The greatest agency put into man's hands is prayer. Prayer is not persuading God. It does not influence God's purpose. It is not winning Him over to our side; never that. He is far more eager for what we are rightly eager for than we ever are. What there is of wrong and sin and suffering that pains you, pains Him far more. He knows more about it.

> *"The door between God and one's own self must be kept ever open. The knob to be turned is on our side."*

He is more keenly sensitive to it than the most sensitive one of us. Whatever of hearts yearning there may be that moves you to prayer is from Him. God takes the initiative in all prayer. It starts with Him. True prayer moves in a circle. It begins in the heart of God, sweeps down into a human heart...so intersecting the earth which is the battlefield of prayer, and then it goes back again to its starting point, having accomplished its purpose on the downward swing.

A man's whole life is utterly dependent upon the giving hand of God. Everything we need comes from Him. Our friendships, ability to make money, health, strength, in temptation, and in sorrow, guidance in difficult circumstances, and in all of life's movements; help of all sorts, financial, bodily, mental, spiritual—all come from God, and necessitate a constant touch with Him. There needs to be a constant stream of petition going up, many times wordless prayer. And there will be a constant return stream of answer and supply coming down. The door between God and one's own self must be kept ever open. The knob to be turned is on our side. He opened His side long ago, and propped it open, and threw the knob away. The whole of life hinges upon this continual intercourse with our wondrous God.

S. D. Gordon, *Quiet Talks on Prayer*

We Need Feelings

"For which cause we do not lose heart; but though our outward man perishes, yet the inward man is renewed day by day. For our light affliction, which is but for a moment, works for us a far more exceeding and eternal weight of glory." 2 CORINTHIANS 4:16, 17

I believe that life without feelings is like a riverbed without water. The water is what makes the river a place of activity and life. You don't want to destroy the water, but you do need to control it. Feelings that are out of control are like the floodwaters of a river. The gushing currents of boisterous waters over their banks can bring death and destruction. They must be held at bay by restrictions and limitations. Although we don't want to be controlled by feelings, we must have access to our emotions. We need to allow ourselves the pleasure and pain of life.

> *"We need to allow ourselves the pleasure and pain of life."*

Emotional pain is to the spirit what physical pain is to the body. Pain warns us that something is out of order and may require attention. Pain warns us that something in our body is not healed. In the same way, when pain fills our heart, we know that we have an area where healing or restoration is needed. We dare not ignore these signals, and neither dare we let them control us.

Above all, we need to allow the Spirit of God to counsel us and guide us through the challenges of realignment when upheavals occur in our lives. Even the finest limousine requires a regular schedule of tune-ups or realignments. Minor adjustments increase performance and productivity.

It is important to understand the difference between minor and major adjustments. The removal of a person from our lives is painful, but it is not a major adjustment. People are being born and dying every day. They are coming and going, marrying and divorcing, falling in love and falling out of love. You can survive the loss of people, but you can't survive without God! He is the force that allows you to overcome when people have taken you under. His grace enables you to overcome!

T. D. Jakes, *365 Days to Healing, Blessings, and Freedom*

Single Hours

"See then that you walk circumspectly, not as fools, but as wise, redeeming the time, because the days are evil. Therefore be not unwise, but understanding what the will of the Lord is." EPHESIANS 5:15-17

The perfect time to make the most of every opportunity is while you are single. Every believer should use time wisely.

Rather than staying home worrying about another "dateless" Saturday night, realize how much valuable time has been entrusted to you at this point in your life. Rather than resent your many single hours, embrace them as a gift from God—a package that contains opportunities to serve Him that are limited only by your own self-pity and lack of obedience.

> *"Rather than resent your many single hours, embrace them as a gift from God."*

Countless single women stay home rather than travel alone into the unknown. They not only miss out on being encouraged by others, but also are not exposed to new relationships when they remain at home tied up by cords of fear and feeling sorry for themselves.

If a single woman allows the fearful prospect of meeting new people and new challenges to keep her at home, she may find herself bored and lonely while all the time missing many satisfying and fulfilling experiences.

Are you busy serving Jesus during your free time, or do you waste hours trying to pursue and snag an available guy?

_____

_____

_____

_____

_____

_____

_____

_____

_____

_____

Debbie Jones & Jackie Kendall, *Lady in Waiting—Meditations of The Heart*

Broken Prayers

"The effective fervent prayer of a righteous man avails much." JAMES 5:16

God answers prayer. Prayer is God and man joining hands to secure some high end. He joins with us through the communication of prayer in accomplishing certain great results. This is the main drive of prayer. Our asking and expecting, and God's doing jointly brings to pass things what otherwise would not come to pass. Prayer changes things. This is the great fact of prayer.

Yet a great many prayers are not answered. Or to put it more accurately, a great many prayers fail utterly of accomplishing any results. Probably it is accurate to say that thousands of prayers go up and bring nothing down. As a result many persons are saying, "Well, prayer is not what you claim for it; we prayed and no answer came; nothing was changed."

> *"Probably it is accurate to say that thousands of prayers go up and bring nothing down."*

From all sorts of circles, and in all sorts of language comes this statement. Scholarly men who write with wisdom's words, and thoughtless people whose thinking never even pricks the skin of the subject, and all sorts of people in between group themselves together here. And they are right, quite right. The bother is that what they say is not all there is to be said. Partial truth is a very mean sort of lie.

The prayer plan like many another has been much disturbed, and often broken. And one who would be a partner with God...must understand the things that hinder the prayer plan. if I am holding something in my life that the Master does not like, if I am failing to obey when His voice has spoken...If that faithful quiet inner voice has spoken and I know what the Master would prefer and I fail to keep in line, then prayer is useless; sheer waste of breathe. And the truth is because I have broken with God, the praying—saying words in that form—is utterly worthless. And if we cannot talk together, working together is out of the question. And prayer is working together with God.

S. D. Gordon, *Quiet Talks on Prayer*

Selfish Sanctity

"You ask, and receive not, because you ask wrongly, that you may consume it upon your passions." JAMES 4:3

"Ye have not because ye ask not"—that explains many parched up lives and churches and unsolved problems: no pipelines run up to tap the reservoir, and give God an opening into the troubled territory. Then he pushes on to say—"Ye ask, and receive not"—ah!.why?... "Because ye ask amiss to spend it on your pleasures." That is to say, selfish praying; asking for something just because I want it; want it for myself.

"He never fails to work whenever he has a half chance."

Here is a wife praying that her husband might become a Christian. "He would go to church with me, and sit in the pew Sunday morning. I'd like that." Perhaps, she thinks, "He would be careful about swearing." She is thinking of herself; not of the loving grieved God against whom her husband is in rebellion…God might touch her husband's heart and say: "I want you to help Me win My poor world back." And the change would mean a reduced income, and a different social position. Oh! She had not meant that! Yes—what she wanted for herself!

To acknowledge that would be to see the mean contemptibility of it. Please notice that the reason for the prayer not being answered here is not an arbitrary reluctance upon God's part to do a desirable thing. He never fails to work whenever he has a half chance as far as it is possible to work. But the motive determines the propriety of such requests. Where the whole of one's life is for Him, these things may be asked for freely as His gracious Spirit within guides. He knows if the purpose of the heart is to please Him.

S. D. Gordon, *Quiet Talks on Prayer*

God's Word on Your Potential

"Fear not therefore, you are of more value than many sparrows."
MATTHEW 10:31

Do you understand how much you are worth? You are equal to the value of your Source. You are as valuable as the God you came from! Stop feeling bad about other people's estimations of your value. You are special. You are worth feeling good about. God's word on your potential is the only evaluation that counts. You are not what your teacher or your spouse or your children or your boss say about you. You are as valuable and capable as God says you are. If you are going to release your full potential, you must understand and accept the value God places upon you and the confidence He has in your abilities.

> *"Your ability depends on your response to God's ability."*

Even as God is the One who set your value, so too He is the only One who is qualified to determine the extent of your potential. The possibilities that lie within you are dependent upon God, because the potential of a thing is always determined by the source from which it came. Even as the potential of a wooden table is determined by the strength of the tree from which it was made, so your potential is determined by God, because you came out of God.

Your ability depends on your response to God's ability. The basic principles that apply to the potential of all things also apply to your potential. God, your Source/Creator, is the Definer of your potential. Because you came from God and share His essence and components, your value and potential are known to Him alone.

God wants you to see yourself and your abilities the way He sees you. He puts great value on you and eagerly encourages each step you take toward using even a small part of your talents and abilities. God believes in you.

Myles Munroe, *Releasing Your Potential*

When the Pressure is On

"And when Peter was come down out of the ship, he walked on the water, to go to Jesus. But when he saw the wind boisterous, he was afraid; and beginning to sink, he cried, saying, 'Lord, save me.'"
MATTHEW 14:29-30

I admire Peter for being the only apostle who was brave enough to ask Jesus if he could get out of the boat and walk on the water.

The apostle Peter was a good example of someone who revealed his true character when the pressure was on. He also showed us that a person can change their character over time. What a difference there is between the man depicted in the Gospels and the mature, bold Peter we read about in the Book of Acts. In Matthew 26:33-35 Peter promised Jesus that he would die before he'd ever fail him. Then just a few hours later, he cursed, swore, and declared, "I don't know the man!" Even so, Peter didn't give up on himself. He didn't quit. And by the time we get to the Book of Acts, we find that an amazing transformation has occurred. Peter won't stop talking about Jesus Christ, no matter what the authorities try to do to him. They put him in jail several times, but he goes right on preaching the Good News. They beat him, but that doesn't stop him either.

> *"He enables us to stand when we'd otherwise fall."*

This brings me to a very important point. When it comes to character, those who belong to Christ have a tremendous advantage over those who don't know Him. That's because He gives us power and strength that are far beyond our normal capabilities. He enables us to stand when we'd otherwise fall, to walk when we'd otherwise be standing still, and to run when we'd otherwise be forced to crawl.

Pat Williams, *American Scandal*

*T*he Fourth Man

"Beloved, do not think it strange concerning the fiery trial which is to prove you, as though some strange thing happened unto you: but rejoice."
I PETER 4:12-13

You may be in a burning fiery furnace right now, because it comes in different ways. A fiery furnace to me may not be one to you. One to you may not be the same to me. But you may be in a condition right now where you're suffering, where you're under a threat where you're about to do something that will compromise your integrity with God, that will cause your faith to weaken and the devil to get an upper hand for temporary gain.

But God knows if you compromise, you will lose what you compromised to get. And God knows if you refuse to compromise—no matter how bleak the circumstances look and how defeat seems to loom so near to you—that you may temporarily lose, but before it's over, you will not lose. God will pick you up. God will restore to you seven times what the devil stole from you.

> *"You're freer in the furnace than you are outside."*

When you live by faith, you're on the winning side. Who is the fourth man? He's the Everlasting God. He's the Eternal Ruler, and the government of our life is upon his shoulder. You're freer in the furnace than you are outside. You are freer when you live by your faith than you are by compromising and seeming to get all the stuff they promised. You're freer.

You have more freedom in your spirit. You have a more peaceful mind. You have a body that rests better. You have a courage that doesn't fail...When you refuse to compromise and live by faith, you're freer...even if they cast you into life's fiery furnaces. You're going to win because the Fourth Man goes into the fiery furnace with you—and brings you out.

Oral Roberts, *Still Doing the Impossible*

Judas Was No Mistake

"Be strong and of a good courage; be not afraid, neither be thou dismayed: for the Lord thy God is with thee whithersoever thou goest." JOSHUA 1:9-KJV

Judas was no mistake. He was handpicked and selected. His role was crucial to the death and resurrection of Christ. No one helped Christ reach His goal like Judas. If God allowed certain types of people to come into our lives, they would hinder us from His divine purpose.

We all want to be surrounded by a friend like John, whose loving head lay firmly on Jesus' breast. We may long for the protective instincts of a friend like Peter, who stood ready to attack every negative force that would come against Jesus. In his misdirected love, Peter even withstood Jesus to His face over His determination to die for mankind. But the truth of the matter is, Jesus could have accomplished His goal without Peter, James, or John; *but without Judas He would never have reached the hope of His calling!*

> *"When you encounter a Judas in your life, remember that it is his actions that carry out the purpose of God in your life!"*

Leave my Judas alone. I need him in my life. He is my mysterious friend, the one who aids me without even knowing it. When you encounter a Judas in your life, remember that it is his actions that carry out the purpose of God in your life! Look back over your life and understand that it is persecution that strengthens you. It is the struggles and the trauma we face that help us persevere.

Thank God for your friends and family and their support, but remember that it is often your relationship with that mysterious friend of malice and strife that becomes the catalyst for greatness in your life! It is much easier to forgive the actions of men when you know the purposes of God! Not only should we refuse to fear their actions—we should release them.

T. D. Jakes, *365 Days to Healing, Blessings, and Freedom*

Sometimes You Have to Get Out of the Kitchen

"But Martha was distracted about much serving, and came to him, and said, 'Lord, do you not care that my sister has left me to serve alone? tell her therefore that she help me.'" LUKE 10:40

The New Testament portrait of Mary and Martha responding to Jesus' visit to their home in Bethany reveals an important principle at work. Both of them were needed. Mary knew how to minister to the divinity of Christ, and she gave it top priority. Martha knew how to minister to His humanity and that was her primary focus. When you get both of these ministries operating in unity in the same house, there is power. Yet there must be balance.

> "He will always put footwashers before food-preparers,"

Martha was so encumbered by her focus on ministry in the natural that she was blind to the priority of the spiritual. She made it difficult for the Spirit to interrupt her kitchen agenda of serving the Lord's natural needs for the sake of the spiritual. On the other hand, Mary was so "heavenly minded" that at times she bordered on the neglectful. If Martha hadn't been there, she would have kept Jesus talking long after dinnertime and into the night without a meal.

Forced to choose between the two, the Lord will always choose the one who sits at His feet in adoration and communes with Him. He will always put foot-washers before food-preparers, but He prefers to have both. Somewhere in the middle of Martha's kitchen and Mary's seat of devotion at Jesus' feet there is a place of divine power. The ideal balance would place both Mary and Martha at Jesus' feet in joyful devotion and communion until the appropriate time; then both would be released in power to serve Him and worship Him in the "kitchen" of life.

Tommy Tenney, *The Daily Chase*

You See What You Believe

"So then faith comes by hearing, and hearing by the word of God."
ROMANS 10:17

It's easy to forget sometimes that the earth is the Lord's and everything in it. He places desires in our hearts, then proceeds to move the universe to grant them. But God knows how forgetful we are. So He sends a friend, a brother or sister, a book, a rainbow, a memory, or a song to remind us that He holds our time, all our time, in His hand.

Change begins with a desire. That desire becomes a choice. That

> *"Change begins with a desire. That desire becomes a choice."*

choice is then placed, by faith, in the hands of Almighty God. Once in His hands, it ceases to be controlled by people or circumstances. What we see begins to lie to us about what we heard God say. How often have you prayed to God for something, looked at your circumstances, your past, or your present situation and decided that your prayer didn't have a future? Sometimes the only thing separating us from what we want is our faith...God doesn't show you something and then speak on it. He speaks, waits for you to believe, then shows you that you did in fact hear Him...Throughout Scripture, God speaks, then allows His words to come to pass. And since we know that He's the same yesterday, today, and forever, we know that He's still operating like that today. He speaks, we hear, we believe, we see. Faith is the substance of things not seen, but faith comes by hearing (see Hebrews 11:1; Romans 10:17). What are you hearing God say that is getting lost under what you see?

Dr. Wanda Turner, *Celebrating Change*

Green Light

"For therein is the righteousness of God revealed from faith to faith: as it is written, 'The just shall live by faith.'" ROMANS 1:17

You feel as though you have been waiting without seeing any results, almost like a car waiting at an intersection. Then the light suddenly changes from red to green and you are free to move. When God changes the light in your life from red to green, you can accomplish things that you tried to do at other times but could not perform... I call those seasons "green light" time...What an exciting time it is to suddenly find your engine kicking into gear and your turbines turning in harmonious production. Your tires screech from a dead stop to jet speed in seconds and bang! You are on the road again.

> *"I want to see you burn some spiritual rubber for Jesus!"*

This is an exciting time for the prepared believer. I believe with all my heart that soon people whom God had waiting their turn will burst to the forefront and pull into the fast lane. Trained by patience and humbled by personal challenges, they will usher in a new season in the cycle of the Kingdom. Are you a part of what God is doing, or are you still looking back at what God has done? I want to see you burn some spiritual rubber for Jesus!

What good is having your season if over your head gather the gloomy clouds of warning that keep thundering a nagging threat in your ears?...First, let me rebuke the spirit of fear. Fear will hide in the closet as we are blessed and make strange noises when no one else is around. We need to declare God to this fear. We dare not fall in love with what God is doing, but we must always be in love with who God is. God does not change . . . He has promised that if we walk uprightly, He will not withhold any good thing from us (see Ps. 84:11). I therefore conclude that if God withheld it, then it was no longer working for my good. I am then ready for the next assignment—it will be good for me.

Multiplied Rewards

"The kingdom of heaven is like a grain of mustard seed, which a man took, and sowed in his field:...but when it is sown, it grows up, and becomes greater than all herbs, and becomes a tree." MARK 4:31-32

I had been raised in a church where the pastors taught giving, but they said nothing about receiving. In fact, they taught the opposite: Giving was a debt we owed to God, but expecting something back was selfish. We should consider our giving only as a sacrifice we had made. I knew something was wrong with this kind of thinking and believing. A new slogan came up inside me: Giving is not a debt you owe, but a seed you sow.

> *"Giving is not a debt you owe, but a seed you sow."*

For the first time I really understood. "Jesus paid it all" on the cross. If we had all the money in the world, we couldn't pay our debt to Him. This eventually led to my discovery; God is a good God.

This idea of giving and receiving brought about a desperately needed change, a fresh breeze of enthusiasm for God, a contagious joy that we could give out of our need and expect the Lord of the harvest to multiply our seed sown and meet the needs for which we had sown.

I wonder about you. Have you subscribed to the general teaching that you are to give sacrificially only and no expect miracle returns? I want to tell you that the eternal laws of God in the Bible say:

Receiving does follow giving
Reaping does follow sowing
Harvesting does follow seedtime
And you are to expect miracle returns!
Including financial!

God has a better way for you to carry on your personal life and work and to be a leader in your community who is respected and who gets results!

_____

_____

_____

_____

_____

Oral Roberts, *Still Doing the Impossible*

*F*rom the Bottom Up

"According to the grace of God which is given unto me, as a wise master builder, I have laid the foundation, and another builds thereon. But let every man take heed how he builds thereupon." 1 CORINTHIANS 3:10

Why do so many people try to convey the image that they have always been on top? The truth is most people have struggled to attain whatever they have. They just try to convince everyone that they have always had it. I, for one, am far more impressed with the wealth of a person's character who doesn't use his success to intimidate others. The real, rich inner stability that comes from gradual success is far more lasting and beneficial than the temperamental theatrics of spiritual yuppies who have never learned their own vulnerabilities. We must not take ourselves too seriously. I believe that God grooms us for greatness in the stockades of struggle.

> *"God grooms us for greatness in the stockades of struggle."*

I have found God to be a builder of men. When He builds, He emphasizes the foundation. A foundation, once it is laid, is neither visible nor attractive, but nevertheless still quite necessary. When God begins to establish the foundation, He does it in the feeble, frail beginnings of our lives. Paul describes himself as a wise master builder. Actually, God is the Master Builder. He knows what kind of beginning we need and He lays His foundation in the struggles of our formative years.

The concern over the future coupled with the fear of failure brings us to the posture of prayer. Often we don't realize how severe our beginnings were until we are out or about to come out of them. Then the grace lifts and we behold the utter devastating truth about what we just came through.

Don't Rob Yourself of Forgiveness

"For if you forgive men their trespasses, your heavenly Father will also forgive you." MATTHEW 6:14

Here is a vital scriptural principle: You are only forgiven as you forgive others. If you cling to unforgiveness toward another person, you are robbing yourself of your own forgiveness from God. Forgiveness toward others doesn't come naturally, it comes supernaturally.

Have you ever had to "work on" having a bad spirit? If you are like every other human being on earth, it just comes naturally to your flesh. We never have to work on being resentful. Have you ever had to tell yourself, "You know, he did me wrong and I'm going to have to work up a good case of resentment against him; it may take me three or four days to get it going good, but I'm going to work up a good case of resentment and get myself a bad spirit"? No, it just doesn't happen that way.

> *"You are only forgiven as you forgive others."*

When resentment rises up, it comes without our even thinking about it; it is virtually instant. Forgiveness, on the other hand, takes a conscious choice and effort on our part. Our job is to work on keeping a good attitude, a sweet spirit, and a pure heart before God and other people. This is impossible unless we learn the power of forgiveness and make right choices along the way.

Tommy Tenney, *The Daily Chase*

Consistently Inconsistent

"Now faith is the substance of things hoped for, the evidence of things not seen." HEBREWS 11:1

We can only move forward when we embrace the truth of the Scripture that exhorts us to "Let this mind be in you, which was also in Christ Jesus:" (Phil. 2:5). Now, the mind of Christ Jesus is illogical and consistently inconsistent and irrational to our earthly rationalizing. It just doesn't make sense sometimes. The mind of Christ surpasses all understanding and operates in the reverse of all we think, for God is a being of grace and mercy and often we are not. God hates sin but loves the sinner. We hate sinners but love sin. God accepts; we reject. God is compassionate and is known to be "the Healer." Man is often brutal and called "a killer." We want God to come on our time, and He comes in His time. We look past people's needs to see their faults. Jesus looked past our faults and saw our need.

> *"The mind of Christ, I found, is beyond my reason."*

The mind of Christ, I found, is beyond my reason. It's absurd, confounding, and puzzling. In fact, the mind of Christ boggles my mind. You will get a headache trying to figure Him out. In times of drought, Jesus says go fishing and let down your nets. We destroy marriages with fornication. Jesus destroys fornication with marriage. Jesus says if you want life, be wiling to die. If you want to rule, be a servant. If you want to be mature in your faith, act like a child. Rejoice in tribulation. Love those who hate you.

If you're crippled, you should know that you can walk. If you believe you're the one doing the walking you're gong to fall. If you want to receive, give. On earth, seeing is believing. In the spirit realm, believing is seeing, because faith is the substance of things hope for, the evidence of things not seen. What a God we serve. And in order to receive a godly blessing, we must think and see the way He does, then do accordingly.

_____

_____

_____

_____

_____

Dr. Wanda Turner, *Celebrating Change*

*H*eaven Hears

"Behold the birds of the air: for they sow not, neither do they reap, nor gather into barns; yet your heavenly Father feeds them. Are you not much better than they?" MATTHEW 6:26

I believe we are much more important to God than we can ever realize. He so much wants to bless us and guide us through troublesome times... A great man of God whom I esteem as a prophet once told me of an incident in his life. This particular event occurred in the 1960's. He was on his way to an Oral Roberts meeting when the Lord spoke to him and told him that he and his wife would be sitting in the second row from the front. When they arrived at the huge auditorium, the only seats they found empty were halfway down the aisle from the platform.

> *"If you are in need of an answer for some facet of your life, hold on—your answer is on the way."*

After they were seated, he asked the Lord, "I thought You said I would be seated in the second row from the front?" Just a moment or two after he had whispered the question, an usher stopped at his seat. This man informed them of some empty seats in the second row and asked if they would like to move.

The next day in prayer he asked the Lord why He would take the time to tell him where he would be sitting at a miracle crusade. The Lord impressed this answer in his spirit: Son, I know everything about you. I know where you are going to be and exactly what you will be doing. My eyes are ever upon you.

If you are in need of an answer for some facet of your life, hold on—your answer is on the way. God will go to whatever measure needed to see that you receive it.

Morton Bustard, *The Impassioned Soul*

*O*pen Communication

"Likewise the Spirit also helps our weaknesses: for we know not what we should pray for as we ought: but the Spirit himself makes intercession for us with groanings which cannot be uttered." ROMANS 8:26

What creates a feeling of wholeness in the heart of the believer is the awareness that while God's standards do not change, neither does His compassion. One thing we search for at every level of our relationships is "to be understood." When I am properly understood, I don't always have to express and explain. Thank You, Lord, for not asking me to explain what I oft can scarcely express!

We quickly grow weary when we are around anyone who demands that we constantly qualify our statements and explain our intent. We want to be near those who comprehend the subtle expressions of affection, intimacy, and need...a touch, a brief hug, a sigh emitted in the stillness of a moment. At this level there is a communication so intense that those who understand it can clearly speak it, even through closed lips... It is with this kind of understanding that God clearly perceives and understands our every need.

> *"Communication cannot be typed or taught; it must be understood."*

I believe that when the Scriptures declare that men "ought always to pray, and not to lose heart" (Luke 18:1b), that they are speaking of living in a state of open communication with God, not necessarily jabbering at Him nonstop for hours.

Let me ask you, would you want someone to talk to you like that? True friends can drive down a road and lapse in and out of conversation, deeply enjoying each other's company—all without any obligation to maintain a steady rhythm of rhetoric. Their communication is just an awareness of the presence of someone they know and understand.

We don't need to labor to create what is already there. I am glad my Savior knows what my speech and my silence suggest. I need not labor to create what we already share in the secret place of our hearts!

_____

_____

_____

_____

_____

T. D. Jakes, *365 Days to Healing, Blessings, and Freedom*

Understand Your Potential

"Let us draw near with a true heart in full assurance of faith."
HEBREWS 10:22A

God is God whether you choose to use His potential or not. Your decision to live with Him or without Him does not affect who He is or what He can do. He is not diminished when you choose to replace Him with other sources.

This is true because your potential is related to God's potential, and God is omnipotent. The combination of omni (meaning "always or all full of") and potent (meaning "power on reserve"—from which we get the word potential) declares that God is always full of power. Or to say it another way, all potential is in God. Thus, people who understand that God contains all the things that He's asking them to do are not afraid to do big things. It's not what you know but who you know that enables you to do great things with God.

> *"God still has the stuff you need to fulfill your potential."*

When you combine the knowledge of God's omnipotence with the knowledge of who you are in God, you can resist all things that seek to overcome you and to wipe out your potential. You can be strong and do great exploits. God is the Source of your potential. He waits to draw from His vast store to enable you to accomplish all that He demands of you.

Myles Munroe, *Releasing Your Potential*

What Are You Hungry For?

"Blessed are they which do hunger and thirst after righteousness: for they shall be filled." MATTHEW 5:6

When you pursue God with all your heart, soul, and body, He will turn to meet you and you will come out of it ruined for the world.

Good things have become the enemy of the best things. ...It's time for you to make your life holy. Quit watching what you used to watch; quit reading what you used to read if you are reading it more than you read His Word. He must be your first and greatest hunger.

> *"You can get so caught up in being "religious" that you never become spiritual"*

If you are contented and satisfied, then I'll leave you alone and you can safely put down this book at this point and I won't ever bother you again. But if you are hungry, I have a promise from the Lord for you. He said, "Blessed are they which do hunger and thirst after righteousness: for they shall be filled" (Mt. 5:6).

Our problem is that we have never really been hungry. We have allowed things of this realm to satisfy our lives and satiate our hunger. We have come to God week after week, year after year, just to have Him fill in the little empty spaces. I tell you that God is tired of being "second place" to everything else in our lives. He is even tired of being second to the local church program and church life! ...

You can get so caught up in being "religious" that you never become spiritual.... I pray that you get so hungry for God that you don't care about anything else. I think I see a flickering flame. He will "fan" that.

Tommy Tenney, *The Daily Chase*

God Works for Your Good

"And we know that all things work together for good to them that love God, to them who are the called according to his purpose." ROMANS 8:28

If no good can come out of a relationship or situation, then God will not allow it. This knowledge sets us free from internal struggle and allows us to be transparent.

"Every good gift and every perfect gift is from above, and comes down from the Father of lights, with whom is no variation, neither shadow of turning." (James 1:17-NKJV)

If you don't understand the sovereignty of God, then all is lost. There must be an inner awareness within your heart, a deep knowledge that God is in control and that He is able to reverse the adverse.... He orchestrates them in such a way that the things that could have paralyzed us only motivate us.

> *"There must be an inner awareness within your heart, a deep knowledge that God is in control and that He is able to reverse the adverse."*

God delights in bestowing His abundant grace upon us so we can live with men without fear. In Christ, we come to the table of human relationships feeling like we are standing before a great "smorgasbord" or buffet table. There will be some relationships whose "taste" we prefer over others, but the richness of life is in the opportunity to explore the options. What a dull plate we would face if everything on it was duplicated without distinction. God creates different types of people, and all are His handiwork.

Even in the most harmonious of relationships there are injuries and adversity. If you live in a cocoon, you will miss all the different levels of love God has for you. God allows different people to come into your life to accomplish His purposes. Your friends are ultimately the ones who will help you become all that God wants you to be in Him. When you consider it in that light, you have many friends—some of them expressed friends, and some implied friends.

T. D. Jakes, *365 Days to Healing, Blessings, and Freedom*

Can You Take the Heat?

"There has no temptation overtaken you except such as is common to man: but God is faithful, who will not allow you to be tempted above that you are able; but will with the temptation also make a way to escape, that you may be able to bear it." 1 CORINTHIANS 10:13

We find ourselves faced with trials when God is testing our faith in Him. When our circumstances change drastically and we can't trace our new situation directly to our disobedience, it is a sure sign that we are being tested or tried. While the purpose of trouble is to change our behavior, the purpose of a trial is to change our mind. We are transformed (changed) by the renewing of our minds when we allow God to take us through a trial.

"Proving our faith" is a concept that many don't understand. Most of us see that and think that God is trying to see if we have faith, so He allows a test. In actuality, you can take that phrase at face value (or faith value). He allows trials to prove that we have a certain amount of faith. Before the trial, He knows you have what it takes to get through it. He just wants you to know that you have reached that level of faith in Him. There is a wonderful illustration of this principle found at the potter's wheel.

> *"When God puts us in the fire, it is not until He is sure we've got what it takes to stand the heat."*

After a potter shapes a pot on a wheel, he puts it in the oven to harden the clay. Most people think that it is the heat from the fire that makes the pot firm. In reality, it is the shape of the pot before you put it into the fire that ensures it will keep its shape. If the pot was not formed correctly on the wheel, it won't stand up to the pressure of the heat. When God puts us in the fire, it is not until He is sure we've got what it takes to stand the heat. That's why God can promise us in His Word that He won't put any more on us than we can bear. In other words, He won't put us in the fire unless He knows we can take it.

God's Heroes

"When Jesus understood it, he said unto them, 'Why trouble the woman? for she has wrought a good work upon me.'" MATTHEW 26:10

God's definition of a hero and ours are probably not the same. Consider what He said about the "sinful" woman who broke the alabaster box to anoint the Lord with oil. If Heaven has a hall of fame, then I can tell you someone whose name is going to be right at the top of the list. It is Mary, the woman with the alabaster box. What is so startling about it is that the disciples were so embarrassed by the woman's actions that they wanted to throw her out, but Jesus made her actions an eternal monument of selfless worship! Jesus didn't intervene because of Mary's talent, beauty, or religious achievements; He stepped in because of her worship. The disciples said, "To what purpose is this waste?" (Mt. 26:8b) Jesus said, "It's not waste; it's worship."

> *"Often dense disciples mislabel things during their political posturing about who sits at the right and who at the left, while Jesus goes "worship hungry.""*

Often dense disciples mislabel things during their political posturing about who sits at the right and who at the left, while Jesus goes "worship hungry." His growling hunger pangs attract an outsider, a "box-breaker," a foot washer! Such worshipers must often ignore the stares and comments of a politically correct church while ministering to Jesus.

He desires our adoration and worship. Heaven's "hall of fame" is filled with the names of obscure people like the one leper who returned to thank God while nine never bothered. It will be filled with the names of people who so touched the heart and mind of God that He says, "I remember you. I know about you. Well done, My good and faithful servant."

Tommy Tenney, *The God Chasers*

*F*ive Essentials

"The light of the body is the eye: if therefore your eye be single, your whole body shall be full of light." MATTHEW 6:22

Light is an essential to the eye. The eye's seeing depends wholly on light. If it does not see light, by and by, it cannot see light. The ear that hears no sound loses the power to hear sound. Light is essential to the healthful eye: sound to the ear: air to the lungs: blood to the heart.

Essential is right habits of prayer. Living a veritable life of prayer. Making prayer the chief part not alone of your life, but of your service. Having answers to prayer as a constant experience. Being like the young man in a conference in India, who said, "I used to pray three times a day: Now I pray only once a day, and that is all day..."

> *"The ear that hears no sound loses the power to hear."*

Life is not mere length of time but the daily web of character we unconsciously weave. Our thoughts, imaginations, purposes, motives, love, will, are the under threads: our words, tone of voice, looks, acts, habits are the upper threads: and the passing moment is the shuttle swiftly, ceaselessly, relentlessly, weaving those threads into a web, and that web is life. It is woven, not by our wishing, or willing, but irresistibly, unavoidably, woven by what we are, moment by moment, hour after hour.

S. D. Gordon, *Quiet Talks on Power*

Release and Resolve

"For even Christ pleased not himself; but, as it is written, 'The insults of them that insulted you fell on me.'" ROMANS 15:3

Buried deep within the broken heart is a vital need to release and resolve. Although we feel pain when we fail at any task, there is a sweet resolve that delivers us from the cold clutches of uncertainty. If we had not been through some degree of rejection, we would have never been selected by God. Do you realize that God chooses people that others reject?! From a rejected son like David to a nearly murdered son like Joseph, God gathers the castaways of men and recycles them for Kingdom building.

> *"If we had not been through some degree of rejection, we would have never been selected by God."*

What frustration exists in the lives of people who want to be used of God, but who cannot endure rejection from men. I admit I haven't always possessed the personality profile that calloused me and offered some protection from the backlash of public opinion. This ability to endure is similar to having a taste for steak tartar—it must be acquired! If you want to be tenacious, you must be able to walk in the light of God's selection rather than dwell in the darkness of people's rejection. These critics are usually just a part of God's purpose in your life.

Focus is everything. If your attention is distracted by the constant thirst of other people, or if you are always trying to win people over, you will never be able to minister to the Lord—not if you are trying to win people. It seems almost as though He orchestrates your rejections to keep you from idolatry. We can easily make idols out of other people. However, God is too wise to build a house that is divided against itself. Against this rough canvas of rejection and the pain it produces, God paints the greatest sunrise the world has ever seen!

T. D. Jakes, *365 Days to Healing, Blessings, and Freedom*

God's System: Faith

"And God is able to make all grace abound toward you, that ye, always having all sufficiency in all things, may abound to every good work."
2 CORINTHIANS 9:8

God designed you to be a limitless person. He pulled you from His omnipotent Self and transferred to you a portion of His potential. He also wired you to operate like He does. When you reconnect with God through faith in Jesus Christ, He empowers you to return to your original mode of operation, which is like His own.

God thinks in terms of potential—of things that are not yet manifested. He relies on what He knows isn't visible yet, instead of what is visible. He is not excited by what you've already done.

> *"The fact that you look more like an undercomer than an overcomer doesn't change the truth that you are an overcomer."*

If you've accomplished something, enjoy it and appreciate it. But don't get so hung up on it that you fail to move on to what you yet can do. Paul wasn't satisfied with what he had attained. He was always looking for the next step. Why? Because the past is no longer motivational.

If God says you are or have something, it's in you somewhere. He sees what people can't see, and He says what He sees. If God says that you are an overcomer, you are an overcomer. The fact that you look more like an undercomer than an overcomer doesn't change the truth that you are an overcomer. Because God says it, it is true.

God's waiting for your potential to be revealed. He says, "You are not what you are acting like. Because you are My child, you have the potential to act better than you're acting. My potential is flowing from Me to you."

_____

_____

_____

_____

_____

_____

_____

Myles Munroe, *Releasing Your Potential*

*T*he Power to Run the Race

"let us lay aside every weight, and the sin which does so easily entangle us"
HEBREWS 12:1B

Are there weights in your life—things you've taken upon yourself—that are not the burden of the Lord? He wants you to lay them aside in exchange for power to run the race! Unnecessary weights will weary your mind and turn you into a zombie in the spiritual world.

God's Word says you can take care of that by unloading or flinging off that weight. If it's a sin, repent of it. If it is a weight or care you have brought on yourself, lay it aside. Are you overloaded with the unrealistic expectations of others? Unload them before you become a slave in the "Kingdom of They-dom." The bottom line is that "the government is on His shoulder," not the shoulders of your critics or would-be slave drivers. (See Isaiah 9:6.) Please God before you please man.

> *"God made us with two ends—one to think with, the other to sit on."*

Have you noticed that whenever you set out to do something for the Lord, it seems like the enemy paints a target on your shield? It is easy to get overloaded when this happens because if the enemy can't get to you by one means, he always tries another. If you feel worn down and short-circuited like a battery that has run dry, then try the power that comes with unloading!

Set your priorities and let Him determine your load.

God made us with two ends—one to think with, the other to sit on. The end you use determines whether you win or lose: Heads you win, tails you lose! Trite as it may sound, if you are so overloaded and burdened with things not of God that you virtually "cannot move," then you will lose. Use your head. Learn the power of unloading and give your burdens to the Lord. Then we can accept the "burden of the Lord" and share the yoke with Jesus. He makes the burden easy to bear, and when He shares the burden, losers become winners every time!

_____

_____

_____

_____

_____

_____

February 28

*P*ain Is Not Forever

"That you may be the children of your Father which is in heaven: for he makes his sun to rise on the evil and on the good, and sends rain on the just and on the unjust." MATTHEW 5:45

Asking 'why' is human. There is no sin in inquiring why trials come and why we have to face the situations that confront us. In His blood-covered, pain-ridden body Jesus looked into the heavens and asked why.

The Bible says it rains on the just and the unjust... The Psalmist David declared, "Many are the afflictions of the righteous: but the Lord delivereth him out of them all" (Ps. 34:19 - KJV). David did not say "from" but "out of." There is a major difference between the two.

"They that sow in tears shall reap in joy. He that goeth forth and weepeth, bearing precious seed, shall doubtless come again with rejoicing, bringing his sheaves with him" (Psalm 126:5-6 - KJV).

> *"We never know Him as the Lily of the Valley until we trod through the deep, lonely valley."*

Notice that David did not say "they that sow with tears," but rather "in tears." That means sowing when it is not convenient, being faithful through times of pain and heartbreak. It implies squaring our shoulders and meeting the task head-on through life's storms and winds of adversity.

There is a reason as well as a reward for enduring such hardship. When all is said and done, we will have experienced a relationship with God we never had before. We never know Him as the Lily of the Valley until we trod through the deep, lonely valley (see Song of Solomon 2:1). God could have spared the three Hebrew boys from having to enter a fiery furnace, but if He had, they would never have seen the fourth man (see Dan. 3:20-25).

Morton Bustard, *The Impassioned Soul*

How Does God Operate?

"... for whatsoever is not of faith is sin." ROMANS 14:23B

God operates by faith. The light in the darkness was not visible before God called it forth, but He believed that light was present in the darkness and, by faith, He spoke it into view. Faith isn't a jump in the dark. It is a walk in the light. Faith is not guessing; it is knowing something.

God made and fashioned you to operate by faith. He designed you to believe the invisible into becoming visible.

> *"Faith isn't a jump in the dark. It is a walk in the light. Faith is not guessing; it is knowing something."*

You may not see what God is calling forth from your life, but God asks you to believe it is there. He created you to operate like He does. If you aren't functioning like God, you are malfunctioning. The manual says, "The just shall live by faith" (Romans 1:17b), and "...whatsoever is not of faith is sin (Romans 14:23b).

God also created us to operate like He does:

Then God said, "Let Us make man in Our image, in Our likeness..." (Genesis 1:26-NIV)

The Hebrew word translated into the English word likeness means "to operate like," not "to look like." God's original design for man requires that we function like God.

Myles Munroe, *Releasing Your Potential*

$\mathcal{M}$y Gratitude

Loving what I have—what I am grateful for:

_____
_____
_____
_____
_____
_____
_____
_____
_____
_____
_____
_____
_____
_____
_____
_____
_____
_____
_____
_____
_____
_____
_____
_____
_____

"Devote yourselves to prayer, being watchful and thankful."
COLOSSIANS 4:2 (NIV)

Just Tell Me—Is That Him?

"And they which went before warned him, that he should hold his peace: but he cried so much the more, "Son of David, have mercy on me." MARK 10: 48

As Jesus passed through the gate, the blind beggar on the side of the road turned to someone standing nearby and asked a question:

"Is that Him? Just tell me, is that Him?"

"Yeah, yeah, Bartimaeus; that's Him."

"Then you better get out of my way because I'm about to lose my dignity."

Hear me, friend. You can't preserve your dignity and seek His Deity. You can't save your face and seek His face. At some point you are going to have to lose your spiritual manners. You will have to leave your Pentecostal, Baptist, or Presbyterian protocol behind you. You need to forget what you are supposed to do when, where, and how. You will have to reduce it down to the basics: "Is that Him? I think He's in the building! I think He's close." I don't know how you feel, but I refuse to let Him get that close to me and pass me by.

> *"God has always preferred spiritual hunger over spiritual ritual."*

Would Jesus pass us by? Absolutely. Jesus would have passed by the disciples when they were rowing a boat across the Sea of Galilee in the darkness of the night, but they cried out to Him (see John 6:16-21.) He would have walked past the blind man, but Bartimaeus called out and kept calling out until Jesus turned aside to see him. Jesus would have walked past the woman with the incurable bleeding problem too, but she stretched out her hand and touched the hem of His garment by faith.

Why don't you forget about your manners right now? It is time to lay aside your religious protocols, the things that dictate what is supposed to happen and when. God has always preferred spiritual hunger over spiritual ritual. Are you going to miss your moment? If you can feel Him edging closer and closer, then don't let Him get this close and pass you by.

Tommy Tenney, *The Daily Chase*

Water In the Desert

"Pray without ceasing." 1 THESSALONIANS 5:17

"Pray without ceasing." Pray in spite of no rain, wind, or fire. Whatever you do, don't curse the snow. Winter's wrath may have canceled important duties and obligations; life may have come to a screeching halt due to the accumulating snow. Just bundle up nice and cozy, prop your feet on the hearth, and sip on some hot chocolate.

Reservoirs today are full of water that melted from yesterday's storm. You are fruitful in summer because you were faithful in winter.

Your checkbook is in the red; your business is limping toward Chapter Eleven. An accident occurred, and midday has suddenly become midnight; your child is in the back of an ambulance being rushed to the hospital. You make a 911 call to Heaven. Rivers of glory flow into your life with miracles caught in their rushing current.

> *"While hell is raging and Heaven appears silent, whisper a prayer. Your answer is not denied, just delayed."*

How is it possible that a river is flowing in your desert? The breath of God swept across a mountaintop and melted a snowcap. Somewhere in the past you prayed a prayer you thought went unanswered. You could not see any form of precipitation—be it rain, sleet, or snow—yet you continued to pray.

You looked in every direction for a sign, but nothing caught your eye. When the earth all around you lay dry and barren, snow was gathering atop mountains. When you pray the will and Word of God, every prayer is answered . . . While hell is raging and Heaven appears silent, whisper a prayer. Your answer is not denied, just delayed.

Morton Bustard, *The Impassioned Soul*

$\mathcal{K}$nock the Limits off Your Life

"Therefore I say unto you, Whatsoever things you desire, when you pray, believe that you receive them, and you shall have them." MARK 11:24

The concept of Mark chapter 11 is that if you ask anything—if you can believe what you desire hard enough—God says it will be done. Somehow God gives us a little glimpse into our potential. Too often we are not willing to believe like God defines believe.

God does not say, "Everything is possible if you get the idea." Things don't become reality because we have an idea. We have to believe in the idea. We have to believe we can do it by committing ourselves to it—abandoning ourselves to it—even if it costs us our lives. That's what it takes to believe in the Lord Jesus Christ—to lose our lives—to abandon ourselves. We must say, "I'm going to go into eternity believing in Jesus. I'm not sure what's out there, but I'm going to ride on that Name and that atonement."

> *"Thinking is great. But all things are possible when we believe."*

Everything is possible if you will abandon yourself to an idea enough that you are willing to lose your life for it.

Jesus said in Mark chapter eleven, "Whatever you desire when you pray, believe you'll receive it, and you will have it." The word desire is the key. Being interested in or attracted to something is not desiring it. To desire means "to crave for something at the expense of losing everything." Thinking is great. But all things are possible when we believe.

_____

_____

_____

_____

_____

_____

_____

_____

_____

_____

_____

Myles Munroe, *Understanding Your Potential*

The **Personal Power Test**

"Finally, my brethren, be strong in the Lord, and in the power of his might. Put on the whole armor of God, that you may be able to stand against the wiles of the devil." EPHESIANS 6:10-11

It takes power to keep the body under control: the mouth clean and sweet, both physically and morally: the eye turned away from the thing that should not be thought about: the ear closed to what should not enter that in-gate of the heart: to allow no picture to hang upon the walls of your imagination that may not hang upon the walls of your home: to keep every organ of the body pure for nature's holy function only—that takes mighty power.

> *"...allow no picture to hang upon the walls of your imagination that may not hang upon the walls of your home."*

It will take a power that some of us have not known to let that glass go untouched, and that quieting drug untasted and unhandled. If the rear end of some pharmacies could speak out, many a story would startle our ears of struggles and defeats that tell sadly of utter lack of power.

It takes power to keep sweet in the home, where, if anywhere, the seamy side is apt to stick out. How many wooden oaths could kicked chairs and slammed doors tell of! After all the home-life comes close to being the real test of power, does it not? It takes power to be gracious and strong, and patient and tender, and cheery, in the commonplace things, and the commonplace places, does it not?

Now, I have something to tell you that to me is very wonderful, and constantly growing in wonder. It is this—the Master has thought of all that! For every subtle, strong temptation, for every cry of need, for every low moan of disappointment, for every locking of the jaws in the resolution of despair, for every disheartened look out into the morrow, for every yearningly ambitious heart there comes tonight that unmistakable ringing promise of His—ye shall have power.

S. D. Gordon, *Quiet Talks on Power*

*F*orgive Yourself!

". . . and him that comes to me I will in no way cast out." JOHN 6:37B

When Jesus prayed, "Father, forgive them," His words reached back in time to enfold the entire history of man before the Lord's incarnation. They covered the "present world" of His day, and reached ahead to the world that would exist after His return to Heaven. Now two thousand years or more after Jesus uttered those words, we are covered with divine forgiveness and pardon.

> *"Forgiveness puts the handcuffs of Heaven on hell itself."*

The day God forgave, flesh was affected, angels were affected, hell was affected, demons were affected, and the devil himself was bound. No matter how bad your life has been, the river of God's forgiveness will flow again into the cold, bitter, and hardened valleys of your heart when you come into the presence of forgiveness.

When forgiveness is present, the enemy of your soul has to back up without a word being said to him. His hands are tied and he cannot work in the presence of forgiveness. Forgiveness puts the handcuffs of Heaven on hell itself.

Jesus transformed the life of Mary Magdalene the prostitute, but she still probably wished that she could undo the mistakes and pain of her past. She couldn't. Mary faced the same choice we all face: She could remain a slave to unforgiveness by clinging to her anger and resentment toward the men who abused her and the people who rejected her; or she could accept God's forgiveness, choose to forgive, and begin a life of freedom. We know the choice Mary made. What about you?

Tommy Tenney, *The Daily Chase*

No Place Like Home

"And when he came to himself, he said, How many hired servants of my father's have bread enough and to spare, and perish with hunger!"
LUKE 15:17

If by chance you slipped out the back door of Father's house and now find yourself in a pigpen, come on home. The devil can keep you there only as long as you allow him to convince you that you have no value. The reason you have taken up residence with hogs and share their supper is you listened to the enemy. He told you that you were worthless. He relentlessly attacked your self-esteem simply because he knew a bargain when he saw one.

> *"The devil has tried to convince you that coming home is complicated. It's actually quite simple. Turn around. The road that led you away will bring you back."*

As he sat in the pigsty, the prodigal son put himself in perspective. The lowest person on Dad's payroll lived a whole lot better than he did. The farmhands who fed the slop to the hogs were not expected to eat it. The greatest night the son had on the road couldn't compare to the dullest day at Dad's place. Life on the outside was not all that it was cracked up to be (see Luke. 15:11-17).

When you have reached the pigpen, you have reached the lowest level. The devil showed you dreams of stardom when all along he intended to dump you into the mire. The friend-turned-enemy never ever thought of you as anything more than a pig.

While you are hanging with hogs, back at home Dad is pacing the floor. His mind is constantly on you. When you packed up and pulled out, he didn't disown you. Everything is in place just as you left it, waiting for your return. For Heaven's sake, don't allow something so valuable to end up in the trash! Hurry on back.

The devil has tried to convince you that coming home is complicated. It's actually quite simple. Turn around. The road that led you away will bring you back.

Morton Bustard, *The Impassioned Soul*

*O*n the Anvil of the Knees

"He went away again the second time, and prayed, saying, 'O my Father, if this cup may not pass away from me, unless I drink it, your will be done.'"
MATTHEW 26:42

One enters with a holy hush over his spirit, and, with awe in his eyes, looks at Jesus in Gethsemane. This great Jesus! Son of God: God the Son. No draftsman's pencil ever drew the line between His divinity and humanity; nor ever shall. For the union of divine and human is itself divine.

How sympathetic those inky black shadows! It takes bright light to make black shadows. Yet they were not black enough. Intense men can get so absorbed in the shadows as to forget the light.

> "True prayer is wrought out upon the knees alone with God."

The extreme grips Him. May there not possibly be some other way rather than this—this! A bit of that prayer comes to us in tones strangely altered by deepest emotion. "If it be possible—let this cup pass." There is still a clinging to a possibility, some possibility other than that of this nightmare vision. And a parenthetical prayer for strength goes up. And the angels come with sympathetic strengthening. With what awe must they have ministered.

By and by a calmer mood asserts itself and out of the a darkness second petition comes. It tells of the tide's turning, and the victory full and complete. A changed petition this! "Since this cup may not pass— since only thus can Thy great plan for a world be wrought out—Thy— will—slowly but very distinctly the words comes—"Thy—will—be—done."

True prayer is wrought out upon the knees alone with God. Shall we not plan to meet God alone, habitually, with the door shut, and the Book open, and the will pliant so we may be ready for this holy partnership of prayer. Then will come the clearer vision, the broader purpose, the truer wisdom, the real unselfishness, the simplicity of claiming and expecting...until the night be gone and the dawning break, and the ink-black shadows be chased away by the brightness of His presence.

_____

_____

_____

_____

_____

S. D. Gordon, *Quiet Talks on Prayer*

*T*hank God for Small Things

"Not that I speak in respect of need: for I have learned, in whatsoever state I am, therewith to be content." PHILIPPIANS 4:11

If you are praying, "Lord, make me bigger," you are probably miserable, although prayerful. Did you know you can be prayerful and still be miserable? Anytime you use prayer to change God, who is perfect, instead of using prayer to change yourself, you are miserable. Stop manipulating God! Stop trying to learn something you can say to God to make Him do what He knows you are not ready to endure or receive. Instead, try praying this: "Lord, make me better." I admit that better is harder to measure and not as noticeable to the eye. But better will overcome bigger every time.

> *"I believe that God grooms us for greatness in the stockades of struggle."*

The real, rich inner stability that comes from gradual success is far more lasting and beneficial than the temperamental theatrics of spiritual yuppies who have never learned their own vulnerabilities. We must not take ourselves too seriously. I believe that God grooms us for greatness in the stockades of struggle.

What a joy it is to be at peace with who you are and where you are in your life. How restful it is to not try and beat the clock with friends or try to prove anything to foes. You will never change their minds anyway, so change your own. I want to be better—to have a better character, better confidence, and a better attitude! The desire to be bigger will not allow you to rest, relax, or enjoy your blessing. The desire to be better, however, will afford you a barefoot stroll down a deserted beach. You can sit in the sand, throw shells into the water, and shiver when the tide rushes up too high. Sing into the wind a song out of tune. It may not harmonize, but it will be full of therapy. There are probably many things you didn't get done and so much you have left to do. But isn't it nice to sigh, relax, and just thank God for the things—the little, tiny, small things—that you know He brought you through.

T. D. Jakes, *365 Days to Healing, Blessings, and Freedom*

You Are Not Junk

"...to whom God would make known what is the riches of the glory of this mystery among the Gentiles; which is Christ in you, the hope of glory."
COLOSSIANS 1:27

There are many people who are being passed by because others don't see what is in them. But God has shown me what's in me, and I know it is in you too. My job is to stop you and say: "Can you see what's in you? Do you know your potential? Do you know that you are not just someone born in a ghetto over the hill? There's a wealth of potential in you."

A sculptor sees so differently. They say Michelangelo used to walk around a block of marble for days—just walking around it, talking to himself. First he would see things in the rock; then he would go and take them out.

> *"When God looks at you, He sees things that everybody else ignores"*

Insight like that of a sculptor is seen in the Bible. When the world dumps and rejects you, and you land on the garbage heap of the world, God walks along and picks you up. He looks deep within you and sees a person of great worth.

Don't ever let anybody throw you away. You are not junk. When God looks at you, He sees things that everybody else ignores. You are worth so much that Jesus went to Calvary to salvage and reclaim you. The Spirit of God connected to your spirit is the only true judge of your worth. Don't accept the opinions of others because they do not see what God sees.

Relinquish What You Don't Understand

"I am crucified with Christ; nevertheless I live; yet not I, but Christ lives in me." GALATIANS 2:20A

The power of relinquishment is the ability to relinquish what we don't understand to a divine mandate. We do not want to walk away from a place in which God sees potential. Where He leads, we must follow, and He will receive all the glory.

Arturo Tuscani was a famous Italian symphony conductor. His specialty was the works of Beethoven. One night in Philadelphia, Pennsylvania, Tuscani conducted the Philadelphia Symphony Orchestra in a program that included the Ninth Symphony, one of the most difficult pieces to direct. It was so majestic and so moving that when the piece was completed, the audience stood for round after round of applause. Tuscani took his bows again and again. He turned to the orchestra; they bowed. The audience continued to clap and cheer. The orchestra members themselves were smiling and clapping. Finally, Tuscani turned his back to the audience, and spoke only to the orchestra. He said, "Ladies, gentlemen—I am nothing. You are nothing. Beethoven is everything."

> *"We do not want to walk away from a place in which God sees potential."*

When you think of this story, remember the divine power of relinquishment. Regardless of how eloquent you are, or how gifted you are with a voice to sing like an angel, throw yourself at the feet of Jesus and let Him take the serpent out of your gift.

When you commit your future to God and let Him set your course, He will direct you to places of unprecedented freedom and usefulness in the Kingdom. First, you must be willing to say with the apostle Paul, "...nevertheless I live; yet not I, but Christ lives in me." Declare to Him, "I am nothing. You are everything. Here I am, and here are my gifts, abilities, and dreams, Lord. I throw it all down at Your feet. I give You all, and I hold nothing back."

Tommy Tenney, *The Daily Chase*

Making It Through The Night

"In this you greatly rejoice, though now for a season, if need be, you are in sadness through many trials: that the genuineness of your faith, being much more precious than of gold that perishes." 1 PETER 1: 6-7A

I am an advocate of praying for divine health and have been blessed by witnessing miracles of healing. Several times in my own life the Lord's healing virtue has been released, bringing a speedy if not instant recovery. However, after living for God for any length of time, we learn that being His children does not exempt us from suffering.

Sometimes it requires all our effort to last through the darkness of night. Perhaps you are in the proverbial nighttime of your life. Things have taken a drastic shift; everything has changed from "going great" to collapsing around you. Instead of days of sunshine and laughter you find yourself in a downpour of despair.

> *"Sometimes it requires all our effort to last through the darkness of night."*

You toss and turn and wonder if the sun will ever shine again. You sincerely want to believe, but you are overwhelmed with doubt because of the continual onslaught of the enemy.

Then somewhere amid the restlessness you hear the chirping of a bird. Another answers. Soon the chirping turns into a song and once again tiny creatures raise their beaks toward heaven in praise of the Creator.

As the sun slowly begins to rise in the east, rays of light beam through the window of your soul and you feel the warmth of a brand new day. You know that it is over. Nighttime does not last forever, and neither do trials.

Morton Bustard, *The Impassioned Soul*

$\mathcal{N}$urturing to Endure Trials

"Blessed is the people that know the joyful sound: they shall walk, O Lord, in the light of they countenance." PSALM 89:15 (KJV)

We often face discouragement in this world. Many have never had anyone who believed in them. Even after achieving some level of success in one area or another, many have not had anyone to point out their potential. Isn't it amazing how we can see so much potential in others, yet find it difficult to unlock our own hidden treasure? Highly motivated people are not exempt from needing someone to underline their strengths and weaknesses. It is impossible to perceive how much stronger we might be if we had had stronger nurturing. Nurturing is the investment necessary to stimulate the potential that we possess. Without nurturing, inner strengths may remain dormant. Therefore it is crucial to our development that there be some degree of nurturing the intrinsic resources we possess.

> *"Nurturing is the investment necessary to stimulate the potential that we possess."*

There is a difference in the emotional makeup of a child who has had a substantial deposit of affection and affirmation. Great affirmation occurs when someone invests into our personhood. I believe that people are the greatest investments in the world. A wonderful bond exists between the person who invests and the one in whom the investment is made. This bond evolves from the heart of anyone who recognizes the investment was made before the person accomplished the goal. Anyone will invest in a sure success, but aren't we grateful when someone supports us when we were somewhat of a risk?

Although it is true that fire will not destroy gold, it is important to note that fire purifies the gold. When God gets ready to polish His gold, He uses fiery trials. The finished product is a result of the fiery process. Whenever you see someone shining with the kind of brilliancy that enables God to look down and see Himself, you are looking at someone who has been through the furnace of affliction.

_____

_____

_____

_____

_____

You Have Part of God

"Do you look on things according to the outward appearance? If any man trusts to himself that he is Christ's, let him of himself think this again, that, as he is Christ's, even so are we Christ's." 2 CORINTHIANS 10:7

You will never discover who you were meant to be if you use another person to find yourself. You will never know what you can do by using what I've done to measure your ability. You will never know why you exist if you use my existence to measure it. All you will see is what I've done or who I am. If you want to know who you are, look at God. The key to understanding life is in the source of life, not in the life itself. You are who you are because God took you out of Himself. If you want to know who you are, you must look at the Creator, not the creation.

> *"If you want to know who you are, you must look at the Creator, not the creation"*

There are three words we use to describe God. First, God is omniscient-which means He is all knowing. Second, God is omnipresent—which means God is present everywhere. Third, God is omnipotent—which means God is always potent. God is always full of power—He has in Him the potential for everything. From the beginning, God gave that same ability to be potent to all His creation. He planted within each person or thing He created—including you—the ability to be much more than it is at any one moment.

You are somebody because you came out of God, and He leaked some of Himself into you.

*T*he Testing Ground

"But let perseverance have its perfect work, that you may be perfect and complete, lacking nothing." JAMES 1:4

When we encounter trouble, God expects us to obey. Trials require us to wait for direction or revelation. God is usually silent during a trial. He seems to be ignoring us as we cry, shout, and beg for some sign, any sign, to tell us what to do. But the purpose of a test in school is to prove what you already know. Would you raise your hand in class during a test and ask the teacher to tell you the answers? You know the answers. You just have to remember them. That's what the Holy Spirit is for. He's your spiritual memory bank. He's also your comfort. He'll tell you not to panic about the test and instead to ask yourself what you're being tested on. You're being tested on what you believe. And once you know what you believe, you can settle, if a little uncomfortably, into your situation until your change arrives. And it will arrive.

> *"Would you raise your hand in class during a test and ask the teacher to tell you the answers?"*

On the way to celebrating that change is a road called "patience" and a place called "time." That's why James tells us to rejoice when we find ourselves in the midst of a trial (see James 1:2) It means a blessing is on the way. As we patiently suffer, allowing our trials to prepare us for change, God uses that time to work every part of that trial for our good. He wants to bless us. He wants to prosper us. He wants to provide for us. But many of us would abort our blessings if God did not prepare us to receive them first.

Think about a weight lifter. He doesn't start off lifting 300 pounds. He learns to lift progressively. Some of us can't handle the $25,000 salary we're making now, and we're asking God to bless us with millions. So He has to test us and take what we already have to teach us how to appreciate it and be a good steward over it. Then He can bless us with more. As we handle what God gives us with wisdom, generosity, and gratitude, He gives us more to handle, in every area of our lives.

_____

_____

_____

_____

_____

Dr. Wanda Turner, *Celebrating Change*

Ask What You Will

"...for truly I say unto you, if ye have faith as a grain of mustard seed, ye shall say unto this mountain, 'Move from here to yonder place;' and it shall move; and nothing shall be impossible unto you." MATTHEW 17:20

We never hear of Jesus moving an actual mountain. But He chooses the thing most difficult for His illustration. Can you imagine a mountain moving off into the sea? If you know mountains down in your country you cannot imagine it actually occurring. "—And shall not doubt in his heart—" That is Jesus' definition of faith. "—But shall believe that what he saith cometh to pass; he shall have it. Therefore, I say unto you, all things whatsoever ye pray and ask for, believe that ye receive them, and ye shall have them." How utterly sweeping this last statement! And to make it more positive it is preceded by the emphatic "therefore—I—say—unto—you." Both whatsoever and whosoever are here. Anything and anybody.

> *"That word abide is a strong word... It means moving in to stay."*

In John 14:13-14: "And whatsoever you shall ask in my name, that will I do, that the Father may be glorified in the Son. If you shall ask anything in my name, I will do it." The repetition is to emphasize the unlimited sweep of what may be asked.

John 15:7: "If you abide in me, and my words abide in you—" That word abide is a strong word. It does not mean that you leave your cards; not to hire a night's lodging; not to pitch a tent, or run up a miner's shanty, or a lumberman's shack. It means moving in to stay. "—Ask whatsoever ye will—" There is nothing said directly about God's will. There is something said about our wills. "—and it shall be done unto you."

If you abide in Me, and My words sway you, please ask what is it your will to ask. And—softly, reverently now—I will lay Myself out to bring that thing to pass for you. That is the force of His words here.

_____

_____

_____

_____

_____

_____

S. D. Gordon, *Quiet Talks on Prayer*

We Need Feelings

"For which cause we do not lose heart; but though our outward man perishes, yet the inward man is renewed day by day." 2 CORINTHIANS 4:16

We went through a phase once when we thought real faith meant having no feelings. Now I believe that life without feelings is like a riverbed without water. The water is what makes the river a place of activity and life. You don't want to destroy the water, but you do need to control it. Feelings that are out of control are like the floodwaters of a river. The gushing currents of boisterous waters over their banks can bring death and destruction. They must be held at bay by restrictions and limitations. Although we don't want to be controlled by feelings, we must have access to our emotions. We need to allow ourselves the pleasure and pain of life.

> *"We need to allow ourselves the pleasure and pain of life."*

Emotional pain is to the spirit what physical pain is to the body. Pain warns us that something is out of order and may require attention. Pain warns us that something in our body is not healed. In the same way, when pain fills our heart, we know that we have an area where healing or restoration is needed. We dare not ignore these signals, and neither dare we let them control us.

Above all, we need to allow the Spirit of God to counsel us and guide us through the challenges of realignment when upheavals occur in our lives. Even the finest limousine requires a regular schedule of tune-ups or realignments. Minor adjustments increase performance and productivity.

It is important to understand the difference between minor and major adjustments. The removal of a person from our lives is painful, but it is not a major adjustment. Whether you realize it or not, people are being born and dying every day. They are coming and going, marrying and divorcing, falling in love and falling out of love. You can survive the loss of people, but you can't survive without God! He is the force that allows you to overcome when people have taken you under.

_____

_____

_____

_____

_____

_____

_____

T. D. Jakes, *365 Days to Healing, Blessings, and Freedom*

Life Is Seasonal

"I am Alpha and Omega, the beginning and the end. I will give unto him that is thirsty of the fountain of the water of life freely." REVELATION 21:6B

In times past when you prayed, rain came pouring down in torrents. Fire from Heaven fell, consuming the sacrifice and bringing vindication to your cause. Gusts of wind blew into your upper room, filling you with power and unspeakable joy.

> *"God knew that you needed a winter to endure your summer."*

Now as you pray, there is not a drop of rain, spark of fire, or enough breeze to alter the flight of a feather. But it's snowing, and perhaps you're complaining, thinking God isn't responding. There is victory in every season of life; you must work with what God gives you.

Job implied that the treasure in the snow is reserved for the day of battle (see Job 38:22-23). God knows that somewhere in life you will be engaged in spiritual warfare. Drought will threaten to destroy your crops. Something totally unexpected will suddenly confront you, not allowing any time for prayer. You are going to need an emergency survival kit to make it. This is the treasure of the snow.

A rose bloomed in your arid desert. A fountain penetrated from beneath the concrete floor of your wilderness, providing sustenance for life's journey. As you stood with mouth agape, luxuriating in the brilliant leaves of fall, God knew that you needed a winter to endure your summer.

Morton Bustard, *The Impassioned Soul*

There's No Retirement In The Bible

"But as it is written, 'Eye has not seen, nor ear heard, neither have entered into the heart of man, the things which God has prepared for them that love him.'" I CORINTHIANS 2:9

There are times when we get tired of our jobs. In fact, we get so tired that we look for retirement. And when we get it, we just want to retire—we want to stop permanently. God says to us: "You have it all wrong. Your thinking is wrong. There is no retirement in the Bible. It is not in My thinking." God doesn't think retirement. The only thing God thinks is rest. Why? Because God knows you have eternity to go just like He does. God wants you to assist Him in creating and developing and dominating and ruling forever and ever and ever. That's a long time. The wealth of your potential is so rich it requires an eternal life to bring it out.

> *"The only thing God thinks is rest"*

We are not going to be in heaven for a million years bowing down around a throne. God doesn't have an ego problem. He doesn't need us to tell Him how nice He is. In fact, He was nice without us. We make Him look pretty bad. We've really messed up God. We came out of God. We are the only ones made in His image, and look what we did. God was better off without us. He doesn't need our praises to make Him feel high.

Now don't get me wrong. I'm not talking down heaven. I'm trying to open your mind. God has so much in store for you. The Holy Spirit will continue to unfold it and reveal it until eternity ends—which it won't. God has placed enough potential in you to last forever. Try to do as much now as you can. Pack as much as you can into the 70 to 100 years you have here. Go for it. Go for a hunk of gold. Go for the mountain that has the gold in it. Go for the whole thing. Because if you can think it, you can do it. God is the limit of your ability. He won't allow you to think it if you can't do it.

No One Hears Like the Lord

"We are of God: he that knows God hears us; he that is not of God does not hear us." 1 JOHN 4:6

I can think of no better illustration of this scripture than the ten lepers in the Bible (see Luke 17:11-19). These ten distraught, grossly afflicted men were entombed by the prison of their own limitations. No matter who they were before, now they were lepers. Like bad apples, they were separated and cast out from friends and family. Pain brings together strange bedfellows. Ten men huddled together on the side of the road heard that Jesus was passing by. The most frightening thing that could happen in any hurting person's life is for Jesus to just pass by. These men, however, seized the moment. They took a risk...they cried out to Him. Desperate people do desperate things. Have you ever had a moment in your life that pushed you into a radical decision? These lepers cried out!

> *"He can hear the desperate cry of someone who has nothing left to lose."*

No one can hear like the Lord does. He can hear your thoughts afar off (see Ps. 139:2), so you know He can hear the desperate cry of someone who has nothing left to lose. When the ten cried, He responded. There were no sparks, no lightning, and no thunder, but the power of His words whisked them off into the realm of miracles. He told them to go show themselves to the priest. Thus they walked toward a goal. Step by step they walked. I don't know which dusty step it was along the way that brought to them a cleansing of their leprous condition. Perhaps, as with most people, it is no one step that brings you to success, but a relentless plowing through of obstacles and insecurities that brings the result of prayers answered and miracles realized.

Nevertheless, somewhere between Jesus' words and their going to the priest, they stepped into the greatest experience of their lives. Where there had been white, encrusted flesh, there was new skin as clear as a baby's. That is the wonderful thing about knowing Jesus—He takes away the old ugly scars of sin and leaves newness and fresh beginnings.

Challenge Tradition

"And it shall come to pass in the last days, says God, I will pour out of my Spirit upon all flesh: and your sons and your daughters shall prophesy, and your young men shall see visions, and your old men shall dream dreams:"
ACTS 2:17

Traditions are powerful enemies of potential because they are full of security. We don't have to think when we do something the way we've always done it. Neither do we receive the incentive to grow and be creative because our new ideas may interfere with the conventional way of doing things.

The tragedy is that the tradition, which probably served its purpose well when it was started, prevents the accomplishment of the purpose for which it was established. Remember, no matter how good the present system, is there's always a better way. Don't be imprisoned by the comfort of the known. Be an explorer, not just a passenger. Don't allow yourself to become trapped by tradition or you will do and become nothing. Your present level of success will be your highest

> *"Don't allow yourself to become trapped by tradition or you will do and become nothing."*

level of success, and God, who is not trapped within tradition, will find someone else to do what you could have done.

Use your imagination. Dream big and find new ways to respond to present situations and responsibilities. Then you will uncover never-ending possibilities that inspire you to reach for continually higher achievements. We are sons of the "Creator," who created us to be creative. Nowhere in Scripture did God repeat an identical act.

Refrain from accepting or believing, "We've never done it that way before." Now is the time to try something different. The release of your full potential demand that you move beyond the present traditions of your home, family, job, and church—in essence, throughout your life. To maximize your life you must be willing to release ineffective traditions for new methods.

We Can Do It!

"Let your light so shine before men, that they may see your good works, and glorify your Father which is in heaven." MATTHEW 5:16

It is wonderful to have a plan, but that means nothing if you have no power to perform the plan and accomplish the purpose. God sends people in and out of your life to exercise your faith and develop your character. When they are gone, they leave you with the enriched reality that your God is with you to deliver you wherever you go! Moses died and left Joshua in charge, but God told him, "As I was with Moses, so I will be with thee" (Josh. 1:5b - KJV). Joshua never would have learned that while Moses was there. You learn this kind of thing when "Moses" is gone. Power is developed in the absence of human assistance. Then we can test the limits of our resourcefulness and the magnitude of the favor of God.

> *"You see more clearly that the people who treated you the worst were actually preparing you for the best."*

As we go further, you may want to reevaluate who your real friends are. You see more clearly that the people who treated you the worst were actually preparing you for the best. They stripped from you the cumbersome weights and entanglements that hindered the birth of inner resilience.

Yes, such friends leave us feeling naked and even vulnerable, but it is through those feelings that we begin to adapt and see our survival instincts peak. There is within the most timid person—beneath that soft, flaccid demeanor—a God-given strength that supersedes any weakness he appeared to have. The Bible puts it this way: "I can do all things through Christ which strengthenth me!" (Phil. 4:13 - KJV)

Greater still is the fact that we gain great direction through rejection. Rejection helps us focus on new horizons without the hindrances of wondering, "What if?"

T. D. Jakes, *365 Days to Healing, Blessings, and Freedom*

You Must Cooperate

"Now unto him that is able to do exceedingly abundantly above all that We ask or think, according to the power that works in us, unto him be glory in the church by Christ Jesus throughout all ages, world without end. Amen."
EPHESIANS 3:20-21

God's potential is far greater than anything we can ask Him to do. Everything that is visible came out of God. Everything that we yet will see is still within Him. Because we came out of God, that same potential is available to us. But there's a catch. God's power must be at work within us before we can tap that power.

When Jesus told His disciples that He was going away, He promised them that the Holy Spirit would come to be with them forever (see John 14:16). Moments before His ascension to Heaven, Jesus also promised that the power of the Holy Spirit (see Acts 1:8) would equip His followers to be His messengers.

> *"When you are in tune with the Holy Spirit, you can do things this world has never seen."*

Is the Holy Spirit present in your life? Are you flowing in a consistent, empowering relationship that undergirds your every thought, dream, and plan? Or are you trying to do great things without the power of the Spirit?

Your cooperation with the work of the Holy Spirit is the means by which God reveals the stuff He took from Himself and gave to you. When you are in tune with the Holy Spirit, you can do things this world has never seen. The power's there. It's up to you whether you make the connection that releases the power. If that power isn't working in you, your potential is being wasted.

Myles Munroe, *Releasing Your Potential*

The Gift of Goodness

"And let us not be weary in well doing: for in due season we shall reap, if we do not lose heart." GALATIANS 6:9

Most of us know instinctively what it means to be good. Being good makes us feel good inside because we know we're pleasing to God. If we're not good, we feel crummy because we know we haven't acted the way God wants us to act. Only those who have seared their consciences through continually bad behavior don't feel a twinge of guilt when they misbehave.

> *"Our small efforts at kindness can change people's lives more than we will ever know."*

The Bible has a great deal to say about being good. In Luke 6:27, Jesus commands us to "do good to them that hate you." The apostle Paul writes, "For we are his workmanship, created in Christ Jesus unto good works, which God has beforehand ordained that we should walk in them." (Ephesians 2:10).

The prophet Micah says, "He has showed you, O man, what is good. And what does the Lord require of you? To act justly and to love mercy and to walk humbly with your God." (Micah 6:8 NIV).

How do you want people to remember the encounters they've had with you? Our small efforts at kindness can change people's lives more than we will ever know. Since it takes so little time and energy to change the world for the better, why not make an effort to do it every day?

Be good. You just might change the world!
Those who say it's easy to be good
have never tried to be good.

—C. S. Lewis

Belief or Unbelief

"For what says the scripture? 'Abraham believed God, and it was counted unto him for righteousness.'" ROMANS 4:3

Each morning we awake and go about our day based on one of two beliefs: Either we believe in God and our every action is motivated by this central value, or we do not really believe and our actions reflect so.

You can be a believer yet act as though there is no God. Whenever you fret over life circumstances, you immediately demonstrate unbelief. Whenever you move out of fear or anxiety, you believe a lie about God's nature.

> *"In what circumstances do you act as an "unbeliever?*

Each day your actions affirm or convict you of your belief system. It reveals who the central focus of your life really is—you or God. It reveals who you place your ultimate trust in–you or God. It is one of the great paradoxes for believers. One day we can believe Him to move mountains. The next day we can question His very existence.

Peter believed God and walked on water.
A sick woman touched the hem of His garment and was healed.
A Canaanite woman believed and freed her daughter from demon-possession.

In what circumstances do you act as an "unbeliever"? Ask God to increase your level of trust so that your actions match up with one who believes every day.

Expressing The Hidden You

"He that sows the good seeds is the Son of man." MATTHEW 13:37B

The tremendous potential you and I have been given is locked inside us, waiting for demands to be made on it. We have a responsibility to use what God stored in us for the good of the world. We dare not leave this planet with it. Many of us are aware of the ability we have inside, but we have been frustrated by our failure to release that ability. Some of us blame our historical circumstances. Others blame social status. Still others transfer the responsibility for their failure and frustration to their lack of formal education or their less than ideal opportunities. Too much of this treasure is buried every day, untapped and untouched, in the cemeteries of our world.

> *"Too much of this treasure is buried every day, untapped and untouched, in the cemeteries of our world."*

Over the years, I have come to realize that no excuse can be given to justify the destruction of the seed of potential that God placed within you. You can become the man or woman you were born to be. You can accomplish the vision you saw. You can build that business you planned. You can develop that school you imagine. You are the only one who can stop you. No matter what your environment, you have the ability to change your attitude and your internal environment until they are conducive to the germination of your potential seed. You must not add to the wealth of the graveyard. You owe it to the next generation to live courageously so the treasure of your potential is unleashed. The world needs what God deposited in you for the benefit of your contemporaries and all the generations to follow.

Tap the untapped. Release the reservoir.

Myles Munroe, *Releasing Your Potential*

The Job of Unloading is Yours

"Therefore...let us lay aside every weight, and the sin which does so easily entangle us, and let us run with perseverance the race that is set before us."
HEBREWS 12:1

Many times these people will say, "I've asked God to take it away and He just won't." You could tell them the truth and say, "No, God said for you to do it. The Scripture says, '...let us lay aside every weight.' The job is in your portfolio, not God's." However, don't be surprised if they reply, "I've tried that. I just can't...."

God would not tell us to "lay aside" something if we were not fully capable of doing it. It is not that we cannot; it is that we will not. We have established habits and imposed things upon ourselves that have nothing to do with the gospel.

> *"You will never come into a dimension of God's power until you learn how to prioritize and unload."*

Balanced priorities are essential. Some of us tend to become consumed with the work of God while actually neglecting our relationship with Him. We get so busy doing the things of God that we sacrifice our walk with God.

You will never come into a dimension of God's power until you learn how to prioritize and unload. Many things in life will come along to deter you from your goal or slow your progress. Nevertheless, God's thermometer stays fixed; the labels on His bottles don't change with circumstances. He is "the same yesterday, and today, and for ever." (Heb. 13:8). His prescription for health in good times and hard times hasn't changed: "I urge therefore, that, first of all, supplications, prayers, intercessions, and giving of thanks, be made for all men;" (1 Tim. 2:1).

The most popular excuse you hear is, "I just don't have time." Yet all of us are given the same number of hours each day. Each of us has 1,440 minutes to "spend" each day. We decide how to use the 86,400 seconds per day, and our management of that time makes all the difference. Some things must be set aside for later, and some things must be unloaded altogether.

Tommy Tenney, *The Daily Chase*

Beauty for Ashes

"And this word, 'Yet once more,' signifies the removing of those things that are shaken, as of things that are made, that those things which cannot be shaken may remain." HEBREWS 12:27

What are ashes? They are the unburned particles and grayish powder left after a thing has been burned. They are the ruins or remains of something destroyed. The furnace of affliction is full of ruined and destroyed lives. To the world, it looks like nothing. In reality, it is the workshop from which God crafts His most miraculous and glorious works of art. Second Corinthians 4:17 sums it up like this: "For our light affliction, which is but for a moment, works for us a far more exceeding and eternal weight of glory;"

> *"In order for gold to be purified, it has to be heated until it melts."*

If you look at God's handiwork throughout Scripture—you'll find that whenever He works with gold, it's always pure gold. In other words, He only uses gold that is free from impurities or other metals. In order for gold to be purified, it has to be heated until it melts and all the impurities, which are not as heavy as the gold itself, rise to the top and are drawn off.

Our affliction, which is "lighter" than the "weight" of the glory of eternal life with God, is brought to the surface when the fire of adversity is allowed to rage in our lives...The crises, the troubles, the losses, the embarrassments, and the struggles . . .usher us into the furnace of affliction. And those troubles and trials that satan has meant to destroy us, instead burn us down to a place where "the things that can be shaken will be shaken so that those that cannot be shaken can remain." But that's where God declares, "I'm going to give you beauty for everything broken, stolen, marred, or desecrated by satan in your life. Everything burned up—dreams, visions, marriages, finances, ministries, health—I'm going to return to you in glorious condition."

Dr. Wanda Turner, *Celebrating Change*

Hard Work—and Then Some

"For we are his workmanship, created in Christ Jesus unto good works, which God has beforehand ordained that we should walk in them."
EPHESIANS 2:10

Excellence never comes cheaply. It involves desire, discipline, and determination.

Renowned baritone Sherrill Milnes is a good example of someone who put in long, hard hours in an attempt to become better at his chosen profession. His wife, Nancy Stokes Milnes, told the New York Opera Newsletter that when she and her husband had dinner with a famous voice coach, they played him a recording Sherill had made when he was in college. Then they asked him, "What do you think about this voice?"

> *"You can't tell people what their dreams are or what the limits of their dreams should be."*

The voice coach shook his head sadly, "Not a chance," he said. "Don't encourage this person. Tell him to get a day job."

When Sherill said, "Why, that's me," the voice coach's jaw dropped. "I'll never discourage another singer again," he said.

Mrs. Milnes writes, "You never can tell. The most gifted person can walk into your studio and achieve very little. Someone whose talent seems okay can work and work until he or she can make it. You can't tell people what their dreams are, or what the limits of their dreams should be. It's up to them to tell you."

James E. Byrnes, who served as secretary of state under Harry Truman, once said that he learned early in life that the difference between those who succeed in life and those who don't is determined by three little words, "and then some." He explained, "The top people did what was expected of them, and then some. They were considerate and thoughtful of others, and then some. They met their obligations and responsibilities fairly and squarely, and then some. They could be counted on in an emergency, and then some."

These are excellent words to live by—and then some.

Pat Williams, *American Scandal*

Marriage is Not a Dream

*"Now no disciplining for the present seems to be joyful, but painful:
nevertheless afterward it yields the peaceful fruit of righteousness unto them
which are trained thereby."* HEBREWS 12:11

Realizing that marriage is not a dream but real life can also help you to wait patiently. Instead of merely being envious, get with a godly woman and see the extra load she carries. Look at all she cannot do, instead of the fact that she has a man in her house. Understand that in reality, married life is not constant communication, daily roses, hugs and kisses, breakfast in bed, and sheer bliss. Marriage is every bit as much work as it is wonderful, even in God's way and time. It is good, but don't be deceived into mistaking it for Heaven.

> *"Although there is a romantic inside every one of us, you must be realistic regarding marriage or the shock could be devastating."*

Since no spouse is perfect, learning to live "as one" is not without its tears. Marriage alone is not a cure-all or answer to every heartfelt need. If you think it is, you had better just keep waiting, for that kind of marriage doesn't exist. Although there is a romantic inside every one of us, you must be realistic regarding marriage or the shock could be devastating.

Developing patience is hard. Getting married ahead of God's timing is worse. God may not work according to your time schedule, but He does have your best interests in mind.

_____

_____

_____

_____

_____

_____

_____

_____

_____

_____

_____

Debbie Jones & Jackie Kendall, *Lady in Waiting—Meditations of The Heart*

God's Instruction Manual

"All scripture is given by inspiration of God, and is profitable for doctrine, for reproof, for correction, for instruction in righteousness: that the man of God may be complete, thoroughly equipped unto all good works." 2 TIMOTHY 3:16

Do you read manuals? Any manufacturer of a piece of equipment—a refrigerator, a microwave, a television, a toaster, —gives you a manual when you buy their product. When you open the manual, the first thing you read is: Before plugging in this product, read this manual carefully. But most of us don't, right? I know I don't.

> *"If you want a piece of equipment to operate at its maximum potential, you have to follow the manufacturer's instructions."*

We are excellent, complexly designed, tremendously built, intricately put together pieces of equipment. But we don't know what we can do. We can't even imagine the full extent of our potential. Knowing this, God sent us a manual that contains a description of our parts. He said, "Now this first part is your spirit and the second part is your soul and the third part is your body. Now here is what the body is supposed to do—here is what the soul can do—here is what the spirit can do." God also tells us the potential of this equipment called human beings. In His manual, He lists all the things we are capable of doing.

When God first presented this piece of equipment called man, something went wrong. Instead of taking it back to the manufacturer to be fixed, we took it to a second-rate, second-class, unskilled technician. And look what he did. He muddled the job. We submitted God's equipment and product to satan, who is an unauthorized dealer with no genuine parts.

But God loved us so much that, even though the warranty had run out, He decided to take back the product. God is starting all over again—and He's putting in His own parts. God is rebuilding and remaking us. He knows us better than anybody else, because He is our Creator. His Word, the Bible, reveals much about His attitude toward our potential.

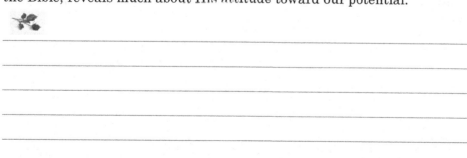

*I*nvestments With No Return

"So the men sat down, in number about five thousand. Then he took the five loaves and the two fishes, and looking up to heaven, he blessed them, ...And they did all eat, and were filled." JOHN 6:10-11

The 5,000 whom Jesus fed with five loaves of bread and two fishes enjoyed the miracles. They were attracted to the spectacular. As long as Jesus was ministering to their needs and not to their souls, they stayed around.

When Jesus began to talk about the Kingdom of God and the cost of discipleship, one by one they began to leave. When it came to giving rather than getting, feeding rather than feasting, and dying rather than dining, they left.

> *"They seemingly are not aware of the fact that while their natural man is fed, their spiritual man is starving."*

This category of people requires a lot of maintenance but has very little impact. The place in the Kingdom where they have arrived tastes good and feels good as long as self-denial is not mentioned. To them, sacrifice is an ancient word that ended at Calvary.

Whenever mountains—intended to build character and increase faith—are in their pathway, they choose an alternate route. They want smooth highways and ideal weather. The multitudes were always sent away whenever challenging situations arose. They were not compatible with storms and cries.

Their perspective of God remains one-dimensional. They leave with their bellies full of fish, thinking that is the ultimate, while robbing themselves of greater revelation of the deity of Christ. They seemingly are not aware of the fact that while their natural man is fed, their spiritual man is starving.

In no way do I want to trivialize the necessities of the natural man. Fish and bread are important. However, the 5,000 stunted their spiritual growth by leaving when they should have stayed. The next dimension of ministry by our Lord was intended to put meat on the bones of their spirit man.

Morton Bustard, *The Impassioned Soul*

$\mathcal{M}$y Gratitude

Loving what I have—what I am grateful for:

_____
_____
_____
_____
_____
_____
_____
_____
_____
_____
_____
_____
_____
_____
_____
_____
_____
_____
_____
_____
_____
_____
_____
_____
_____
_____
_____
_____
_____

"I urge therefore, that, first of all, supplications, prayers, intercessions and giving thanks, be made for all men;" 1 TIMOTHY 2:1

*F*ullness of the Stature

"He that believes on me, as the scripture has said, out of his heart shall flow rivers of living water." JOHN 7:38

Would you care to have a flood tide of love flush the channel ways of your life like that? It would clean out something you have preferred keeping. It would with quiet, ruthless strength, tear some prized possessions from their moorings and send them adrift down stream and out. Its high waters would put out some of the fires on the lower levels. Better think a bit before opening the sluice-ways for that flood. But ah! it

> *"Floods are apt to do peculiar things."*

will sweeten and make fragrant. It will cut new channels, and broaden and deepen old ones. And what a harvest will follow in its wake. Floods are apt to do peculiar things. So does this one. It washes out the friction-grit from between the wheels. It does not dull the edge of the tongue, but washes the bitter out of the mouth, and the green out of the eye.

Note some of the changes in the personality which attend the Spirit's unrestrained presence. Without doubt the face will change, though it might be difficult to describe the change...The real secret of winsome beauty is here. That new dominant purpose will modulate the voice, and the whole expression of the face, and the touch of the hand, and the carriage of the body. And yet the one changed will be least conscious of it, if conscious at all. It is of peculiar interest to note the changes in the mental makeup. It may be said positively that the original group of mental faculties remain the same. There seems to be nothing to indicate that any change takes place in one's natural endowment. No faculty is added that nature had not put there, and certainly none removed. But it is very clear that there is a marked development of these natural gifts, and that this change is brought about by the putting in of a new and tremendous motive power, which radically affects everything it touches.

S. D. Gordon, *Quiet Talks on Power*

$\mathcal{L}$iving Forward, Understanding Backward

"Faithful is he that calls you, who also will do it." I THESSALONIANS 5:24

When I was in my 20's, I participated in a wilderness training course in a desert and mountain area. For our "final exam," we were blindfolded, placed in the back of a pickup truck, and taken to a remote area. We were dropped off and told to meet back at the camp in three days. With our food and water on our backs, we began our trek. It had just snowed that morning, so the way was difficult. There were times when we did not think we could go another foot. Exhaustion and frostbitten feet were taking their toll. However, we finally made it to our base camp successfully, and to our surprise, we were the first ones among the other patrols to make it back.

> *"Trust Him with the outcome of where you find yourself today."*

At the conclusion of our journey, we were able to stand on top of a ridge, look behind us and see the beautiful terrain that we had just scaled. The pain of what we had just endured seemed to subside. We could not believe we had actually walked through those valleys and snowcapped hills. There was a sense of accomplishment.

Life is very much like this. It is often lived forward, but understood backward. It is not until we are down the road a bit that we can appreciate the terrain God has allowed us to scale and the spiritual deposits He has made in our life as a result. When you begin to realize some of this, you sit back and breathe a sigh of relief because you know that God was in control all along. It didn't seem like it at the time, but He was.

Are you in the midst of a difficult journey that seems almost impossible to continue? Be assured that God is providing grace even now to equip you for that journey. There will be a time when you can say, "Wow, look at what God has done because of what I gained through that valley." Trust Him with the outcome of where you find yourself today.

Os Hillman, *Today God is First*

$\mathcal{A}$ Seed is the Promise of a Tree

"...for the things which are impossible with men are possible with God"
MARK 10:27

The entire creation possesses this principle of potential. Everything has the natural instinct to release its ability. The plant and animal kingdoms abound with evidences of this fact. The Creator designed everything with this principle of potential, which can be simplified to the concept of a seed. The biblical document states that God created everything with "seed in it according to their kinds" (Genesis 1:12-NIV). In essence, hidden within everything is the potential to fulfill itself and produce much more than we see.

> *"You can become all God designed you to be if you are willing to defy the norm and dare to believe God's assessment of your ability."*

You have the ability to accomplish everything your God-given purpose demands. Your Creator has given you the responsibility of releasing this precious seed in obedience to His commands. The releasing of your potential is not up to God but you.

Although I have said that everyone possesses great potential and the capacity to release this awesome ability, I also believe, with great sadness, that not everyone will become all the Creator intended them to be. Too many people are mere products of their environments, allowing themselves to be victimized by the opinions of others and the assessments of human analysis. I also believe, however, that anyone, of any age, and in any circumstances, can transform himself if he wants to. You can become all God designed you to be if you are willing to defy the norm and dare to believe God's assessment of your ability. It's not what you don't know that hurts you. It's what you know that just ain't so. Nothing is impossible to him who believes.

A seed, until it is released,
is only a promise of a tree.

_____

_____

_____

_____

_____

_____

Myles Munroe, *Releasing Your Potential*

Lacking Nothing

"But my God shall supply all your need according to his riches in glory by Christ Jesus." PHILIPPIANS 4:19

God wants us to succeed in every area of our lives, including our finances, in order to do His work worldwide. This is based first on our needs being met. Over and over this Scripture moved me: "Do not let this Book of the Law depart from your mouth; meditate on it day and night, so that you may be careful to do everything written in it. Then you will be prosperous and successful." (Josh. 1:8 NIV).

God's prosperity for each of us is having more than enough to do what the Lord has called us to do. If our heart is truly in sowing and reaping, God will asolutely meet all your needs according to His riches (not man's alone) in glory (See Galations 6:7; Phillipians 4:19; Matthew 17:29.)

> *"Let no debt remain outstanding, except the continuing debt to love one another."*

Misfortune pursues the sinner, but prosperity is the reward of the righteous (Proverbs 13:21 NIV).

One of Satan's greatest weapons against us is fear. His greatest natural weapon is getting us to go into debt that is over our faith and our common sense.

Talk about fear! Debt tends to fill us with fear that crushes and consumes. We're subject to the lender, with its interest and monthly payments, whether we have it or not. It can separate us from trusting a loving God and carrying out His true purpose for our lives. It is a many-tentacled monster that lives to wrap itself around us, pulling us under to a place where the pressure is so great we cannot breathe.

I've learned not to look to anyone else to provide wealth for me. We should look to God as our Source of provision. "Commit to the Lord whatever you do, and your plans will succeed" (Proverbs 16:3 NIV). Again I say, God is your Source, not man.

Oral Roberts, *Still Doing the Impossible*

Change—The Ally of Peace

"For he has said, 'I will never leave you, nor forsake you.'" HEBREWS 13:5B

When we decide to accept and embrace change in our lives, according to the will of God, we are met with an immediate sense of peace. That peace is our indication that we have stopped struggling with God and that He has let us know we're on the right track. If you take nothing else from this work, take this: Always follow your peace.

I should tell you here that peace and quiet are not the same thing, any more than solitude and loneliness are, or happiness and joy. Happiness is a state of well-being that has to do with what's "happening" in your life. Joy is that unspeakable understanding that all is well, no matter what is happening. Loneliness is the sadness that overcomes one who wishes he or she was not alone. Solitude is that "aloneness" that we seek out in order to find out who we are in God. And quiet is no more than a lack of audible noise. Peace, on the other hand, is the absence of all unnecessary internal "noise." It is that gift that makes the voice of God ring clearly in us.

> *"Always follow your peace."*

Peace is the chief ally of effective change. And it is the first thing the enemy will try to disrupt when you are trying to make changes in your life. His assignment is to throw as much "noise" at you as he can to distract you from the right choice and steer you toward the wrong one. I thought that all my battles would end when I decided to embrace the changes God had in store for me. But I quickly realized that between "deciding" and "doing," there was a whole new series of encounters with satan to deal with. In other words, first there are the challenges to change. Then there are the challenges of the change. It makes sense. Any decision you make in obedience to God will bring you closer to Him.

Dr. Wanda Turner, *Celebrating Change*

Searchlight Sights

"Finally, my brethren, be strong in the Lord, and in the power of his might. Put on the whole armor of God, that you may be able to stand against the wiles of the devil." EPHESIANS 6:10

Coming into Cleveland harbor one evening, just after nightfall, a number of passengers were gathered on the upper deck eagerly watching the colored breakwater lights and the city lights beyond. Suddenly a general curiosity was aroused by a small boat of some sort, on the left, scudding swiftly along in the darkness like a blacker streak on the black waters. A few of us who chanced to be near the captain on the smaller deck above, heard him quietly say, "Turn on the searchlight." Almost instantly an intense white light shone full on the stranger-boat, bringing it to view so distinctly that we could almost count the nail-heads, and the strands in her cordage.

> *"Turn on the searchlight."*

If some of us have made the prayer—Lord Jesus, show me what there is in my life that is displeasing to Thee, that Thou wouldst change—we will appreciate something of the power of that Lake Erie searchlight. There is a searchlight whiter, more intense, more keenly piercing than any other. Into every heart that desires, and will hold steadily open to it, the Lord Jesus will turn that searching light. Then you will begin to see things as they actually are. Many a hidden thing, which you are glad enough to have hidden, will be plainly seen. How is it possible, you will be ready to ask, for me to lead the life the Master's ambition has planned for me, with such mixed motives, selfish ambitions, sinfulness and weakness as I am beginning to get a glimpse of—how is it possible?

There is one answer to that intense heart-question, and only one. We must have power, some supernatural power, something outside of us, and above us, and far greater than we, to come in and win the victory within us and for us.

S. D. Gordon, *Quiet Talks on Power*

*E*arth's Museum of Potential

"Now there are diversities of gifts, but the same Spirit. And there are differences of administrations, but the same Lord.". 1 CORINTHIANS 12:4-5

The voice over the intercom announcing that we had finally begun our descent after ten hours of flying startled me from my restless sleep. With a deep sense of anticipation, It was my first trip to the great South American country of Brazil.

Seven days into my stay, my host and translator took me on a tour of their beautiful capital, Brasilia. After visiting the well-organized city and government buildings and touring the stately monuments of the picturesque city, we entered one of my favorite places to visit—the

> *"Each of us comes into this world with an assignment to fulfill."*

national museum. As I viewed, studied, and admired the tremendous historical pieces and the priceless testimonies of the glory of this nation's past and present, I was once again reminded that each painting, sculpture, and specimen was the product of the release of someone's potential. Although many of the artists are dead, their works are not. Display after display gave evidence to potential that had not been buried with the artists.

Throughout time, the great and small works of individuals—be they paintings, books, music, poetry, drama, architecture, inventions, or the development of theories—have affected the lives of many. All who have helped to shape our society's destiny—the giants who teach us and inspire us—used their potential with a passion and refused to let circumstances dictate their future. Their released potential is the world's inheritance.

I believe earth itself is a museum. Each of us comes into this world with an assignment to fulfill. God commissions us to leave for the following generations something from which they can learn and be inspired. The abilities to complete these assignments lie within us. The tools are our natural talents, gifts, and ambitions. Each of us comes into this world with an assignment to fulfill.

Myles Munroe, *Releasing Your Potential*

God's Balance Sheet

"...for where your treasure is, there will your heart be also." MATTHEW 6:21

According to my study of the bible, spirits of lack, poverty, and greed roam the earth putting husband against wife, children against parents, and even shepherds against their sheep. As a result, marriages fail, relationships crumble, and ministries are destroyed.

The good news, however, is that the greatest book ever written on stewardship is in our hands. The Bible provides us with a poignant five thousand year history of man's struggles...and provides relevant answers to every financial question you and I will ever encounter.

> *"If we mismanage what the Lord has entrusted to us...then our work will also be in bondage."*

Over two thousand verses in Scripture, as well as two-thirds of the parables, reveal lessons to us about finances and stewardship. They show us how to see the invisible and do the impossible financially. God uses the spiritual to teach us about the material and the supernatural to teach us about the natural.

You may ask, "But why would the Lord use the supernatural to teach about our finances?"

He looks deep into our hearts and knows, "for where your treasure is, there will your heart be also" (Mt. 6:21). If we mismanage what the Lord has entrusted to us; if our personal finances are a mess; then our work will also be in bondage. It's true that you can gain without following the Bible principles of giving and receiving, of sowing and reaping.

But in the final analysis, your wallet will still have holes in it.

Oral Roberts, *Still Doing the Impossible*

The Extra Mile

"And whosoever shall compel you to go a mile, go with him two."
MATTHEW 5:41

This verse is found in the Sermon on the Mount. What did Jesus mean by this? During Christ's earthly ministry Palestine was under Roman occupation, and the law stipulated that a Roman soldier could ask a citizen in an occupied country to carry his belongings for one mile. If you were a Jew working in your field and a Roman said, "Hey you! I need some help over here," you had to drop whatever you were doing and hop to it. After a mile you were free to go.

I can't imagine that too many Jews joyfully carried the heavy loads of their oppressors. Most of them were probably grumbling under their breath the whole time, wishing there was something they could do to get even. But Jesus said, "Do double what the Roman soldier asks of you. Carry his load for two miles!" What Jesus said applies to all areas of life. He was also saying:

> *"God notices, and He will make sure that none of your efforts are wasted."*

"Do more than the boss asks of you."
"Be willing to come in early and work late."
"Work through lunch once in awhile, even if no one asks you to."
"Don't ever be content with doing the bare minimum."
"If someone needs a volunteer for that difficult job, be willing to raise your hand."

Why should we do these things? Not to get credit or to have others notice us and thank us. This is simply what God expects His people to do. I know it's difficult when you work your fingers to the bone and nobody notices, but remember that God notices, and He will make sure that none of your efforts are wasted.

Pat Williams, *American Scandal*

How Will You Be Remembered?

"I shall not die, but live, and declare the works of the Lord." PSALM 118:17 (KJV)

Come with me in your imagination to the funeral of a loved one. Picture yourself driving to the funeral parlor or the church, parking your car and getting out. As you walk inside the building, notice the flowers and the soft organ music. See the faces of friends and family as you move through the room. Feel the shared sorrow of losing and the joy of having known that radiates from the hearts of the people there.

As you walk to the front of the room and look inside the casket, you come face to face with yourself. This is your funeral, five years from today. All these people have come to honor you and to express feelings of love and appreciation for your life. As you take a seat and wait for the service to begin, you look at the program in your hand. Five persons will speak. The first speaker is from your family, immediate and extended—your children, brothers, sisters, nephews, nieces, aunts, uncles, cousins, and grandparents who have come from all over the country to attend. The second speaker is to be one of your friends, someone who can give a sense of what you were

> *"I firmly believe that the greatest tragedy in life is not death, but life...life that fails to fulfill its purpose and potential."*

as a person. The third speaker is from your work or profession. The fourth speaker is from your church or some community organization where you were involved in service. The fifth and final speaker is your spouse.

Now think deeply. What would you like each of these speakers to say about you and your life? What kind of husband or wife, father or mother would you like their words to reflect? What kind of son or daughter or cousin? What kind of friend or working associate?

Before you read further, take a few minutes to seriously consider these questions. I firmly believe that the greatest tragedy in life is not death, but life...life that fails to fulfill its purpose and potential.

_____
_____
_____
_____
_____
_____

Myles Munroe, *Releasing Your Potential*

All They Want to Do Is "Date" God

"Now the purpose of the instruction is love out of a pure heart, and of a good conscience, and of faith sincere." I TIMOTHY 1:5

There is something in us that makes us afraid of the commitment that comes with real intimacy with God. For one thing, intimacy with God requires purity. The days of fun and games in the Church are over. What do I mean by "fun and games"? If your definition of fun is "low commitment and lots of thrills and chills," then all you've ever wanted to do is "date God." You just wanted to get in the backseat with Him. Do I need to draw a picture? God is tired of us wanting to get our thrills from Him without putting on the ring of commitment! Some are more enamored with the "goose bumps" than the glory! They're addicted to the anointing, liking the feeling of being blessed, receiving the "gifts" like a religious "gold-digger," happy with chocolates, flowers, and jewelry. The last time I checked He was still looking for a bride, not a girlfriend; one who will "stick" with Him.

> *"If your definition of fun is 'low commitment and lots of thrills and chills, then all you've ever wanted to do is 'date God.'"*

I'm afraid that many people in the Church have simply approached God to get what they can from Him without committing anything in return... We've often placed the cart before the horse. We say, "We want revival," and never mention intimacy. We seek revival without seeking Him. That's a lot like some stranger of the opposite sex walking up to you and saying, "I want kids. What do you say? I don't really know you and I'm not even sure I like you. Of course, I don't want all the commitment that goes with marriage, but I really do want children. How about it?"

Children in and of themselves do not make a household! They are the natural by-product of a loving relationship and intimacy in a marriage. What we really need to be seeking is a real relationship with God. It's a natural outgrowth of the process of intimacy.

Tommy Tenney, *The God Chasers*

*B*e as Little Children

"Are not two sparrows sold for a copper coin? and one of them shall not fall on the ground without your Father. But the very hairs of your head are all numbered. Fear not therefore, you are of more value than many sparrows."
MATTHEW 10:29-31

"I have an important business meeting in the morning. Would you please set the alarm for 5:30 a.m.?" I said to my wife.

"Oh, that won't be necessary. Just tell the Lord what time you want to wake up. He does it for me all the time," my wife said.

I rolled my eyes in disbelief. "Well, I'd feel more comfortable if we set the alarm."

"Okay, ye of little faith. But just to prove my point I am going to ask the Lord to wake us up just before 5:30."

The next morning I awoke before the alarm went off. I looked at the clock. It read 5:15. I looked at my wife, who had just awakened at the same time with an I-told-you-so smile.

> *"The idea of "bothering God" for such a trivial matter seems foolish and presumptuous"*

Sometimes we wrongfully view God as someone we go to for only the "big things." The idea of "bothering God" for such a trivial matter seems foolish and presumptuous. However, when you were a child and had to get up in the morning for school, didn't your mom or dad come wake you up? They were your parents, and you could come to them with the most trivial concerns or requests. Why would our heavenly Father be any less approachable? We often operate with an unwritten code that says our needs must have a certain degree of importance or crisis before we come to God with them. This is not God's character towards us.

Does the Lord desire this level of intimacy with you and me? The apostle Paul exhorted us to "pray without ceasing" (I Thessalonians 5:17). There is never a caution to pray only about matters of great importance.

Today, go to God with matters that you might view as trivial and would normally avoid bringing to God. Ask God to increase your level of intimacy with Him. You may even be able to get rid of your alarm clock.

Os Hillman, *Today God is First*

Developing Patience

"For, if God so clothe the grass of the field, which today is, and tomorrow is cast into the oven, shall he not much more clothe you, O you of little faith?"
MATTHEW 6:30

Developing patience is hard...You don't know what tomorrow holds, but you do know who holds tomorrow. Say this with the psalmist:

> *"Are you trying to involve yourself in matters that are too great for you?"*

"O Lord, my heart is not proud, nor my eyes haughty; nor do I involve myself in great matters, or in things too difficult for me. Surely I have composed and quieted my soul; like a weaned child rests against his mother, my soul is like a weaned child within me. O [substitute your name], hope in the Lord from this time forth and forever." (Psalm 131 NAS).

The place of rest that the psalmist found was a result of the choice he made. This quietness of soul did not come naturally to him. He actively chose to take himself out of involvement and quiet his soul (his mind, will, and emotions). He chose to put his hope in God. Are you trying to involve yourself in matters that are too great for you? Can you see into a man's heart? Can you know the future? You know Someone who does know men's hearts and the future. Patiently rest against His chest. He will bring you the peace you need. This attitude of patience is not something that will just happen.

By an act of your will you must choose to trust God regardless of what happens. Patiently wait for His best... Regardless of what you see or what you feel, God is in full control of your situation.

_____

_____

_____

_____

_____

_____

_____

_____

_____

The Secret Path to His Presence

*"There came unto him a woman having an alabaster jar of very precious
ointment, and she broke open the jar, and poured it on his head,
as he sat at the table."* MARK 14:3

They say that Simon was or had been a leper . . . but even so, Simon
the Pharisee was still a spiritual leper because he was afflicted with the
disfiguring sin of hypocrisy.

"Now when [Simon] the Pharisee which had invited
him saw it, he spoke within himself, saying, "This
man, if he were a prophet, would have known who
and what manner of woman this is that touches
him: for she is a sinner." (Luke 7:37-39)

> *"God's
> acceptance
> means you can
> ignore all the
> other voices..."*

You can always count on some Pharisees with
the leprosy of hypocrisy showing up to look with
disdain as you rush in to throw your best at the Lord's feet, but who
cares? Who knows what problems will be lifted from your shoulders in
that moment? Who knows what worries, fears, and anxieties will fade
away when you hear Him say, "I accept you."

In God's eyes, we are all lepers in the spirit realm. God's acceptance
means you can ignore all the other voices that say, "I reject you." I don't
mean to be rude, but who cares how many other lepers reject you when
you have been healed and accepted by the King?

Mary's harshest critics weren't the Pharisees or Sadducees. The
disciples of Jesus were ready to throw her out when Jesus quickly
intervened.

Then Jesus said, "Let her alone: for the day of my burial has she kept
this. For in that she has poured this ointment on my body,

"Truly I say unto you, Wheresoever this gospel shall be preached
throughout the whole world, this also that she has done shall be spoken of
for a memorial of her." (Mark 14:6-9).

Tommy Tenney, *The Daily Chase*

The Lap of Complacency

*"He giveth power to the faint; and to them that have no might
he increaseth strength."* ISAIAH 40:29 (KJV)

Complacency is an arrogant sin. It is arrogant because it publicly chooses not to acquiesce to God's request for change. It is sin because it is dishonest and deceitful. It parades as everything but what it is. On the surface, complacent people look content. They appear confident. To the untrained spiritual eye, they portray faith. In truth, that contentment is apathy, the confidence is pride, and the faith is in fact fear.

Complacency is defined as "a feeling of quiet pleasure or security often while unaware or unconcerned with unpleasant realities." It is self-satisfaction. In our context, complacency is the act of avoiding change for one of three reasons: 1) We don't know what lies ahead and we are afraid. 2) We know what's ahead and we don't like it. 3) We don't care what's ahead. We'd rather plot our own course.

> "Complacency is the act of avoiding change ."

When we avoid change because of our fear, we have made God to be a liar. When we complicate matters by pretending to be satisfied where we are, we have made ourselves to be liars. God did not give us a spirit of fear, but we do find ourselves in possession of it often. In Scripture, "Fear not" is usually the first thing God has to tell His people before they have to deal with change. Try doing a Bible study of every instance where God told His people, either directly or through prophets, not to be afraid. I promise that it can keep you busy for years.

God is not concerned that we have fear. He expects that. But He is concerned with how we handle it. Complacency is often a ploy to keep us from facing the fear of change, which is, in reality, giving in to fear, which is abandoning our faith. And that is of great concern to God.

Dr. Wanda Turner, *Celebrating Change*

*T*he Source of All Potential

"In the beginning was the Word, and the Word was with God, and the Word was God. The same was in the beginning with God. All things were made by him; and without him was not anything made that was made." JOHN 1:1-3

Everything that was and is was in God. Before God created anything, there was only God. Thus, God had within Him the potential for everything He made. Nothing exists that was not first in God. God is the source of all life, because before anything was, God is.

"In the beginning God created the heavens and the earth" (Genesis 1:1 - KJV). He pulled everything that He made out of Himself. Indeed, the beginning was in God before it began. God started start. If the book of Genesis had started with Genesis 1:0, it might have read, "Before there was a beginning, there was God. Before there was a creation, there was a Creator. Before anything was, there was God."

> *"Everything in the world we know was in God before it came to be seen."*

God did not begin when the beginning began. He was in the beginning before the beginning had a beginning. "In the beginning was the Word, and the Word was with God, and the Word was God" (John 1:1). Everything in the world we know was in God before it came to be seen. "All things were made by him; and without him was not anything made that was made" (John 1:3). Thus, God is the source of all potential. He is everything we haven't seen yet.

When we describe this characteristic of God, we say that He is omnipotent. Omni means "always" and potent means "full of power." God is always full of power. He can always do more than He has already done.

Myles Munroe, *Releasing Your Potential*

So Close . . . But Still So Far

"And, being assembled together with them, commanded them that they should not depart from Jerusalem, but wait for the promise of the Father, which, he said, 'you have heard of me.'" ACTS 1:4

We'll start off in hot pursuit, full of energy and expectation, enthusiastic for the journey, barely able to contain ourselves. We imagine what it will be like when we reach our goal. Perhaps we even start running...hoping that by hastening our steps, we'll arrive even earlier. We're not really sure exactly where we're going and we don't know how much further we have to go, but around every corner lies the tantalizing hope that perhaps we've almost made it.

Enthusiasm won't keep us going for long, though. Aching feet and tired bodies overpower hope and weary spirits and exhausted minds disable faith as corner after corner yields no sign that we're any closer than when we began. Reality sets in, and the joy of the journey evaporates like a morning mist. The temptation is to just give up—to conclude that we'll never reach the goal, or that we've been going the wrong way the whole time.

> *"You could be sulking in the very shadow of your desired destination!"*

Perhaps you've been there. Maybe you're reading this devotional exhausted and sprawled out on a park bench of your own—dejected and determined that you will not take one more step. You thought that your Father knew where He was taking you, but obviously this isn't where you wanted to be. You could be sulking in the very shadow of your desired destination! So close...yet so far away!

There will be times when we'll want to quit—when the road ahead of us seems so long and so difficult that we don't believe we'll ever make it. Those are the times when God can develop our character. Gifts can be given, but character must be developed. We enjoy receiving the gifts...but we don't enjoy our transit times in the "wilderness."

_____

_____

_____

_____

_____

_____

Tommy Tenney, *The Daily Chase*

Making a Living vs. Living to Make it.

"Now he that plants and he that waters are one: and every man shall receive his own reward according to his own labor." I CORINTHIANS 3:8

Work should never be something you do just to make money or to pass the time. If you hate your job and are just counting the days to retirement, then you're not doing what you should be doing. Only when you find something that you love to do and then do it with all the energy God gave you will your work become the rich, rewarding profession God intended it to be.

I can think of few things sadder than putting in eight or nine hours a day doing something you really don't want to do. What a waste of the time and talent God has given you! If you find that you spend your entire workweek looking forward to Friday, then you owe it to yourself to look for something else to do with your life.

> *"I can think of few things sadder than...doing something you really don't want to do."*

Writer Mamie McCullough says, "We often feel hard work is a curse to be endured. Nothing could be further from reality! The truth is, work is a blessing." She goes on, "Work is often an antidote for whatever ails us...a precious gift that enhances your well being. Be thankful if you have useful work to do. It is a blessing above all others."

That reminds me of a story about Thomas Edison, who was known for spending one hundred hours or more in his laboratory each week. Once, after a particularly long, hard day, Edison came home to a sympathetic wife who told him he'd been working too hard. "You need to take a vacation," she told him.

"But where on earth would I go?" he asked.

"Just decide where you would rather be than anyplace else on earth," she told him.

The great inventor nodded, "Very well. I'll go there tomorrow."

The next morning he got up and went back to his laboratory.

Pat Williams, *American Scandal*

Making Adjustments

"Cast the net on the right side of the ship, and you shall find." JOHN 21:6A

A former client of mine was the marketing director of a large food brokerage company and told me a story about one of their client grocery stores located in the upper Midwest. It seems that the store could not understand why at a certain time every winter sales plummeted. They studied their product line and interviewed customers. They did everything possible to uncover the mystery. Finally, someone made a remarkable discovery that changed everything.

> *"Adjusting our lives to God is the first thing that has to happen."*

It seemed that whenever it was really cold outside, the manager raised the temperature in the store. When customers came into the store it was too warm for them, so they removed their coats and placed them in their shopping carts. This meant less room for food and resulted in reduced sales overall. They lowered the temperature of the store, and as a result, the sales climbed back to the levels they were accustomed to. Their adjustment resulted in restoring sales levels.

Jesus stood on the shoreline and watched Peter and a few of the disciples fish. Jesus yelled from the shoreline asking if they had caught anything. They had not. He then suggested they cast their line on the other side of the boat. Without knowing the person who was addressing them, they took His advice. They began catching so many fish they could not bring them in.

Adjusting our lives to God is the first thing that has to happen in order to begin experiencing Him in our daily lives. For some, it is simply following the advice of those above us. For others, it may require a major change in our job situation. Still, for others it could mean making changes in relationships. Whatever the case, you can be sure that until we adjust our lives to God we will not receive His full blessing. Ask Him today where you need to adjust to Him.

Os Hillman, *Today God is First*

$\mathcal{K}$now Your Purpose

"In him also we have obtained an inheritance, being predestined according to the plan of him who works all things according to the purpose of his own will." EPHESIANS 1:11

When a manufacturer proposes a new product, he first clarifies the purpose of that product. Then he designs the features to accomplish his intent. Therefore, a car manufacturer will first decide whether the vehicle is to be a racecar, a delivery van, or a family car. Once the vehicle's purpose has been established, the engineer will incorporate various features to meet that purpose.

Before you were born, God had a plan and a purpose for your life. Then, in accordance with that plan, He gave you special abilities and aptitudes to enable you to accomplish everything that He intended. If you are going to release your potential, you must first discover God's plan for your life. Knowing and living within God's purpose is the difference between using and abusing the gifts and capabilities God built into you.

> *"If you are going to release your potential, you must first discover God's plan for your life."*

You must understand your resources. Manufacturers also determine the resources that are necessary for a product to perform correctly and efficiently. A car manufacturer might specify the octane of the gasoline to be used, the pressure of the air in the tires, or the weight of the oil for the engine.

God's pattern for your life also includes specifications for the spiritual, physical, material, and soul resources that are necessary for you to live a fulfilling and productive life. Until you learn what resources God has arranged for you to enjoy, and what benefits He planned for you to receive from each resource, your potential will be stunted and your performance will be less than it could be.

_____

_____

_____

_____

_____

_____

_____

Myles Munroe, *Releasing Your Potential*

Cultivating Excellence

"But by the grace of God I am what I am: and his grace which was bestowed upon me was not in vain; but I labored more abundantly than they all: yet not I, but the grace of God which was with me." I CORINTHIANS 15:10

I've never viewed myself as an extraordinarily talented person. Whatever I accomplished was achieved through hard work, and plenty of it!

I suppose you could say that I am a classic over-achiever. I have an incessant inner drive that pushes me on. The only way I know how to succeed is to outwork other people. And do you know what? It works well. I recommend it!

> *"Drive and dedication are far more important than talent when it comes to winning top honors."*

Sadly, many people in this world work just hard enough to get by. They hang on to their jobs because there's no real reason to fire them, but there's no reason to promote them either. Such are many of the people you will pass on your way up the ladder, if you're willing to work hard.

Author/motivational speaker Zig Ziglar says: "We need to teach our children that, for eight hours a day, competition is extremely tough; but when we work one more hour, 90 percent of the competition will drop out. At that point, we have an open door to greater productivity and a promotion."

Recently I came upon another remarkable piece of research done by Dr. Benjamin Bloom, professor of education at the University of Chicago and Northwestern University. His five-year study showed that drive and dedication are far more important than talent when it comes to winning top honors. He found that very few of those who are now at the top of their chosen professions demonstrated exceptional natural talent or ability for what they do.

Pat Williams, *American Scandal*

You Are Not Alone

"Blessed be God, even the Father of our Lord Jesus Christ, the Father of mercies, and the God of all comfort;" 2 CORINTHIANS 1:3

I remember when our car broke down. It didn't have too far to break down because it already was at death's door. The only way to fix that car was to commit the body to the ground and give the engine to the Lord. At the time, though, I needed to get uptown to ask the electric company not to cut off the only utility I had left. I caught the bus to town. I walked into the office prepared to beg, but not prepared to pay. I pleaded with the young lady; I promised her money. Nothing seemed to move her, and she cut it off anyway. I was crushed. I had been laid off my job, and my church was so poor it couldn't even pay attention. I was in trouble. I walked out of the utility office and burst into tears. I don't mean the quiet leaking of the tear ducts, either. I mean a deluge of sobbing, heaving, quaking, and wailing. I looked like an insane person walking down the street. I was at the end of my rope.

> *"The only way to fix that car was to commit the body to the ground and give the engine to the Lord."*

To this melodramatic outburst God said absolutely nothing. He waited until I had gained some slight level of composure and then spoke. I will never forget the sweet sound of His voice beneath the broken breathing of my fearful frustration. He said, in the rich tones of a clarinet-type voice, "I will not suffer thy foot to be moved!" That was all He said, but it was how He said it that caused worship to flush the pain out of my heart. It was as if He were saying, "Who do you think that I am? I will not suffer thy foot to be moved. Don't you understand that I love you?" I shall never forget as long as I live the holy hush and the peace of His promise that came into my spirit. Suddenly the light, the gas, and the money didn't matter. What mattered was I knew I was not alone. He sat down beside me and we rode home smiling in each other's face. It was the Lord and I.

T. D. Jakes, *365 Days to Healing, Blessings, and Freedom*

$\mathcal{A}$ God Kind of Faith

"Whatsoever things you desire, when you pray, believe that you received them, and you shall have them." MARK 11:24

If I give you a tree as a gift and I tell you it is an avocado tree, you will tell every person who asks you what kind of tree is in your front yard that it's an avocado tree. Now you haven't picked any avocados from that tree, but you still dare to say it's an avocado tree. Why? Because you have faith in me that the tree is what I say it is. You believe that somewhere in that tree there are many avocados. Faith is simply believing and acting on the words and integrity of another. Faith in God is to believe and act on what He says.

The words of Jesus as recorded in the Gospel of Mark admonish us to have faith in God.

> *"Put your faith in God, because it's your faith in Him that will accomplish the moving of mountains."*

And Jesus answering said unto them, "Have faith in God. For truly I say unto you, If you have faith, you shall not only do this which is done to the fig tree, but also if you shall say unto this mountain, 'Be removed, and be cast into the sea'; and shall not doubt in his heart, but shall believe that those things which he says shall come to pass; he shall have whatsoever he says. Therefore I say unto you, Whatsoever things you desire, when you pray, believe that you receive them, and you shall have them." (Mark 11:22-24)

What Jesus is really saying is, "Have the God kind of faith." Don't put your faith in your own faith or in the faith of other people or in the mountains or in anything that you expect to happen because of your faith. Put your faith in God, because it's your faith in Him that will accomplish the moving of mountains. You can't speak to the mountain and expect it to move unless you are connected to God. Apart from Him you don't have the power to complete such monumental tasks.

Myles Munroe, *Releasing Your Potential*

Kindness Doesn't Cost

". . . bearing with one another, and forgiving one another, if any man has a quarrel against another: even as Christ forgave you, so also do you."
COLOSSIANS 3:13

A mature person understands that it's okay to be kind. They don't go around with a brash, tough-guy attitude, pushing people out of their way and demanding, "You looking at me?"

When are we finally going to figure out that the very best way to help ourselves is to help other people? Jesus wasn't kidding around when He said that we get back what we give, that we reap what we sow, and that we will be treated the same way we treat others.

Kindness is one of the greatest ways to preach the Gospel without saying a word. Kindness draws people to you. Besides, the person who is always kind to others shows that he has faith in God's ability to make things turn out as they should. On the other hand, a man or woman who thinks they have to be tough to make it in this world is demonstrating a lack of faith. That kind of thinking is in line with Darwin's "survival of the fittest." It doesn't square with this Bible admonition to clothe ourselves with kindness.

> *"A little thing can make a big difference in someone's life."*

Although I don't always succeed, my intention is to do something especially kind every day. I give a compliment or a word of encouragement when I can. When I'm eating out, I tell the servers that I appreciate the good service they give me. When I hear something good about someone, I share it with that person. In rush-hour traffic I'll slow down so the guy next to me can change lanes and not miss his exit. These are little things, but a little thing can make a big difference in someone's life.

You can't claim to be kind unless you are habitually kind...you show kindness without even thinking about it. —Rick Warren

Being Least Isn't Bad

"Therefore take unto you the whole armor of God, that you may be able to withstand in the evil day, and having done all, to stand." EPHESIANS 6:13

John the Baptist was called the forerunner of Christ. It is quite obvious from the Scriptures that John did not purchase his wardrobe from any of the high-end clothiers. He lacked social graces, and his diet did not impress me in any way.

However, when he spoke, people listened. John drew a larger crowd in the desert than we can attract to our modern, air-conditioned edifices. They did not come for the music or a program; they attended his crude, arid, uncomfortable services and listened to fearless, sin-rebuking preaching because he was a man sent from God.

> *"The good news is, if you are not pleased with where you find yourself, you can change to another any time you choose."*

One would think this was the ultimate, that John the Baptist had to be the greatest. Not so. God has a place reserved for us in the Kingdom that exceeds John's. He was born with the Spirit; you and I are born of the Spirit.

I do not deem myself worthy to be in the same room with John the Baptist. Nonetheless, according to the Scriptures, if I hold the title as being the least in the Kingdom of God, then I have excelled beyond John. If this is the least I can be, than I am in awe when I think of what more I can be.

"Verily I say unto you, Among them that are born of women there hath not risen a greater than John the Baptist notwithstanding: he that is least in the kingdom of heaven is greater than he." (Matthew 11:11).

The good news is, if you are not pleased with where you find yourself, you can change to another any time you choose.

_____

_____

_____

_____

_____

_____

Morton Bustard, *The Impassioned Soul*

There Have Always Been God Chasers

"One man of you shall chase a thousand: for the Lord your God, he it is that fighteth for you, as he hath promised you." JOSHUA 23:10 (KJV)

God is just waiting to be caught by someone whose hunger exceeds his grasp. God chasers have a lot in common. Primarily, they are not interested in camping out on some dusty truth known to everyone. They are after the fresh presence of the Almighty. Sometimes their pursuit raises the eyebrows of the existing church, but usually they lead the church from a place of dryness back into the place of His presence. If you're a God chaser, you won't be happy to simply follow God's tracks. You will follow them until you apprehend His presence.

> *"God chasers don't want to just study from the moldy pages of what God has done; they're anxious to see what God is doing."*

The difference between the truth of God and revelation is very simple. Truth is where God's been. Revelation is where God is. Truth is God's tracks. It's His trail, His path, but it leads to what? It leads to Him. Perhaps the masses of people are happy to know where God's been, but true God chasers are not content just to study God's trail, His truths; they want to know Him. They want to know where He is and what He's doing right now.

Sadly, today the bulk of the Church is like some proverbial detective holding a magnifying glass in his hand and studying where God has been. Unfortunately, the Church today spends countless hours and much energy debating where God has been, how heavy He was when He was there, and even His gender. To true God chasers, all these things are immaterial. They want to run hard and hot on this trail of truth until they arrive at the point of revelation, where He presently exists.

A true God chaser is not happy with just past truth; he must have present truth. God chasers don't want to just study from the moldy pages of what God has done; they're anxious to see what God is doing.

Tommy Tenney, *The God Chasers*

The Past Is Not the Present

"Then he arose, and rebuked the wind and the raging of the water: and said unto the sea, "Peace, be still." And the wind ceased, and there was a great calm." MARK 4:39

Have you allowed God to stand at the bow of your ship and speak peace to the thing that once terrfied you? We can only benefit from resolved issues. The great tragedy is that most of us keep our pain active. Consequently, our power is never activated becaue our past remains unresolved. If we want to see God's power come from the pain of an experience, we must allow the process of healing to take use far beyond bitterness into a resolution that releases us from the prison and sets us free.

> *"You discuss the past as if it were the present because the past has stolen the present right out of your hand!"*

God's healing process makes us free to taste life again, free to trust again, and free to live without the restrictive force of threatening fears. Someone may say, "I don't want to trust again." That is only because you are not healed. To never trust again is to live on the pinnacle of a tower. You are safe from life's threatening grasp, but you've become locked into a time warp. You always talk about the past because you stopped living years ago. Listen to your speech. You discuss the past as if it were the present because the past has stolen the present right out of your hand! In the name of Jesus, get it back!

Are you ready to live, or do you still need to subject all your friends to a history class? Will you continue your icessant raging and blubbering about that which no one cane change—the past?

I am only trying to jump-start your heart and put you back into the presence of a real experience, far from the dank, dark valley of regret and remorse. It is easy to unconsciously live in an euphoric, almost historial, mirage that causes current opportunities to evade you.

T.D. Jakes, *Naked and Not Ashamed*

No End to The Wait

"The unmarried woman cares for the things of the Lord, that she may be holy both in body and in spirit; but she that is married cares for the things of the world, how she may please her husband." 1 CORINTHIANS 7:34B

Take courage, single friend. You are not alone in your wait; neither are you alone in the feelings and struggles you encounter. Many godly women have waited and won. Many women have lost hope and compromised. Wait patiently and win triumphantly the future your Father has planned for you. It will always be designed with you in mind and is worth being patient to discover.

"Here comes the bride all dressed in...chains!" Hey, wasn't that supposed to be "all dressed in white"? The last word in the chorus was changed to "chains," not because the bride is marrying a member of a motorcycle gang, but because she made the unwise choice of marrying an unbeliever. The chains symbolize what she has to look forward to as a believer married to an unbeliever. The Word of God speaks clearly about a partnership with an unbeliever

> *"Many godly women have waited and won. Many women have lost hope and compromised."*

Ruth was a wonderful example of a Lady of Patience. Ruth did not allow her circumstances or lack of male companionship to cause her to be impatient. Instead she concentrated on developing companionship with her heavenly Father and chose to let Him bring a husband to her if He saw fit. Concern over the ticking of her "biological clock" did not make her fearful of the future. Instead she concentrated on being a lady of character, not on getting a man. She took one day at a time, knowing that God was not bound by circumstances nor her age. She used the wait to become the woman God wanted her to be. At the end of this personal preparation God chose to provide her with a husband.

Debbie Jones & Jackie Kendall, *Lady in Waiting—Meditations of The Heart*

*E*verything Has Potential

"But now being made free from sin, and becoming servants to God, you have your fruit unto holiness, and the end everlasting life." ROMANS 6:22

All men are sent to the world with limitless credit, but few draw to their full extent. It is a tragedy to know that with over five billion people on this planet today, only a minute percentage will experience a significant fraction of their true potential. Perhaps you are a candidate for contributing to the wealth of the cemetery. Your potential was not given for you to deposit in the grave. You must understand the tremendous potential you possess and commit yourself to maximizing it in your short lifetime. What is potential, anyway?

> *"Potential never has a retirement plan."*

Potential is dormantability, reserved power—untapped strength, unused success—hidden talents capped capability. All you can be but have not yet become...all you can do but have not yet done...how far you can reach but have not yet reached...what you can accomplish but have not yet accomplished. Potential is unexposed ability and latent power.

Potential is therefore not what you have done, but what you are yet able to do. In other words, what you have done is no longer your potential.

The greatest tragedy in life is not death, but a life that never realized its full potential. You must decide today not to rob the world of the rich, valuable, potent, untapped resources locked away within you. Potential never has a retirement plan.

_____

_____

_____

_____

_____

_____

_____

_____

_____

Myles Munroe, *Understanding Your Potential*

$\mathcal{P}$etty Aggravations

"He that is faithful in that which is least is faithful also in much: and he that is unjust in the least is unjust also in much." LUKE 16:10

Anybody can be kind and gentle when they are having a good day. There's no reason to tell a lie when the truth is on your side. You won't be tempted to steal your neighbor's Ford Escort with one hundred thousand miles on the odometer if you have a brand-new Jaguar parked in your garage. It's no big deal to let someone go first when you're not in a hurry.

The true test of a person's character is how they react when they're not having a good day—when they didn't get enough sleep the night before, or when they have an upset stomach or a headache. Their character involves what they say when the truth is only going to reveal that they messed up in some way, when a slight "bending of the truth" is going to get them out of a difficult situation. You might feel differently if you were the one trying to nurse a few more miles out of that little Escort, while your neighbor was tooling around town in that brand-spanking new Jag.

> *"People of true character are better able to weather the storms of life."*

People of true character are better able to weather the storms of life. They don't lose their tempers when they're stuck in a traffic jam on the way to work or loaf around in the office all day because they know the boss is out of town. Chuck Colson hit the nail right on the head when he said, "Far from being trivial, minor tests of character are the best basis on which to predict future behavior."

"Therefore, my beloved brethren, let every man be swift to hear, slow to speak, slow to anger: for the anger of man does not work the righteousness of God..." (James 1:19 TSB)

_____

_____

_____

_____

_____

_____

_____

Pat Williams, *American Scandal*

My Gratitude

Loving what I have—what I am grateful for:

_____
_____
_____
_____
_____
_____
_____
_____
_____
_____
_____
_____
_____
_____
_____
_____
_____
_____
_____
_____
_____
_____
_____
_____

"I will restore to you the years that the locust hath eaten."
JOEL 2:25

"And the Lord shall guide thee continually; and satisfy thy soul in drought, and make fat thy bones; and thou shalt be like a watered garden, and like a spring of water, whose waters fail not."

ISAIAH 58:11 (KJV)

*P*rayer of Surrender

"Rejoice evermore. Pray without ceasing. In everything give thanks: for this is the will of God in Christ Jesus concerning you." I THESSALONIANS 5:16-18

My God, I want to give myself to you. Give me the courage to do this. My spirit within me sighs after you. Strengthen my will. Take me. If I don't have the strength to give You everything, then draw me by the sweetness of Your love. Lord, who do I belong to, if not to You? What a horror to belong to myself and to my passions! Help me to find all my happiness in You, for there is no happiness outside of You.

> *"Do the things of this world mean more to me than You?"*

Why am I afraid to break out of my chains? Do the things of this world mean more to me than You? Am I afraid to give myself to You? What a mistake! It is not even I who would give myself to You, but You who would give Yourself to me. Take my heart.

What joy it is to be with You, to be quiet so that I might hear Your voice! Feed me and teach me out of Your depths. Oh God, You only make me love You. Why should I fear to give You everything and draw close to You? To be left to the world is more frightening than this! Your mercy can overcome any obstacle. I am unworthy of You, but I can become a miracle of Your grace. –Archbishop Fenelon

Spiritual Eye Wash

"And the world passes away, and the lust thereof: but he that does the will of God abides forever." 1 JOHN 2:17

In order to have "eyes of faith," you may have to use a spiritual eye wash to remove the debris that the enemy has dropped into your eyes. The Lady of Faith will have times when her secure eyes of faith begin to blink into an anxious twitch of insecure, sensual sight. She can admit her insecurity to her heavenly Fiancé and He can calm the twitching eyes. Spending some quality time in the Word is the best "eye wash" for "eyes of faith."

> *"Spending some quality time in the Word is the best 'eye wash' for 'eyes of faith.'"*

A lady of faith...can only be content in this trying situation if she has her "eyes of faith" properly focused on the ultimate relationship—with her heavenly Bridegroom. Datelessness is a common type of debris that irritates the "eyes of faith," but the eye wash treatment—quality time with Jesus and reading His Word—is always effective.

"And it shall come to pass, if thou shalt hearken diligently unto the voice of the Lord thy God, to observe and to do all his commandments which I command thee this day, that the Lord thy God will set thee on high above all nations of the earth: And all these blessings shall come on thee, and overtake thee, if thou shalt hearken unto the voice of the Lord thy God." (Deuteronomy 28:1-2 - KJV)

Deuteronomy 28:2, 15, and 32 show that God has always desired to bless His people, but He will not force them to do what is best. In His Word He has often warned us to wait, to be careful, and to trust Him. He will not make us wait. His heart of love begs us to listen and obey so He may bless us and the dear ones who will one day look to and follow us. You must choose to wait patiently for God's best.

Debbie Jones & Jackie Kendall, *Lady in Waiting—Meditations of The Heart*

Survive the Crash of Relationships

"Therefore also it is contained in the scripture, 'Behold, I lay in Zion a chief cornerstone, elect, precious: and he that believes on him shall not be put to shame.'" 1 PETER 2:6

Normally, anytime there is a crash, there is an injury. If one person collides with another, they generally damage everything associated with them. In the same way, a crashing relationship affects everyone associated with it, whether it is in a corporate office, a ministry, or a family. That jarring and shaking does varying degrees of damage to everyone involved. Whether we like to admit it or not, we are affected by the actions of others to various degrees.

> *"We must learn to live life with a seat belt in place, even though it is annoying to wear."*

What is important is the fact that we don't have to die in the crashes and collisions of life. We must learn to live life with a seat belt in place, even though it is annoying to wear. Similarly, we need spiritual and emotional seat belts as well. We don't need the kind that harness us in and make us live like a mannequin; rather, we need the kind that are invisible, but greatly appreciated in a crash.

Inner assurance is the seat belt that stops you from going through the roof when you are rejected. It is inner assurance that holds you in place. It is the assurance that God is in control and that what He has determined no one can disallow! If He said He was going to bless you, then disregard the mess and believe a God who cannot lie. The rubbish can be cleared and the bruises can be healed. Just be sure that when the smoke clears, you are still standing. You are too important to the purpose of God to be destroyed by a situation that is only meant to give you character and direction.

Lift your voice above the screaming sirens and alarms of men whose hearts have panicked! Lift your eyes above the billowing smoke and spiraling emotions. Pull yourself up—it could have killed you, but it didn't. Announce to yourself, "I am alive. I can laugh. I can cry, and by God's grace, I can survive!"

T. D. Jakes, *365 Days to Healing, Blessings, and Freedom*

*T*he Principle of Experience

"Jesus said unto him, 'If you can believe, all things are possible to him that believes.'" MARK 9:23

Experience may be defined as "the observation of facts as a source of knowledge and skill gained by contact with facts and events." By its very nature, experience is a product of the past and is, therefore, limited to and controlled by previous exposure. In spite of the fact that experience may be valuable for making decisions and judgments concerning the future, it is important to know that any significant measurement of growth, development, expansion, or advancement will require experience to submit to the substance of the unknown through faith.

Unfortunately, experience has compelled many promising people to cower in the shadows of fear and failure because they were not willing to venture out into the uncharted frontiers of new possibilities. Experience is given not to determine the limits of our lives, but to create a better life for us. Experience is a tool to be used! In essence, experience does not cancel capacity.

> *"In essence, experience does not cancel capacity."*

At any point in our lives, we are the sum total of all the decisions we have made, the people we have met, the exposure we have had, and the fats we have learned. In essence every human is a walking history book. Nevertheless, we must keep in mind that our personal history is being made and recorded every day, and must be careful not to allow our past to determine the quality of our future. Instead, we must use our experience to help us make better decisions, always guarding against the possibility that it may limit our decisions. Remember, your ability is never limited by your experience.

Determine not to let your past experience limit your capacity. Be grateful for the lessons of the past, then accelerate with confidence on to the autobahn of life, being careful to obey only those signs that have been established by your Creator.

Myles Munroe, *Maximizing Your Potential*

*T*he Path of Christ

"And when he had called the people unto him with his disciples also, he said unto them all, 'Whosoever will come after me, let him deny himself, and take up his cross daily, and follow me.'" MATTHEW 16:24

God will eventually test you in all areas of your life, but He will not let your trials become greater than you can bear. Let God use trials to help you grow. Do not try to measure your progress, your strength, or what God is doing. His work is not less efficient because what He is doing is invisible. Much of God's work is done in secret because you would not die to yourself if He always visibly stretched out His hand to save you. God does not transform you on a bed of light, life, and grace. His transformation is done on the cross in darkness, poverty, and death.

> *"His path winds up in the side of a steep mountain"*

Christ did not say, "If anyone will come after me, let him enjoy himself, let him be gorgeously dressed, let him be drunk with delight." He never even said, "Be glad that you are perfect and that you can see how well you are doing." No, Jesus said, "If anyone will come after me, let him deny himself, take up his cross and follow me." His path winds up in the side of a steep mountain where death will be present on every hand. (See Matthew 16:24)

You do not yet see the lovely side of following Christ. You see what He takes away, but you do not see what He gives. You exaggerate the sacrifices and ignore the blessings.

Listen to what I have to say. It is not easy to hear, but it will feed your spirit. Do not listen to the voice that suggests that you live for yourself. The voice of self-love is even more powerful than the voice of the serpent. If the world never asked for anything more than what you could give out of love, wouldn't it be a better master? —Archbishop Fenelon

_____

_____

_____

_____

_____

_____

_____

Gene Edwards, *100 Days in the Secret Place*

*I*nward Beauty

"We look not at the things which are seen, but at the things which are not seen: for the things which are seen are temporal; but the things which are not seen are eternal." 2 CORINTHIANS 4:18B

The key to beauty is found in First Peter 3:4: "but let it be the hidden man of the heart, in that which is not corruptible, even the beauty of a meek and quiet spirit, which is in the sight of God of great value." This kind of beauty can only get better the older it gets.

When you look at the virtuous woman of Proverbs 31:10-31, you will see God's picture of a beautiful woman. There are 20 verses describing her. Only one verse mentions her outward appearance. If you were to spend 1/20 of your time on outward physical beauty and the other 19/20 on developing the other qualities God describes as beautiful, such as wisdom, kindness and godliness, you would become the excellent woman Proverbs 31:10 says a man should try to find.

King Solomon said in Proverbs 31:30 (NIV) "Charm is deceptive, and beauty is fleeting; but a woman who fears the Lord is to be praised."

> *"There are many women who fear pimples, wrinkles, flabby thighs, and crow's feet, but very few women who really fear the Lord."*

For the lips of a strange woman drop as an honeycomb, and her mouth is smoother than oil: But her end is bitter as wormwood, sharp as a two-edged sword.

(Proverbs 5:3,4 - KJV)

There are many women who fear pimples, wrinkles, flabby thighs, and crow's feet, but very few women who really fear the Lord. With which are you attractive to men: the snares of Proverbs 5 or the beauty of First Peter 3:4?

Debbie Jones & Jackie Kendall, *Lady in Waiting—Meditations of The Heart*

Nowhere to Hide

"I will arise and go to my father, and will say unto him, 'Father, I have sinned against heaven, and before you, and am no more worthy to be called your son.'" LUKE 15:18-19A

There is no tiptoeing around the presence of God with pristine daintiness—as if we could tiptoe softly enough not to awaken a God who never sleeps nor slumbers. We shuffle in His presence like children who were instructed not to disturb their Father, although God isn't sleepy and He doesn't have to go to work. He is alive and awake, and He is well. We blare like trumpets announcing our successes, but we whisper our failures through parched lips in the shadows of our relationship with Him. We dare not air our inconsistencies with arrogance because we know we are so underdeveloped and dependent upon Him for everything we need.

> *"When a man hides himself from God, he loses himself. What good is it to know where everything else is, if we cannot find ourselves?"*

His holiness is our objective; we have aspired to acquire it for years, but none have attained it. Surely there is some qualitative relationship that we imperfect sons can master in the presence of our Holy Father! I, for one, need a Father whose eyes can see beyond my broken places and know the longing of my heart.

It is the nature of a fallen man to hide from God. If you will remember, Adam also hid from God. How ridiculous it is for us to think that we can hide from Him! His intelligence supersedes our frail ability to be deceptive. Adam confessed (after he was cornered by his Father), "I heard Thy voice in the garden, and I was afraid, because I was naked; and I hid myself" (Gen. 3:10 · KJV). Do you see what the first man did? He hid himself. No wonder we are lost. We have hidden ourselves.

When a man hides himself from God, he loses himself. What good is it to know where everything else is, if we cannot find ourselves? Like the prodigal son in chapter 15 of Luke, in our desperation we need to come to ourselves and come out from under the bushes where we have hidden ourselves. We need to become transparent in the presence of the Lord.

T. D. Jakes, *365 Days to Healing, Blessings, and Freedom*

*L*ife is More than Shelter, Food or Security

"Therefore I say unto you, Be not anxious for your life, what you shall eat, or what you shall drink; nor for your body, what you shall put on." MATTHEW 6:25

Maslow, one of the greatest influences on the thought patterns of psychology in our world, theorized that man is driven by his base needs. He believed that your most immediate need becomes your controlling factor. Therefore, your first instinct is to find shelter, secondly food and thirdly security or protection. Then you begin to move up the ladder of becoming self-realized and self-actualized, of getting self-esteem and all the rest of that stuff. According to this theory, human beings are driven by their base needs.

In the sixth chapter of Matthew, Jesus challenges that thought pattern. He instructs us to live from the perspective of what exists that we cannot see, instead of being totally caught up in the details and needs of our daily lives. God lives and thinks in the potential. He always sees things that have not yet been manifested.

> *"Stop Worrying"*

Faith too lives in the potential not in the present. Jesus simply asks us to have faith—to believe in God's goodness and care.

In teaching His followers that food, drink, clothes and shelter are not the most important things in life, Jesus directly contradicts the psychological theories of our world. He dares you to follow God and think in the opposite. God doesn't start with your wants, but with who you are.

According to God, Maslow was wrong—and I go with God. There are people who have everything, but they still don't know who they are. People accumulate things with the hope that the things will make them somebody. But you don't become somebody by accumulating things. Ask the guy at the top who can't sleep. Ask the guy who has everything except peace and love and joy in his heart. Maslow was wrong. God desires to give you self-worth and self-esteem first. He wants you to know who you are first.

_____

_____

_____

_____

_____

_____

Myles Munroe, *Understanding* Your Potential

The Buck Stops Here

"Be not deceived; God is not mocked: for whatsoever a man sows, that shall he also reap." GALATIANS 6:7

Sometimes it seems that we are living in a world full of victims. Everyone has a problem and somebody to blame for their problem. However, people of character understand that they alone are responsible for their actions.

Think about this for a moment. The first law of physics tells us that every action brings about an equal and opposite reaction. In other words, everything you do has consequences attached to it. This is not limited to the physical realm. It is also true in spiritual matters, for the Bible says, "A man reaps what he sows" (Galatians 6:7).

> *"Everything you do has consequences attached to it."*

If you drink and become an alcoholic, you have no one to blame but yourself. If you smoke cigarettes and develop lung cancer, that is cause-and-effect in action. Nobody is responsible for what you do but you.

Admittedly there are many things we can't control. We can't control the weather. We can't control the family into which we are born. We can't control the passage of time. Sometimes we can't control much of anything except our attitude, but if we all took responsibility for the things we can control, our society would instantly change for the better.

America needs people who are willing to stand up and take responsibility for their actions. She also needs men and women who are willing to see that they are at least partly responsible for the actions of others.

I don't want to see America become a nation of snoops and snitches, but neither do I want us to become a nation of cowards. We must not be a people who are unwilling to get involved, who turn and look the other way when we see something wrong because we don't want to bother anyone.

Pat Williams, *American Scandal*

Delayed Results

"You ask, and receive not, because you ask wrongly, that you may consume it upon your passions." JAMES 4: 3

Answers to prayer are delayed, or denied, out of kindness, or that more may be given, or, that a far larger purpose may be served. But deeper down by far than that is this: God's purposes are being delayed; delayed because of our unwillingness to learn how to pray, or our slowness—I almost said—our stupidity in learning. It is a small matter that my prayer be answered, or unanswered, not small to me, everything perhaps to me, but small in proportion. It is a tremendous thing that God's purpose for a world is being held back through my lack.

> *"A strong will perfectly yielded to God's will, or perfectly willing to be yielded, is His mightiest ally in redeeming the world."*

The thought that prayer is getting things from God is so small, pitiably small, and yet so common. The true conception, understandable that prayer is partnership with God in His planet-sized purposes, and includes the "all things" beside, as an important detail of the whole.

The results He longs for are being held back, and made smaller because so many of us have not learned how to pray simply and skillfully. We need training. And God understands that. He Himself will train. But we must be willing, actively willing. And just there the great bother comes in. A strong will perfectly yielded to God's will, or perfectly willing to be yielded, is His mightiest ally in redeeming the world.

The real reason for the delay or failure lies simply in the difference between God's viewpoint and ours. In our asking either we have not reached the wisdom that asks best, or, we have not reached the unselfishness that is willing to sacrifice a good thing, for a better, or the best; the unselfishness that is willing to sacrifice the smaller personal desire for the large thing that affects the lives of many.

_____

_____

_____

_____

_____

_____

S. D. Gordon, *Quiet Talks on Prayer*

$\mathcal{A}$ Second Chance to Find Who You Are

"And God shall wipe away all tears from their eyes; and there shall be no more death, neither sorrow, nor crying, neither shall there be any more pain: for the former things are passed away." REVELATION 21:4

If you are wrestling with the curse and stigma of public opinion, if people have categorized you for so long that you have accepted your origin for your prophecy—I still have good news for you. You don't have to stay the way you are. The Potter wants to put you back together again. Do you believe that God is a God of second chances? If you do, I want to unite my faith with yours, because I believe He gives second chances.

> *"... when you were wandering in search of yourself like the prodigal son, God knew who you really were all the time."*

This good news is that God changes names. Throughout the Scriptures He took men like Abram, the exalted father, and transformed his image and character into Abraham, the father of many nations. Jacob, the supplanter, became Israel, the prince. A name is an expression of character; it means no more than the character behind it. Now, I don't want everyone to run to the courthouse and change his name. However, I do want you to realize that there is a place in your walk with God—a place of discipleship—whereby God radically changes your character. With that change He can erase the stigma of your past and give you, as it were, a fresh name in your community—but most importantly, in your heart. You see, my friend, when you were wandering in search of yourself like the prodigal son, God knew who you really were all the time. When you finally came to yourself, He was there. I recommend you get on your knees and wrestle with Him in prayer until you can arise knowing what He knows. Rise up from prayer knowing who you really are in the spirit and in the Kingdom.

T. D. Jakes, *365 Days to Healing, Blessings, and Freedom*

*T*he Step Ladder of Success

"Behold, the kingdom of God is within you." LUKE 17:21B

Success is an enemy of potential. When we complete a task and quit because we think we've arrived, we never become all we are. If, for example, you graduate from college and teach first grade for the rest of your life when God wanted you to be a high school principal, you forfeit much of your potential because you stopped at a preliminary success. Leave your success and go create another one. That's the only way you will release all your potential. We must beware that a small success does not keep us from accomplishing our larger goal or purpose.

> *"Leave your success and go create another one."*

In a similar manner, we must be careful to judge our successes by God's standards, not by the world's. Success in the world's eyes is not really success because the world does not now what true success is. True success is being right with God and completing His assignment and purpose for our lives. It's knowing God and obeying Him. Thus, we cannot succeed without discovering and doing what God asks of us. Without God, everything we do is nothing.

Therefore, do not be intimidated by your lack of achievement in the world's eyes. The power of God within you is greater than any other power. When you're hooked up to God and you're obeying His directives, you will achieve success by His standards. Refuse to allow the world's measurements of success to encourage or discourage you because God's standards are the only criteria that matter. Follow Him as He leads you from success to success. To maximize your life you must never allow temporary achievements to cancel eternal fulfillment.

Myles Munroe, *Maximizing Your Potential*

The Habit of Peace

"Therefore, my beloved brethren, let every man be swift to hear, slow to speak, slow to anger: for the anger of man does not work the righteousness of God." JAMES 1:19

I've had people say to me, "I'm just a hot-headed guy. I have a quick temper. There's nothing I can do about it." My reaction is always the same: "Yes, there is something you can do about it. You can learn to control your temper, even in the most stressful and difficult situations."

The last thing a basketball team needs is a guy who's going to get angry in a critical situation. I've seen so many games turn on a situation like that. It doesn't really matter how much talent a player has. If he's a hot-headed troublemaker, no one's going to want him on their team. This holds true in sports, business, and other areas of life.

> *"The good news is that you really can change the way you act."*

If you're naturally a quick-tempered person, that may not be what you want to hear, but the good news is that you really can change the way you act. Like everything else we are discussing in this chapter, peace comes primarily through knowing God and experiencing His daily presence in our lives. But it's also true—that having a peaceful frame of mind can be a habit. Author Brian Tracy says, "You can learn any habit that you consider desirable or necessary if you work at it long enough and hard enough."

That doesn't mean it's easy to learn a new habit. You may have to work terribly hard at it. I've heard it said that you have to do something nineteen times before it becomes a habit. I have no idea where they came up with nineteen times, and I think it's more than that for me. I also know that it is much easier to learn a good new habit than it is to "unlearn" an old, bad one. As someone has said, "A bad habit is like a soft, warm bed. Easy to get into, but not so easy to get out of."

Pat Williams, *American Scandal*

Following Only the Father's Commands

"Ask me of things to come concerning my sons, and concerning the work of my hands command ye me." ISAIAH 45:11 (KJV)

Have you ever thought about a typical day in Jesus' life? Perhaps He might have had questions like these, "Who am I going to heal today? Who will I visit today? Which person will I deliver from demons this day?" The demands on Jesus' time were great. Yet we see that Jesus allocated His time very deliberately. We don't get the idea that Jesus was flustered or stressed from the activity he was involved in. He often sought times of prayer and reflection away from the disciples. His life appeared to have a balance of quiet moments and active ministry into the lives He came in contact with.

> *"Our lives will become less cluttered, less stressful, and more fulfilling when we follow the model Jesus provided"*

How do we determine what we will be involved in each day of our lives? What keeps us in sync with the will of our heavenly Father for the daily tasks He calls us to? Jesus tells us that He was only involved in those things the Father was involved in. Nothing more, nothing less. So often we determine our participation in an activity based on whether we have the time to do it or whether we desire to participate. The real question we should ask is, "Does the Father want me to participate in this activity?"

Our lives will become less cluttered, less stressful, and more fulfilling when we follow the model Jesus provided. It may not always please everyone. Jesus never sought to please everyone. Ask the Lord each day this week how you and He are to spend your time. Yield your schedule to Him. Let Jesus direct your every activity. You may discover that He desires you to cut back some things in order to spend more time alone with Him. He will be faithful to show you. And you will become more fulfilled because you are centered in His will for you.

He's Looking In Your Direction

"But God has chosen the foolish things of the world to shame the wise; and God has chosen the weak things of the world to shame the things which are mighty." 1 CORINTHIANS 1:27

Dead circumstances cannot hold down the body of someone who has been chosen! If no one else embraces these bleeding, purple heart soldiers, perhaps they should rally together and find comfort in the commonality of their mutual experience.

I must confess that more than once I have seen His hand pick up the pieces of this broken heart and restore back to service my crushed emotions and murky confidence, while I stood in awe at the fact that God can do so much with so little.

> *"God is still in the business of recycling human lives!"*

The greatest place to preach isn't in our great meetings with swelling crowds and lofty recognitions. The greatest place to preach is in the trenches, in the foxholes and the hog pens of life. If you want a grateful audience, take your message to the messy places of life and scrape the hog hairs off the prodigal sons of God, who were locked away in the hog pens by the spiritual elite.

It is here in these abominable situations that you will find true worship being born, springing out of the hearts of men who realize the riches of His grace. No worship seminar is needed for someone whose tearstained face has turned from humiliation to inspiration. Their personal degradation has become a living demonstration of the depths of the unfathomable love of God! My friend, this is Davidic worship! This is the praise of David, whose critical brothers and distracted father helped him become the canvas on which God paints the finest picture of worship these weary eyes have ever witnessed!

It is time for us to redefine and redirect our gaze to find the heroes of God among us. We must not forget that God purposely chooses to use misplaced and rejected people, and He may be looking in our direction.

*T*he Yardstick of Success

"For we dare not make ourselves of the number, or compare ourselves with some that commend themselves." 2 CORINTHIANS 10:12

One of the most significant mistakes humans make is comparison—the measuring of oneself against the standards, work, or accomplishments of another. This exercise is fruitless, demeaning, and personally tragic because it places our true potential at the mercy of others, giving them the right to determine and define our success.

True success is not measured by how much you have done or accomplished compared to what others have done or accomplished; true success is what you have done compared to what you could have done. In other words, living to the maximum is competing with yourself. Success is satisfying your own personal passion and purpose in pursuit of personal excellence. In fact, you must always remember to perform for an audience of one, the Lord your Creator.

> *"True success is what you have done compared to what you could have done."*

"For if a man thinks himself to be something, when he is nothing, he deceives himself. But let every man test his own work, and then shall he have rejoicing in himself alone, and not in another. For every man shall bear his own burden" (Galatians 6:3-5).

Consciously applying this principle to our lives can do much to free us from the immobilizing culture and environment of our society which strives to control us through comparison. From the early years of childhood, we are compared to our sisters and brothers, the neighbor's children, or some other person. This comparative spirit continues on into our teen and adult years, developing into a sophisticated dehumanizing state of competition. The result is traumatizing because we spend most of our lives trying to compete with others, comparing our achievements with those of our peers, and attempting to live up to their standards of acceptance. Instead of being ourselves, we become preoccupied with being who others dictate we should be.

Myles Munroe, *Maximizing Your Potential*

Change Starts With You

"But now we are delivered from the law, that being dead wherein we were held; that we should serve in newness of spirit, and not in the oldness of the letter." ROMANS 7:6

Is there something you've always dreamed of doing but never had the nerve to try? Today is the day to begin working toward the fulfillment of that dream! I urge you to take a few moments right now to think about where you want to go and what it's going to take to get there. Let yourself dream big! Get out a piece of paper and write it all down.

Here's something else to remember from playwright August Wilson: "You are responsible for the world you live in. It's not the government's responsibility. It is not your school's, your social club's, your fellow citizen's, your church's, or your neighbor's. It is yours...utterly and singularly yours."

> *"If you really want to change the world, the best place to start is with yourself!"*

I know I'm repeating myself here, but I feel I must say it again: Begin to pursue your dreams now! Don't be like the Anglican bishop, buried in London's Westminster Abbey, who has these words written on his tomb:

When I was young and free, and my imagination had no limits, I dreamed of changing the world. As I grew older and wiser, I discovered the world would not change, so I shortened my sights somewhat and decided to change only my country. But it, too, seemed immovable. As I grew into my twilight years, in one last, desperate attempt, I settled for changing only my family...those closest to me, but, alas! they would have none of it. Now, as I lie on my deathbed I suddenly realize: If I had only changed myself first, I would have changed my family by example. From their inspiration and encouragement I would have been able to better my country and the world.

The lesson is a simple one. If you really want to change the world, the best place to start is with yourself!

Pat Williams, *American Scandal*

*D*issatisfaction With a Fraction

"And you, child, shall be called the prophet of the Highest: for you shall go before the face of the Lord to prepare his ways." LUKE 1:76

One of life's great tragedies is that the majority of the world's population is composed of individuals who have negotiated an agreement with mediocrity, signed a contract with the average, and pledged allegiance to the ordinary. They have resolved never to be more than society has made them or do more than is expected. What a tragedy of destiny. God expects more! Remember, we cannot become what we were born to be by remaining what we are.

Inside of every human being is a deep call of destiny to do something worthwhile with our lies. The urge to accomplish great things and engage in significant endeavors is the germ of purpose planted by God in the heart of man. Why then do we settle for so little? Why do we abandon our dreams and deny our purpose? Why do we live below our privilege, buried in the cemetery if wishful thinking and empty regrets?

> *"Remember, we cannot become what we were born to be by remaining what we are."*

As we have seen, one reason we fail to progress in fulfilling our purpose is satisfaction with our present measure of success. The belief that we have arrived is the deterrent that keeps us from getting to our destination. A second part of the answer lies in the fact that we have accepted the present state of our lives as the best we can do under the circumstances.

Remember, you will never change anything that you are willing to tolerate. Your creator wants you to consciously choose to fulfill your purpose and maximize your potential because in so doing you will bring glory to His name. Unfortunately, history gives evidence of only a few rare individuals who, driven by a passion to achieve a cherished vision in their hearts, initiated their own deliverance, rose above the tide of the norm, and impacted their generations and ours.

Myles Munroe, *Maximizing Your Potential*

Don't Lose Your Fire

"I know your works, that you are neither cold nor hot: I would you were cold or hot." REVELATION 3:15

I love to surround myself with people who can stir up the fire in me. Some people in the Body of Christ know just what to say to ignite the very fire in you. However, no one can ignite in you what you do not possess! If the cold winds of opposition have banked the fire and your dream is dying down, I challenge you to rekindle your desire to achieve whatever God has called you to do. Don't lose your fire. You need that continued spark for excellence to overcome all the blight of being ostracized.

> *"Rekindle your desire to achieve whatever God has called you to do."*

Fire manifests itself in two ways. First, it gives light...Second, fire gives heat. Every man and woman of God must also remember that fire needs fuel. Feed the fire. Feed it with the words of people who motivate you. Feed it with vision and purpose. When stress comes, fan the flames. Gather the wood. Pour gasoline if you have to, but don't let it die!

Sometimes just seeing God bless someone else gives you the fortitude to put a demand on the promise that God has given you. I don't mean envy, but a strong provocation to receive.

If seeing others blessed makes you want to sabotage their success, then you will not be fruitful. I have learned how to rejoice over the blessings of my brother and realize that the same God who blessed him can bless me also. Other people's blessings ought to challenge you to see that it can be done.

T. D. Jakes, *365 Days to Healing, Blessings, and Freedom*

Claiming Joy!

"For I consider that the sufferings of this present time are not worthy to be compared with the glory which shall be revealed in us." ROMANS 8:18

Joy doesn't come from having more money than anyone else. It isn't the feeling you get when you receive the promotion that your co-worker really wanted. It doesn't spring out of an absence of troubles in your life, but rather from an understanding that God is using whatever troubles you experience to strengthen your character and make you a better human being.

Joy is an inner sense of peace, contentment, and happiness that stays with you even when things aren't going your way. Joy is keeping a smile on your face when people look at you and ask, "What in the world have they got to be smiling about?"

> *"God is still in charge of everything in the universe—including your own life."*

For the most part, joy comes from God's presence in your life. It's impossible not to have joy if you're walking with God on a daily basis. But joy also comes from maintaining an attitude of gratitude, from doing what the old song says:

> Count your many blessings, name them one by one.
> And it will surprise you what the Lord has done.

How do you choose joy in a world that is confronted by terrorism, violence, and suffering on a daily basis? The only way I know is simply to remind yourself several times a day that God is still in charge of everything in the universe—including your own life. Even when life seems like a trip through a minefield, you can rest in the knowledge that Jesus, the Good Shepherd, knows where every single one of those mines is buried. You can trust Him to lead you safely, even through "the valley of the shadow of death."

When things look bleak, remember that God has a happy ending planned for all of this.

Pat Williams, *American Scandal*

$\mathcal{F}$rom Thought to Action

"Now unto him that is able to do exceedingly abundantly above all that we ask or think, according to the power that works in us, unto him be glory in the church by Christ Jesus throughout all ages, world without end. Amen."
EPHESIANS 3:20-21

A thought is a silent word, so a word is an exposed thought. Everything in life starts in the thought form—it's a thought first. After it's said, it is no longer a thought. It becomes a word. The next step is an idea. An idea is the concept of the thought—it has moved into a reality. Ideas are potentials.

> *"Take your ideas and turn them into imagination."*

The third level of operation is what I call imagination. Imagination changes an idea into a plan. If you have an idea it can come and go. You have many ideas in a day—what to cook, what to wear, what to do. You may decide the night before what you are going to wear in the morning and then wake up with a different idea.

Ideas change. But if an idea develops into an imagination, it means the idea has become a plan. It is still not written or drawn, but it is in your head. Imagination is therefore a plan that is not documented. It is a visual display of your thoughts and ideas. Ephesians 3:20 challenges us to believe God is able and willing to do "exceeding abundantly far beyond all we can think or imagine." He dares us to use our imaginations.

If you want to be successful in life, take your ideas and turn them into imagination; then take imagination and duplicate it physically. Put it down. Let it become a plan of action.

Myles Munroe, *Understanding Your Potential*

"Milk Babies" in Padded Pews

"Therefore laying aside all malice, and all deceit, and hypocrisies, and envies, and all evil speakings, as newborn babies, desire the pure milk of the word, that you may grow thereby." I PETER 2:1-2

Too many of us have become "milk babies" who want to sit on padded pews in an air-conditioned and climate-controlled building where someone else will pre-digest what God has to say and then regurgitate it back to us in a half-digested form. (We're afraid of getting "spiritual indigestion" from messages we think are "too rough" to handle). Tender tummies are unused to tough truth!

> *"Tender tummies are unused to tough truth!"*

We have to face the fact that we have become addicted to all the things that accompany church, like the choirs and the music. God is tired of having long distance relationships with His people. He was tired of it thousands of years ago in Moses' day, and He is tired of it today. He really wants to have intimate, close encounters with you and me.

The solution is hunger and desperation for God Himself without intermediaries. We need to pray, "God, I'm tired of everybody else hearing from You! Where is the lock on my prayer closet? I'm going to lock myself away until I hear from You for myself!" We make a great deal out of reading the Word and that is important. But we need to remember that the early Church didn't have access to what we call the New Testament for many years. They didn't even have the Old Testament Scriptures because those expensive scrolls were locked up in synagogues.

The only Scriptures they had were the verses from the law, the Psalms, and the prophets that had been passed down orally from grandfathers and grandmothers—and that only if they were Jewish believers. So what did they have? They walked and talked with Him in such a rich level of intimacy that it wasn't necessary for them to pour over dusty love letters that were written long ago. They had God's love notes freshly written on their hearts.

Tommy Tenney, *The God Chasers*

Pray No Matter the Season

"And he said unto them, "It is not for you to know the times or the seasons, which the Father hath put in his own authority." ACTS 1:7

As a child of God, you will experience winter seasons in your Christian walk. You quite possibly may be there now. It's neither time to plant nor time to reap. Your rose garden has become frozen tundra. Dark brown topsoil, rich with nutrients, has become permafrost.

What is one supposed to do in the dead of winter? Consistency must be kept in every season of life. It is imperative that you maintain your prayer life, although it is not the fruit-bearing season.

> *"When we pray the will and Word of God, every prayer is answered."*

At times we feel as if our prayers do not ascend beyond the ceiling above our head, but this is not the case. When we pray the will and Word of God, every prayer is answered.

"Pray without ceasing." The admonition here is not that one pray 24 hours, 7 days a week. It would be an impossible task for many people to engage in intercessory prayer while at work with the types of jobs they have. We cannot shirk our responsibilities in life and survive. Paul is encouraging us to pray and not be discouraged. In other words, pray until it happens.

Regardless of how the enemy tries to discourage you from praying, badgering you with doubt and unbelief, continue to make your petition known. When ferocious winds of opposition are howling, hold firmly to the promises of God's Word and refuse to let go.

Morton Bustard, *The Impassioned Soul*

*F*inish What You Start

"Forgetting those things which are behind, and reaching forth unto those things which are before, I press toward the goal for the prize of the high calling of God in Christ Jesus." PHILIPPIANS 3:13-14

Tremendous strength can be gained from time spent meditating on and soaking in God's Word. There are so many promises of God's help and blessings upon His people.

When Henry Ford was still at the helm of the company that bears his name, an ambitious young employee sought him out and asked, "How can I make my life a success?"

Ford didn't even have to think about it. He quickly answered, "When you start something, finish it."

> *"If the going's getting easier, you ain't climbing."*

You have to keep going until you cross the finish line! You need to be able to say, along with the apostle Paul, "I have fought a good fight, I have finished my course, I have kept the faith" (2 Timothy 4:7).

If you're having a tough time right now, that probably means you're doing something right. You're not going to face that much adversity if you just drift along with the current, going wherever life takes you. It's only when you're battling your way to higher ground that life becomes difficult. It's only when you speak up for what's right and speak out against what's wrong that you're going to have opposition.

I'm sure you've heard it said that the darkest hour is just before the dawn. I also believe that the road is roughest just before the finish line. That's why I love the sign I once saw in the office of former college basketball coach Lefty Dreisell: "If the going's getting easier, you ain't climbing."

It is easy to start on a task, but God needs people who can last on the job when the going gets difficult, and who can finish what they set out to do. —Halford E. Luccock

God Has A Plan

"Consider the ravens: for they neither sow nor reap; which neither have storehouse nor barn; and God feeds them: how much more are you better than the birds?" LUKE 12:24

Not too long ago a construction crew that was building a road through a rural area came to a tree with a nest full of baby birds. The project superintendent marked the tree so that it wouldn't be cut down until the fledglings had flown from the nest.

A few weeks later, as work on the road progressed, the construction crew came back to that tree, and the superintendent was lifted up in a bucket truck so he could see if the nest was empty. It was, and he ordered his crew to cut the tree down. As it toppled to the ground, the empty nest bounced out of its branches. One of the workmen noticed that a piece of paper, with a few words written on it, was sticking out of it.

"He careth for you."

It was nothing, just part of the scraps of material that had been used to build the nest. But for some reason the workman bent down to take a closer look. He discovered that the paper was torn from a Sunday school book, and that it bore these words: "He careth for you."

What a lesson! God does care for the birds of the air, and He will care for you and me too. You are more valuable than sparrows and crows and starlings and wrens. You are more valuable than hawks.

God has a plan for all of us, but He expects us to do our share of the work. —Minnie Pearl, Comedienne

Pat Williams, *American Scandal*

Dividends From a High Price

"Trust in the Lord with all thine heart; and lean not unto thine own understanding. In all thy ways acknowledge him, and he shall direct thy paths." PROVERBS 3:5,6 (KJV)

Does your relationship with Jesus reflect reckless abandonment to Him, or does it reflect only tokenism, a superficial effort toward following Jesus?

The depth of your relationship with God is up to you. God has no favorites; the choice to surrender is yours. A.W. Tozer so brilliantly stated in his book The Pursuit of God: "It will require a determined heart and more than a little courage to wrench ourselves loose from the grip of our times and return to Biblical ways."

> *"Choose right now to put mediocrity behind you."*

Ruth had just such a determined heart, and the Lord honored her faith to move away from all that was familiar and take a journey toward the completely unknown. Ruth did not allow her friends, her old surroundings, nor her culture's dead faith to keep her from running hard after God. She did not use the excuse of a dark past to keep her from a bright future that began with her first critical choice: reckless abandonment to Jesus Christ.

Have you made this critical choice or you have settled for a mediocre relationship with Jesus? Amy Carmichael, one of the greatest single woman missionaries who ever lived, once remarked, "The saddest thing one meets is the nominal Christian."

Choose right now to put mediocrity behind you; courageously determine to pursue Jesus with your whole heart, soul, and mind.

Supernatural, Not Spectacular

"When I was a child, I spoke as a child, I understood as a child, I thought as a child: but when I became a man, I put away childish things."
1 CORINTHIANS 13:11

Jesus commissioned the 70 to go in groups of two and minister salvation, healing, and deliverance.

"And the seventy returned again with joy, saying, Lord, even the devils are subject unto us through thy name. And He said unto them, I beheld Satan as lightning fall from heaven. Behold, I give unto you power to tread on serpents and scorpions, and over all the power of the enemy: and nothing shall by any means hurt you. Notwithstanding in this rejoice not, that the spirits are subject unto you; but rather rejoice, because your names are written in heaven" (Luke 10:17-20-KJV).

> *"To know God is to know power, but to know power does not mean you know God."*

As important as it is to place emphasis on the supernatural, it is also necessary to realize that demonstration without dedication is dangerous. I am not implying that the 70 were transgressors; I am saying that it is possible to be used by God and not be devoted to Him. They were like children playing with toys; they did not understand the purpose of power.

Possessing power and not purity is like being a vigilante with a dangerous weapon. Eventually someone is going to be fatally wounded. There are far too many casualties caused by those who operated in the gifts but who did not manifest any fruit of the Spirit.

If we see only the hand of God and fail to seek the heart of God, we will be susceptible to repeating the same mistake the 70 made.

To know God is to know power, but to know power does not mean you know God. A sure way to guard oneself against erring in this area is to follow Paul's teachings in First Corinthians 13. When compassion for the needs of others becomes our motive, we are safe-guarded from failure.

Morton Bustard, *The Impassioned Soul*

Live Day by Day

"And such trust have we through Christ toward God: not that we are sufficient of ourselves to think anything as of ourselves; but our sufficiency is of God." 2 CORINTHIANS 3:4-5

Your spiritual walk is a little too restless and uneasy. Simply trust God. If you come to Him, He will give you all that you need to serve Him. You really need to believe that God keeps His word. The more you trust Him, the more He will be able to give you. If you were lost in an uncrossable desert, bread would fall from heaven for you alone.

"Fear nothing but to fail God. And do not even fear that so much that you let it upset you. Learn to live with your failures, and bear with the failures of your neighbors. Do you know what would be best for you? Stop trying to appear so mentally and spiritually perfect to God and man. There is a lot of refined

> *"Fear nothing but to fail God."*

selfishness and complacency in not allowing your faults to be revealed. Be simple with God. He loves to communicate Himself to simple people. Live day by day, not in your own strength, but by completely surrendering to God."

–Archbishop Fenelon

$\mathcal{R}$uin Everything That Isn't God

"Wait on the Lord: be of good courage, and he shall strengthen thine heart: wait, I say, on the Lord." PSALM 27:14 (KJV)

Let me ask you a question: How long has it been since you came to church and said, "We are going to wait on the Lord"? I think we are afraid to wait on Him because we're afraid He won't show up. I have a promise for you: "They that wait upon the Lord shall renew their strength." (Is. 40:31a-KJV). Do you want to know why we've lived in weakness as Christians and have not had all that God wanted for us? Do you want to know why we have lived beneath our privilege and have not had the strength to overcome our own carnality? Maybe it's because we haven't waited on Him to show up to empower us, and we're trying to do too much in the power of our own soulish realm...

> *"He is not going to pour out His Spirit where He doesn't find hunger. He looks for the hungry."*

As far as I can tell, there is only one thing that stops Him. He is not going to pour out His Spirit where He doesn't find hunger. He looks for the hungry. Hunger means you're dissatisfied with the way it has been because it forced you to live without Him in His fullness. He only comes when you are ready to turn it all over to Him. God is coming back to repossess His Church, but you have to be hungry.

How long has it been since you've been so hungry for God that it consumed you to the point where you couldn't care less what people thought of you? I challenge you right now to forget about every distraction, every opinion, but one.

Tommy Tenney, *The God Chasers*

*D*o The Pigeon Walk

"For we hear that there are some which walk among you disorderly, working not at all, but are busybodies. Now them that are such we instruct and call on by our Lord Jesus Christ, that with quietness they work, and eat their own bread." 2 THESSALONIANS 3:11-12

Have you ever noticed the funny way a pigeon walks? His head moves forward, he stops, then he takes a step. I have read that a pigeon's eyes do not focus unless his head is still...therefore, he focuses—then steps. We could learn a lot from this "pigeon walk."

> *"It really doesn't matter how much we 'know'—it matters how much we 'live.'"*

Sometimes our lives seem to get out of control and our hearts are injured and our steps unsure. We lose focus and life comes apart at the seams. This Journal is designed to help us keep focus—step by step and day by day.

Proverbs 3:5-6 (NIV) are key words to live by with regard to our steps. "Trust in the Lord with all your heart...." How much misdirection and pain could we avoid if we trusted in and were daily assured of our God's awesome love for us? "And do not lean on your own understanding...." What trouble could we avoid if we went to the all-knowing God for daily direction and wisdom instead of fretting, planning and, worrying? "In all your ways acknowledge Him..." This is our focus for each step. And the promise? "He will make your paths straight."

It really doesn't matter how much we "know"—it matters how much we "live." This type of journaling through the years has helped me to live more of what I know. I pray that, as you use this spiritual journey tool, you will catch yourself refocusing before each step.

May God richly bless your "walk" with Him!   — Debby Jones

_____
_____
_____
_____
_____
_____
_____
_____

I Am Come In My Father's Name

"I am come in my Father's name, and you do not receive me: if another shall come in his own name, him you will receive." JOHN 5:43

There is nothing quite like trouble to bring out your true identity. Aren't you glad that you are not limited to public opinion? God's opinion will always prevail. Those three Hebrews came out of the furnace without a trace of smoke. That old king tried to change the name on the package, but he couldn't change the contents of the heart! Can you imagine those

> *"If you are to fight the challenge of this age, then shake the enemy's names and insults off your shoulder."*

boys shouting when they came out? One would say, "Who is like God?" Another would lift his hands and say, "Jehovah is gracious!" The other would smell his clothes, touch his hair, and shout, "Jehovah has helped!"

If you have agonized on bended knees, praying at the altar to know the purpose and will of God for your life, and His answer doesn't line up with your circumstances, then call it what God calls it! The doctor might call it cancer, but if God calls it healed, then call it what God calls it. The word of the Lord often stands alone. It has no attorney and it needs no witness. It can stand on its own merit. Whatever He says, you are! If you are to fight the challenge of this age, then shake the enemy's names and insults off your shoulder. Look the enemy in the eye without guilt or timidity and declare:

"I have not come clothed in the vesture of my past. Nor will I use the opinions of this world for my defense. No, I am far wiser through the things I have suffered. Therefore I have come in my Father's name. He has anointed my head, counseled my fears, and taught me who I am. I am covered by His anointing, comforted by His presence, and kept by His auspicious grace. Today, as never before, I stand in the identity He has given me and renounce every memory of who I was yesterday. I was called for such a time as this, and I have come in my Father's name!"

_____

_____

_____

_____

_____

_____

T. D. Jakes, *365 Days to Healing, Blessings, and Freedom*

$\mathcal{M}$y Gratitude

Loving what I have—what I am grateful for:

_____

_____

_____

_____

_____

_____

_____

_____

_____

_____

_____

_____

_____

_____

_____

_____

_____

_____

_____

_____

_____

_____

_____

_____

"Their duty was...to stand every morning to thank and praise the Lord, and likewise at evening," 1 CHRONICLES 23:28, 30-(NKJV]

Releasing Your Potential

"...I will pour out of my Spirit upon all flesh: and your sons and your daughters shall prophesy, and your young men shall see visions, and your old men shall dream dreams." ACTS 2:17

The poorest man in the world is the man without a dream. The most frustrated man in the world is the man with a dream that never becomes reality. I am certain that every individual on this planet—no matter which race, culture, nationality or socio-economic status—has had a dream of some sort. The ability of children to dream is a natural instinct instilled by the Creator. No matter how poor or rich we are, whether we were born in the bush village of an underdeveloped nation or amidst the marble floors of the aristocracy of society, we all have childhood dreams. These dreams are visual manifestations of our purpose, seeds of destiny planted in the soil of our imagination.

> *"The poorest man in the world is the man without a dream."*

I am convinced that God created and gave us the gift of imagination to provide us with a glimpse of our purpose in life and to activate the hidden ability within each of us. Purpose is the reason why something was made. It is the end for which the means exists. It is the source of the dream and the vision you carried in your heart from childhood. It is the key to your fulfillment. It is a fact that every manufacturer makes a product to fulfill a specific purpose, and every product is designed with the ability to fulfill this purpose. In essence, the potential of a product is determined by its purpose. This is true of everything God created, including you.

Your life has the potential to fulfill your purpose. If, however, you imprison that potential, you rob your life of its purpose and fulfillment. You and every other individual on this planet possess an awesome treasure. Much talent, skill and creativity have been lost to the world for want of a little courage.

Myles Munroe, *Releasing Your Potential*

*I*nstant Faith, Instant Healing

"Therefore do not cast away your confidence, which has great repayment of reward. For you have need of endurance, that, after you have done the will of God, you might receive the promise." HEBREWS 10:38

Everything in life has a point where you can contact it. The light switch is the point of contact to the power plant so that when you touch the switch the lights come on. Turning the key in your car is the point of contact that turns the motor on and the cart starts, ready for you to drive.

Likewise, God's healing power has a point of contact which [is something] you *do*, When you *do* one of these, you release your faith directly to God, making contact with the power that spins the universe. Throughout the Bible God tells us the just shall live by faith. I also tell people, "We live by faith or die by doubt."

> *"Faith is not something you have to get. It's something you already have."*

Your faith begins to move, to act, when the power of God supernaturally empties you of doubt and fills you with a knowing. You come into a state of knowing that you know that you know. In that instant you cannot doubt!

Never, never doubt your own faith. You may wonder if you have faith. You do, for Paul said, "...according as God has dealt to every man the measure of faith." (Rom. 12:3).

Faith is not something you have to get. It's something you already have. Act on it by releasing it to God. That's when your healing starts.

You Could Never Repay Me, but You Are Forgiven

"And his fellow servant fell down at his feet, and begged him, saying, 'Have patience with me, and I will pay you all.'" MATTHEW 18:29

There is power in forgiveness. Do you remember Jesus' parable about the man who owed his king ten thousand talents? Scholars place widely varying values on this amount, but all of them agree it was an impossibly high amount for any employee to ever pay back. If we take a middle-of-the-road estimate, then this servant owed his king ten million dollars.

> *"Our sins will always find us out.."*

When the king ordered that the man and his family members be sold to recover the debt, the man begged him, "Forgive me! I'll repay you someday." The king said, "No. You'll never be able to repay me. I'll forgive the whole debt. You are forgiven." Can you imagine how happy that man must have been? His ten-million-dollar debt had been forgiven and marked "Paid in Full"!

This happy man had also been owed some money, so he decided to seek out a fellow servant who owed him "a hundred pence" or only 20 dollars. After being forgiven for a ten-million dollar debt, surely this man went to tell the good news to his debtor and forgive his tiny debt as well...or did he? The Bible says, "and he laid hands on him, and took him by the throat, saying, 'Pay me that you owe'" (Mt. 18:28b).

This man who had been forgiven for a multi-million dollar debt showed no mercy to the man who owed him only 20 dollars; instead he had him thrown into jail until he could repay his debt. Our sins always find us out. The man's fellow servants were so angry when they saw what he did that they told the king. The king canceled the man's pardon and placed him in the hands of tormentors or torturers until he repaid his debt. Jesus bluntly warned His listeners then and now: "So likewise shall my heavenly Father do also unto you, if you from your hearts do not forgive every one of you his brother their trespasses" (Mt. 18:35).

If you have that kind of spirit, cancel it.

_____

_____

_____

_____

_____

_____

Tommy Tenney, *The Daily Chase*

Singleness of Heart

"Bring ye all the tithes into the storehouse, that there may be meat in mine house, and prove me now herewith, saith the Lord of hosts, if I will not open you the windows of heaven, and pour you out a blessing, that there shall not be room enough to receive it." MALACHI 3:10 (KJV)

Women and men of God, let me say this to you. There is a purpose for everything, even singleness. Don't waste your bachelor and bachelorette days looking forward to wedded bliss. If you do, your married days will be anything but blissful. Single people have time to spend hours praying and studying the Word. Married people don't. Single people can drop everything and fly halfway across the world on a mission trip that will change their lives. Married people can't. Single people can fellowship till the wee hours of the morning. Take it from me, married people have curfews. Singleness is a blessing that you should not waste. Use your singleness to let God define, then refine, you so that you won't go looking for somebody else to tell you who you are or what you're worth.

> *"All I had to do was be willing to change, again and again."*

To be honest, there were times when I wasn't even sure I wanted to be married again...I wanted so desperately to ask God if I could have some guarantees to go with His promises, a little more concrete idea of His plans for me. But during that difficult time, my sense of God was so real, so clear. In my heart, I know He had spoken. And I knew if He had spoken, then He would perform, and all would be revealed to me in due season.

Often, as if sensing my trepidation, the Lord would whisper, "Behold, I shall do a new thing." I would look up at the Lord and say, "Lord, can't You see I'm still trying to recover from the old thing?"...I worried God with endless questions about where He was taking me and what He was doing with me. Finally, I realized that God really wasn't trying to destroy or hurt me. He was trying to bless me beyond measure. All I had to do was be willing to change, again and again.

Dr. Wanda Turner, *Celebrating Change*

Rush Hour Character

"For we ourselves also were once foolish, disobedient, deceived, serving various lusts and pleasures, living in malice and envy, hateful, and hating one another." TITUS 3:3

I'm always amazed at how people act in traffic, especially during rush hour. They shout at each other over the smallest infractions, flipping each other off for no good reason and refusing to yield an inch. Can you imagine what a horrible place this world would be if people acted like that all the time? What if folks ran up and down the aisles in the grocery store trying to fill their carts before other folks took all the good products?

> *"Character is the sum total of our everyday choices."*

Imagine how it would be if people refused to be courteous to each other when they were walking city sidewalks, if they yelled and cursed and constantly tried to cut in front of others.

I have no idea why driving brings out the worst in human nature. I just know that it does. Somebody who can't control his temper in rush hour might say, "Aw, that's just me. That's the way I am, and there's not much I can do about it." Wrong.

Someone has said, "Character is the sum total of our everyday choices." The great American philosopher Henry Ford explained it this way: "Life is a series of experiences...each one of which makes us bigger, even though it is sometimes hard to realize this. For the world was built to develop character, and we must learn that the setbacks and griefs which we endure help us in our marching onward."

Old Henry probably said that because he knew that the automobile was going to give all of us plenty of opportunities to develop character!

Pat Williams, *American Scandal*

The Entrance Key

"I count not myself to have apprehended: but this one thing I do, forgetting those things which are behind, and reaching forth unto those things which are before, I press toward the goal for the prize of the high calling of God in Christ Jesus." PHILIPPIANS 3:13-14

The summer home of Thomas Alva Edison is located in Fort Myers, Florida. Today it serves as a museum to display many of his inventions. One of his earliest inventions, the phonograph, can be seen here.

When you observe the phonograph, you can see teeth marks in the wood. As a lad, Thomas was running to catch a train when the conductor pulled him aboard by his ear. That incident left him hearing-impaired.

In order for Mr. Edison to know whether or not his invention worked, he bit into the wood and felt the vibration—the creator delighting in his creation.

God's yearning for man's adoration conveyed Him from Heaven to earth. Deity cloaked Himself in a robe of humanity and paid sin's penalty in order to hear praise's symphony. Instead of teeth marks we see nail prints—the Creator delighting in His creation.

> *"Religious politics and pleasing our peers are viable opponents to knowing Christ."*

The prerequisite that warrants His presence is not large crowds in stained-glass cathedrals. An IQ in the upper triple digits is not necessary.

In this dog-eat-dog world it is easy to lose focus on things that matter most. The whirlwind of daily living has a way of subtly dominating our lives. Our commitment to Christ can slowly erode away unnoticed

Religious politics and pleasing our peers are viable opponents to knowing Christ. I need various things, but one thing only justifies my utmost desire, and this is the one thing I will seek after.

Morton Bustard, *The Impassioned Soul*

We Don't Have a Lock on God

". . . that he might present it to himself a glorious church, not having spot, or wrinkle, or any such thing; but that it should be holy and without blemish."
EPHESIANS 5:27

We do not have a lock on God because we're not married to Him yet. He is still just looking for a bride without spot or wrinkle, and we need to remember that He already left one bride at the altar and He'll leave another.

I believe that God will literally destroy the Church as we know it if He has to so He can reach the cities. He is not in love with our imperfect versions of His perfect Church; He is only out to claim the house that God built. If our foul-smelling, manmade monstrosity stands in the way of what He wants to do, then He will move our junk pile aside to reach the hungry. His heart is to reach the lost, and if He spared not His own Son to save the lost, then He won't spare us either.

> *"If our foul-smelling, manmade monstrosity stands in the way of what He wants to do, then He will move our junk pile aside to reach the hungry."*

We must move into agreement with what God wants to do. The same Bible you and I carry to church services week after week says, "If we don't praise Him, then the rocks will cry out." If the Church won't praise Him and obey Him, then He will raise up people who will. If we won't sing of God's glory in the streets of the cities, then He will raise up a generation that is nonreligious and uninhibited and reveal His glory to them. His problem is that we suffer from the spiritually fatal disease of reluctance. We're just not hungry enough!

God is not coming to people who merely seek His benefits. He's coming to people who seek His face.

Tommy Tenney, *The God Chasers*

*H*is Script

"And he said unto them, 'Is a lamp brought to be put under a tub, or under a bed? and not to be set on a lampstand?'" MARK 4:21

God providentially directed Ruth to the field of Boaz. You find this divine encounter in the second chapter of Ruth, verse 3 (NAS): "...and she happened to come to the portion of the field belonging to Boaz...." The verb happened in Hebrew means "chanced upon." This leaves no room for manipulation. She had a chance and her chance transported her into the center of God's will and right to Boaz's field.

> *"You have nothing to fear except getting in His way and trying to "write the script" rather than following His."*

If Jesus wants you married, He will orchestrate the encounter. You have nothing to fear except getting in His way and trying to "write the script" rather than following His. Jesus does have your best interest at heart. He desires to bless you by giving you the best. Sometimes what you perceive as the best is nothing more than a generic version. Consider His wisdom and love in comparison to your own wisdom and self-love. In whom are you going to trust—all Wisdom and Everlasting Love or little ol' finite you?

Ever since the Garden of Eden, women have often felt they could and should know as much as God. Much pain in our world has resulted from dependence on our wisdom rather than on our Father's.

Don't Bury Your Potential

"Therefore did my heart rejoice, and my tongue was glad; moreover also my flesh shall rest in hope: because you will not leave my soul in Hades."
ACTS 2:26-27

It was a cool, wet, rainy September Sunday afternoon in the historic city of London. After I had walked for a few minutes, the pathway meandered to the entrance of an old cemetery. What an awesome experience it was to read and study the many names, dates, and quotes as these silent stones spoke. Names like John Hill 1800-1864, Elizabeth Robinson 1790-1830, and so on gave evidence of the years of British history buried there.

> *"How can you rest in peace if you died with all your potential inside?"*

Then I came upon a small grave, perhaps three feet in length, that read, "Markus Rogers, 1906-1910." Written below the name was the quote, "Gone but not forgotten." A brief calculation revealed that this was the resting place of a four-year-old child. Many questions and thoughts raced through my mind: Who were the child's parents? What was the cause of death? What special natural talents and gifts did he possess that were never displayed and never benefited anyone? What inventions or discoveries could he have shared with the human race?

As silence answered, I suddenly applied the questions to the many tombstones that surrounded this child's resting place. Some of the others had recorded life spans of thirty, forty, sixty, and even seventy-five years. Then I wondered: How can you rest in peace if you died with all your potential inside?

Immediately a quiet voice screamed in my head: Is it not a greater tragedy if those who lived to old age also carried their books, art, music, inventions, dreams, and potential to the grave?

One of my greatest fears is that many who still walk the streets of our world, perhaps some who are reading this devotional, will also deposit in the cemeteries of their communities the wealth of potential locked inside them. I trust that you will not allow the grave to rob this world of your latent, awesome potential.

Myles Munroe, *Releasing Your Potential*

Delayed Blessing

"For where two or three are gathered together in my name, there am I in the midst of them." MATTHEW 18:20

The crusade was scheduled for 16 days. Each night at the crusade tent quickly filled up, with hundreds standing all around the outside. By raising the side curtain, we could handle several thousand more people.

By the final day the crusade was stirring the city, jammed with record crowds, and the results before our eyes were truly astonishing. God was moving. The pastors met me the afternoon before the closing service and asked me to continue the crusade three more days. "Brethren," I said, "my wife is scheduled to give birth to our third child next Wednesday I am duty bound to drive home after tonight's service."

> *"Come into agreement by faith that God will intervene and do the impossible."*

"We understand that," the chairman said. "But if you could give us just three more days, we believe more than a thousand more souls will be saved ...would you be willing to phone your wife and ask her to postpone the baby's birth beyond Wednesday?" Postpone the baby's birth! Talk about seeing the invisible!

"All right," I said, I'll phone Evelyn." Predictably she said, "Oral, are you out of your mind? I can't tell this baby when to be born... What are you asking me to do?"

"Come into agreement by faith that God will intervene and do the impossible by letting you have the baby a little late." There was silence on the other end of the phone. Then, "All right, Oral, If you pray with me...I'll agree that God will postpone the birth until Friday night and that the baby will be born by midnight."

At twenty minutes before midnight Richard Lee Oral Roberts, Still Doing the Impossible was born, his little fists clenched as if to say, "Here I come! I'm ready to take on the world."

I often recall the supernaturalness surrounding his birth—how his mother and I saw the invisible and watched the impossible happen.

Oral Roberts, *Still Doing the Impossible*

Sit in the Lap of the Blesser

"I know your works: behold, I have set before you an open door, and no man can shut it: " REVELATION 3::8

God is saying to us, "I have set before thee an open door." This is one of those seasons when God seems to be throwing open the door of Heaven and saying, "Come in to a new place of intimacy and communion with Me." You don't need to worry about the blessings if you sit in the lap of the Blesser! Just tell Him that you love Him and every blessing you ever imagined will come to you. Seek the Blesser, not the blessing!

Too often God's people can be guided only by the written Word or the prophetic word. The Bible says He wants us to move beyond that to a place marked by a greater degree of tenderness of heart toward Him and by a deeper maturity that allows Him to "guide us with His eye" (see Ps. 32:8-9 · KJV). In the kind of home in which I was raised, my mom or dad could just look at me a certain way and get the job done. If I was straying down the path of childhood foolishness, they didn't always have to say anything. Just the look in their eyes as they glanced or glared toward me would give me the guidance that I needed. Do you still need to hear a thundering voice from behind the pulpit? A biting prophetic utterance to correct your ways? Or are you able to read the emotion of God on His face?

> *"How long has it been since your hunger caused you to crawl up in His lap."*

God is everywhere, but He doesn't turn His face and His favor everywhere. That is why He tells us to seek His face. Yes, He is present with you every time you meet with other believers in a worship service, but how long has it been since your hunger caused you to crawl up in His lap, and like a child, to reach up and take the face of God to turn it toward you? Intimacy with Him! That is what God desires, and His face should be our highest focus.

Yesterday is Gone

"Brethren, I count not myself to have apprehended: but this one thing I do, forgetting those things which are behind, and reaching forth unto those things which are before..." PHILIPPIANS 3:13

In order to get on with life, we must get to a new place in our hearts where we are willing to "remember not the former things," For unless you are willing to release the old, you can never come into the new. In fact, the greatest enemy of the new is the old. The greatest enemy of our destiny is our history.

Forgiving begins with a decision to let go of or put behind us people, places and things too painful to lie with. When we forgive, we make a decision in our hearts to set people free who hurt us, angered us, or armed us. We are motivated in part by the understanding that our heavenly Father forgives us as we forgive others. That means He forgives us in the same manner that we forgive others. If I am zealous about holding on to wrongs done to me, how much more zealous would God be when it came to excusing me?

> *"The greatest enemy of our destiny is our history."*

I was ready to reach forth for the things that were before me. I was ready to go get all the blessings God laid out in His Word yesterday for my tomorrow, which included His plan to prosper, help, heal, and keep me. I began to remember that I had the destiny that was spoken of in Jeremiah 29:11. He knows the thoughts that He thinks toward me. They are thoughts of peace and not evil, to give me a future and a hope.

When you make up your mind to forget those things that are behind, God doesn't waste any time filling up those empty spaces with His Word. I had new "baggage." Big, pretty Louis Vuitton steamer trunks, full of the Holy Ghost and light as a feather. In them were peace, joy, comfort, power, strength, hope, confidence, faith, and love. And I could go into them and pull out whatever I needed.

_____

_____

_____

_____

_____

_____

Dr. Wanda Turner, *Celebrating Change*

Getting Up and Doing it Again

"Therefore, my beloved brethren, be you steadfast, immoveable, always abounding in the work of the Lord, Inasmuch as you know that your labor is not in vain in the Lord." I CORINTHIANS 15:58

What do you want to be in life? Are you willing to work hard to get there? Are you willing to keep going after you get knocked down once or twice? If somebody tells you that you don't have what it takes to succeed, will you give up, or will you do everything you possibly can to prove them wrong?

> *"Wherever you want to go, you can get there from here, if you give it all you've got."*

As a writer you get used to rejections—sort of. The truth is that rejection always hurts. Some people are simply not going to be interested in whatever you have to say or do. When that happens, you have to have the attitude that you know more about your worth than those who have rejected you.

Over thirty publishers rejected Theodore Geisler, better known as Dr. Seuss, before his first book was finally published and became a runaway bestseller. Jan Karon, whose "Mitford" books have sold hundreds of thousands of copies, did not write her first novel until she was in her fifties. Painter Grandma Moses did not become successful until she was well past retirement age.

Yes! Wherever you want to go, you can get there from here, if you give it all you've got. A woman once rushed up to violinist Fritz Kreisler after an inspiring concert and gushed, "I'd give my life to play as beautifully as you do."

"I did," Kreisler replied.

Many other famous men and women have attributed their success not to genius or talent but hard work.

What is Wisdom?

"Where is the wise? where is the scribe? where is the disputer of this world? has not God made foolish the wisdom of this world?" I CORINTHIANS 1:20

God considers foolishness any wisdom that does not fulfill its original purpose. So if you are wise and you can really figure things out, but you use it to steal, God says, "You are foolish." If you are a very skillful musician, but you use it to create lewdness and sensuality, and to cause people to go into perversion, then God calls that foolishness. If you know that the power you have to believe was given to you by God, but you prefer to believe there is no God, God Calls you a fool. For when you use the belief God has given to you to say you don't believe in Him, your wisdom becomes foolishness.

The fool says in his heart, "There is no God." He takes the ability God gave him to believe and uses that belief power to not believe in God. God says, "That's foolishness!"

> *"God considers foolishness any wisdom that does not fulfill its original purpose"*

Although God calls the wisdom of the world foolishness, it is still wisdom. It's a perverted wisdom used by the chief of perverters to blind us to its very foolishness. For who could believe God would use a crucifixion to bring salvation to the world. That is not the way we expect Him to work. We look for miraculous signs and unusual insights to indicate the presence and working of God. What wisdom would choose a poor carpenter to bring the greatest gift the world has ever known? Surely not the wisdom of the world, which looks to the wealthy and the well-educated. But for those who believe in Jesus Christ, God's apparent foolishness is revealed as true wisdom.

The wisest of human thoughts appears puny beside this foolishness of God, and the greatest of man's strengths pales beside Christ's weakness. What is a stumbling block or pure foolishness for those who don't believe in Christ stands, for the Christian, as a towering source of truth, strength and hope. That is wisdom.

Myles Munroe, *Understanding Your Potential*

Virtue Is Irresistible

"Whose adorning let it not be that outward adorning of braiding the hair, and of wearing of gold, or of putting on of apparel;" 1 PETER 3:3

If you attract a person with only your looks, then you are headed for trouble, since looks don't last. As time goes on, we all end up looking like oysters. Therefore, what you look like on the inside is far more important than what you look like on the outside.

What enabled Ruth to catch Boaz's attention? Was it her gorgeous hair or beautiful eyes? No! The answer is found in Boaz's response to her question in Ruth chapter 2.

> *"A woman of virtue is irresistible to a godly man."*

"So she fell on her face, bowed down to the ground, and said to him, 'Why have I found favor in your eyes that you should take notice of me, since I am a foreigner?' And Boaz answered and said to her, 'It has been fully reported to me, all that you have done for your mother-in-law since the death of your husband, and how you have left your father and your mother and the land of your birth, and have come to a people whom you did not know before.'" (Ruth 2:10-11 NKJV)

Boaz was attracted to the virtue or character displayed in Ruth's life. A woman of virtue is irresistible to a godly man.

Live Effectively

"For it had been better for them not to have known the way of righteousness, than, after they have known it, to turn from the holy commandment delivered unto them." 2 PETER 2:21

Through these devotionals, you are being made aware of the great treasure you possess, which is your potential. I have addressed millions of people on this issue of living effectively. Repeatedly I have stressed that it is better to have never been born than to live and not fulfill the purpose for which you were given life. This truth is echoed in Ecclesiastes.

"A man may have a hundred children and live many years; yet no matter how long he lives, if he cannot enjoy his prosperity and does not receive proper burial, I say that a stillborn child is better off than he. It comes without meaning, it departs in darkness, and in darkness its name is shrouded. Though it never saw the sun or knew anything, it has more rest than does that man" (Ecclesiastes 6:3-5 NIV).

> *"It is better to have never been born than to live and not fulfill the purpose for which you were given life."*

This passage asserts that it would be better for an individual never to have been born than for him to live on this planet many years and not fulfill the purpose for which God gave him birth. In essence, when you become aware of the tremendous potential that resides within you, you are obligated to release that wealth to the world around you.

*T*rue Riches

"From everyone who has been given much, much will be demanded; and from the one who has been entrusted with much, much more will be asked."
LUKE 12:48 (NIV)

Because you are in the Lord's work, in all of your financial dealings, you must—you must—accept the fact that you will be held to a higher standard by both man and God. You must avoid at all cost financial dilemmas that others commonly experience (such as going deeply into debt or making unwise investment decisions),

> *"Only to the degree that we can handle financial matters, will the Lord let us handle spiritual matters."*

You and I must live our financial lives as if every day the local newspaper printed a copy of our personal financial statements and checkbook on the front page.

This may seem to be a hard teaching. But only to the degree that we can handle financial matters, will the Lord let us handle spiritual matters. In Luke 16:1-13 Jesus makes it clear that our stewardship of money is related to the Lord's trusting us with the "true riches" of spiritual things.

God's Word says, "Get wisdom, get understanding; do not forget my words or swerve from them. Do not forsake wisdom, and she will protect you; love her, and she will watch over you. Wisdom is supreme, therefore get wisdom" (Proverbs 4:5-7 NIV).

_____

_____

_____

_____

_____

_____

_____

_____

_____

_____

_____

Oral Roberts, *Still Doing the Impossible*

Can God Interrupt Your Schedule?

"Take my yoke upon you, and learn of me; for I am meek and lowly in heart: and you shall find rest unto your souls. For my yoke is easy, and my burden is light." MATTHEW 11:29-30

Think about all the "baggage" you carry around with you. Ask yourself, "Is all this necessary?" It may be legitimate, but it is still a weight, nonetheless. Schedules have become our slave-drivers and we have become "must do list" addicts! We are afraid to do anything or go anywhere without first checking our palm PCs, appointment books, electronic organizers, or on-line time management programs. Ask yourself: "Can God interrupt me? Have I made it impossible for the Almighty to get my attention without triggering a major catastrophe or sending fire down from Heaven?"

> *"We need to stay open to divine interruption at any time."*

We need to stay open to divine interruption at any time. Some of the greatest "God experiences" in our lives can happen when we have something else planned. Pray that when God interrupts your schedule, you will be sensitive enough to realize it is God and obey Him rather than your appointment book! If you decide to pursue your own agenda instead of Him, don't be surprised if you "run into a brick wall" and wake up with a headache saying, "Oh, God. What went wrong?" His response will be simple, "You did. You went wrong when you didn't inquire of Me and seek My face."

We must not be guilty of putting the secondary above the primary. Our primary purpose in life is to praise and worship God.... It is possible to succeed in the secondary and fail in the primary, but this is not "true success" by eternity's measure.

Tommy Tenney, *The Daily Chase*

Wisdom by the Buckets

"If any of you lacks wisdom, let him ask of God, that gives to all men liberally, and does not find fault; and it shall be given him. But let him ask in faith, nothing wavering." JAMES 1:5-6

God knows that every change He seeks to make in our lives will be met with opposition from the enemy. Satan will try to cloud your mind by distracting you from the real issues at hand. He will try to throw carefully crafted logic in the face of a word of prophecy you may have received.

> *"Ask God for wisdom and He will send it down in buckets, no questions asked."*

I don't care how big your Bible is; you will forget sometimes what the Word of God says about you and to you. That's why one of the items in the Holy Spirit's job description is to bring things to your remembrance. And He will do that sometimes by putting you before wise counselors, people who know you and know God's Word.

One of the worst things you can do in uncertain times is isolate yourself from counsel. If you're not sure who to go to, James tells us to ask God for wisdom and He will send it down in buckets, no questions asked. Wisdom nullifies uncertainty. It gives us clarity and makes sense according to the mind of God. Earthly rationale only takes into account what we see. That's why we are faced with so much uncertainty when we lean to our own understanding. Facts don't always mix with faith. The heart of God often contradicts the mind of men. That's why He so often moves us "beyond the expectations of men."

I began to see that He really had made a way in the wilderness and rivers in the desert for me. He didn't say He would make a puddle in the desert. His Word promises rivers—large, running streams, wide and flowing into bays, gulfs, seas, and even oceans. When we follow God on the path to change, we have access to the rivers and everything they flow into. In other words, God will begin to connect you to people, places, and things that will bless you because of your obedience to Him.

When we embrace change according to the will of God, He obligates Himself to watch over us as we make the transition.

Dr. Wanda Turner, *Celebrating Change*

God Encounters Of the First Kind

"Therefore I say unto you, Her sins, which are many, are forgiven; for she loved much: but to whom little is forgiven, the same loves little." LUKE 7:47

Often I see the aisles of churches strewn with people who have climbed into the lap of the Father. I see them hiding their faces underneath benches and pews as they seek the face of God. Something is happening in the Church today, and it has nothing to do with the hype and manipulation of man. Aren't you sick of all that? Aren't you hungry for an encounter with God that's not contaminated by the vain promotions and manipulations of fleshly leaders? Don't you long to have God just introduce Himself to you? You are not alone. There was one woman who marked the road of repentance with her tears and dismantled her glory for the Lord. (Luke 7:37-39).

> *"You may be only a few spiritual inches away from the encounter of a lifetime."*

"And, behold, a woman in the city, which was a sinner, when she knew that Jesus sat at the table in the Pharisee's house, brought an alabaster jar of ointment, and stood at his feet behind him weeping, and began to wash his feet with tears, and did wipe them with the hairs of her head, and kissed his feet, and anointed them with the ointment" (Luke 7:37-38).

You may be only a few spiritual inches away from the encounter of a lifetime. If you want to see the face of God, then just follow Mary to the feet of Jesus. Pull out your alabaster box of precious sacrificial praise and worship. You've been holding your treasure back for too long, but there is One here who is worthy of it all. Don't hold anything back!

_____

_____

_____

_____

_____

_____

_____

Tommy Tenney, *The Daily Chase*

No Shortcuts to Success

"For the laborer is worthy of his wages." LUKE 10:7

Late in his life, artist Pablo Picasso was having dinner with some friends in a small café. Although the other patrons recognized him immediately, most of them kept their distance out of respect for his privacy. But one man strode over to Picasso's table, shoved a napkin in front of him, and said, "Sketch something." When the great artist looked shocked, the man persisted. "Go ahead. I'll pay you for it, of course."

> "Dreaming about it won't get you there."

Without saying a word, Picasso took a piece of charcoal out of his pocket and quickly made a crude sketch of a goat. When he had finished, he held it out to the man. "There," he said. "You owe me one hundred thousand dollars."

"One hundred thousand dollars!" the man exclaimed. "Why, it only took you a few seconds to draw that picture."

"Oh no, you're wrong about that," Picasso said, as he crumpled up the napkin and stuck it in his pocket. "It took me forty years." In other words, it was practice and hard work—and plenty of it—that had made Pablo Picasso one of the world's most famous and best-paid artists.

Too many in our society have forgotten that you cannot get where you want to go without working hard to get there. Dreaming about it won't get you there. Neither will cutting corners and looking for shortcuts. Excellence and greatness always have a personal price tag!

"Now he that plants and he that waters are one: and every man shall receive his own reward according to his own labor" (1 Corinthians. 3:8).

Pat Williams, *American Scandal*

It's Not Over Till It's Over

"When Jesus heard that, he said, 'This sickness is not unto death, but for the glory of God, that the Son of God might be glorified thereby.'" JOHN 11:4

It is easy to allow yourself to feel forsaken by God when an area of your life is tested. Jesus gave you a promise, though, that He would never forsake you (see Heb. 13:5). The time when you feel that God is nowhere to be found is when He is the closest, for in those times you are not walking by feeling but by faith.

Notice that Shadrach, Meshach, and Abednego did not find the fourth man in the king's court or chambers. They found Him in the furnace (see Dan. 3:25). John the Revelator noticed something about the feet of Jesus:

> *"Never forget—when you are down to nothing, God is up to something."*

"His head and His hairs were white like wool, as white as snow; and His eyes were as a flame of fire; and His feet like unto fine brass, as if they burned in a furnace; and His voice as the sound of many waters." (Revelation 1:14-15 - KJV)

Never forget—when you are down to nothing, God is up to something... No situation is beyond the grasp of God. While you are in panic, God is at peace. The situation that threatens to finish you off is not causing as much as one bead of perspiration on the brow of Christ. Instead of becoming history, you will make history. The thing that should bury you instead will bless you.

He will come right on time, bare His mighty right arm of power, and show Himself to be Lord of all. Hold on, dear child. There is a new day dawning.

_____

_____

_____

_____

_____

_____

_____

Will Your Ability Be Lost to the World?

"He answered and said unto them, 'Because it is given unto you to know the mysteries of the kingdom of heaven, but to them it is not given.'"
MATTHEW 13:11

You possess awesome potential within waiting to be activated and released. The release of your potential demands that you refuse to be satisfied with your latest accomplishment. Only then will you tap into the vast bill of credit with which you were born. Because potential, by definition, is the large, unknown bank of resources you were given at birth, what you have accomplished is no longer your potential. Releasing your potential requires a willingness to move beyond the familiar into the realm of possibilities. The release of your potential demands that you refuse to be satisfied with your latest accomplishment.

> *"The release of your potential demands that you refuse to be satisfied with your latest accomplishment.."*

If you attempt new things and make choices that stretch your horizons, you will embark on an exciting journey. You will begin to see the marvelous being God created you to be—a being filled with more capabilities than you ever dreamed possible. The journey begins when you gain an understanding of what potential is and how you can release it. For once you understand the magnitude of the wealth God gave you, to turn from consciously and conscientiously unwrapping God's gift is to abort your potential and refuse to fulfill the purpose for which He gave you life. The knowledge of what you have failed to use to benefit yourself, your contemporaries, and the generations to follow will judge you on the great day of accountability. Potential is given to be released, not wasted.

Myles Munroe, *Releasing Your Potential*

Stringing Together a Pearl Necklace

"Seeing you have purified your souls in obeying the truth through the Spirit unto sincere love of the brethren, see that you love one another with a pure heart fervently." 1 PETER 1:22

The qualities Ruth and Rebekah displayed do not come from the jewelry store; neither are they activated the day someone places an engagement ring on your finger. Virtue is developed over time as you allow God's Spirit to do a special work in your life.

It is the Holy Spirit, not you, who produces the godly character you seek. These pearls of character are listed in Galatians 5:22-23 as "...love, joy, peace, patience, kindness, goodness, faithfulness, gentleness, self control...." As these qualities develop, your life will become like a beautiful necklace strung with the pearls of godly character.

> *"If you want a cheap imitation, a modeling or charm school will be sufficient for what you seek."*

Galatians 5:19-21, however, describes some "beads" with which many singles choose to adorn their lives instead. They are "...immorality, impurity, sensuality, idolatry, sorcery, enmities, strife, jealousy, outbursts of anger, disputes, dissensions, factions, envying, drunkenness, carousing, and things like these...." If you see that you have a bad bead in your strand of pearls, it must be removed and replaced with the character quality that pleases God.

To tap into pearl-producing power, Ephesians 5:18 says, "...be filled with the Spirit." To be filled, something must first be empty. To be filled by the Spirit you must be empty of yourself and full of God. You give the Holy Spirit complete and total control of your life.

_____

_____

_____

_____

_____

_____

_____

_____

_____

_____

Debbie Jones & Jackie Kendall, *Lady in Waiting—Developing Your Love Relationships*

You Can't Hurry God

"Nevertheless not my will, but yours, be done." LUKE 22:42B

Sometimes God shows you something that will come to pass in the future. If it's not time for it, don't run through the camp shouting, "I'm anointed!" Make sure you relinquish your "right" to hurry God along or to help Him plan out your destiny. He doesn't need our help. God's promises are not tied to time. They are tied to God alone, and He is timeless. He can do a quick work.

> "God's promises are not tied to time."

If you feel discouraged in this area, remember Moses. When he obeyed God and extended the rod over the Red Sea, the waves split open and the children of Israel walked across to victory. That sounds nice, doesn't it? Now do the math and take courage in God's ability to "hurry things along" when He is ready to do so.

There were between three and five million Israelites, so God didn't struggle to provide a few muddy single-file footpaths for those people. If the Israelites crossed that distance in one night, then they marched five thousand abreast (side by side) along a dry, smooth roadway the width of a 48-lane highway! God opened up the largest freeway in history to get millions of Israelites across the Red Sea, and He did it in a brief period of time. When God gets ready, He can do a quick work. God delivered the Israelites from four hundred years of bondage in one night!

We must have the spirit of selflessness manifested in the prayers Jesus taught us to pray and modeled before us: "nevertheless not my will, but yours, be done." (Luke. 22:42b). "Your kingdom come. Your will be done on earth, as it is in heaven." (Matthew 6:10)

Tommy Tenney, *The Daily Chase*

*T*error—A Crisis of the Soul

"There is no fear in love; but perfect love casts out fear: because fear has torment. He that fears is not made perfect in love." 1 JOHN 4:18

Terror is that complication that carries us to the very limits of our mind's ability to think, our body's ability to act, and our heart's ability to receive and express the love of God. Terror is described as a crisis of the soul; a time when we are facing something heretofore unknown and not experienced, and God is asking us to go through it anyway. When we face terror, we have met something we cannot think our way past or around. We can't change our circumstances to avoid it because God has ordered our every step to it and has left us no way of escape.

> *"When we face terror, we have met something we cannot think our way past or around."*

When God inflicts this agent of change, He is aware that you have never been down this particular path before. He leaves you open and vulnerable to the spirit of fear. When terror strikes, it is for the sole purpose of stretching the boundaries of your love for God and your ability to allow His perfect love to cast out fear. First John 4:18 says that with fear comes "torment." That torment is the punishment inflicted by fear on your heart, making it weak, draining it of its desire to fight. When God allows terror to test us, it is for the purpose of perfecting our hearts.

Here is the key to making it through tests of terror. We have to seek help from God. Terror brings us to the limits of our faith, our knowledge, and our strength. And when we reach that point, there are only two things we can do: We can give in to the fear that threatens us, or we can give up and let God take over in us and for us.

_____

_____

_____

_____

_____

_____

_____

_____

_____

Dr. Wanda Turner, *Celebrating Change*

An Attitude of Maturity

"Brethren, be not children in understanding: howbeit in malice be you children, but in understanding be mature." I CORINTHIANS 14:20

When you were a child, did your mother ever tell you to act your age? Mine did. A mature person is able to wait their turn. They understand that they are not going to get everything they want out of life. They are able to delay gratification.

The mature businessperson or entrepreneur understands that it takes time to build a profitable company, and that you can't expect to start turning multi-million dollar profits overnight. They take the long-range view of things, preferring long-term stability and growth over being a flash-in-the-pan that is here today and gone tomorrow.

> *"The mark of a truly mature person is the ability to exercise self-discipline in every area of life."*

My good friend, speaker-author Jay Strack, works with thousands of young people every year. He says that a person reaches maturity "when the little girl or little boy decides to sit down permanently, and the young woman or young man decides to stand up permanently."

In her book, The Best of Dear Abby, the late advice columnist Abigail Van Buren says that a class of sixth graders from Milwaukee asked for her definition of maturity: "Maturity is the ability to do a job whether you're supervised or not; to finish a job once it's started; to carry money without spending it; and to bear injustice without wanting to get even."

What Dear Abby is saying here is that the mark of a truly mature person is the ability to exercise self-discipline in every area of life. I have interviewed dozens of leaders in various careers and the vast majority of them credit their success to consistency. They do not see themselves as incredibly brilliant or as inherently better than other people. Most consider themselves to be average people who have worked consistently and with great effort to reach their goals.

Pat Williams, *American Scandal*

The Value of Words

"Neither shall you swear by your head, because you cannot make one hair white or black. But let your communication be, Yes, yes; No, no: for whatsoever is more than these comes of evil." MATTHEW 5:36-37

Imagine for a moment that you are living in Jesus' time. It is before Jesus has begun His public ministry. He is a carpenter in your local town of Nazareth. You have asked Jesus to make a table for you. You're on a deadline and you must have it in a week. You agree on the price of $100 for the table and the date of one week for completion. A week later you arrive to pick up the table. You lay your money down on the table and Jesus says, "Mr. Johnson, I am sorry but the table is not ready. I ran into complications. Also, I can no longer honor the price I gave you. It is now $150 instead of $100."

> *"I quickly learn whose words have substance behind them."*

Two years later you hear about this same Jesus who is preaching to the local townspeople. How are you going to view this Jesus? You probably won't give much credence to His message because of your personal experience. Our lives have an ability to reinforce the message we stand for, or they can violate it and make it totally ineffective. This literally happens all over the world in different settings with Christian businesspeople. Our message becomes ineffective because we have not done what we said.

I know people who, when they tell me they plan to do something, I can expect them to follow through about 50 percent of the time. I am sure you have had the same experience. Words and commitments are made with little meaning behind those words. However, I know others who will follow through almost every time. The only time they don't is when something falls outside their control. I quickly learn whose words have substance behind them.

Do your words mean anything to those who hear them? Ask the Lord today to show you how you are doing in this area.

What's Your View?

"Brethren, I count not myself to have apprehended: but this one thing I do, forgetting those things which are behind, and reaching forth unto those things which are before, I press toward the goal for the prize of the high calling of God in Christ Jesus." PHILIPPIANS 3:13-14

"I [Naomi] went out full, but the Lord has brought me back empty. ...the Lord has witnessed against me and the Almighty has afflicted me." (Ruth 1:21 NAS)

> *"Nothing and no one can give you a clearer picture of the true God than slipping under His wings and discovering for yourself Who God really is."*

Would you be devoted to a God like Naomi's? In Naomi's bitterness, she no longer referred to God as "the Lord" as she had in verses 8 and 9, but with a title that can cause one to feel alienated and insignificant—"the Almighty." Though Ruth clung to Naomi as a mother, she did not accept her mother-in-law's view of God for herself.

"If we think of Him (God) as cold and exacting, we shall find it impossible to love Him, and our lives will be ridden with servile fear."*

Your past experiences, present circumstances, or your parents' devotion or lack thereof may cause you to have an incorrect view of God. But nothing and no one can give you a clearer picture of the true God than slipping under His wings and discovering for yourself Who God really is, the refuge for which you long. He desires for you to come again "into the garden" and walk with Him in complete Fellowship. This is the fullness of devotion.

*A.W. Tozer, *The Root of the Righteous* (Camp Hill, Pennsylvania: Christian Publishing, Inc. 1985).

What Is Potential?

"For unto whomsoever much is given, of him shall be much required: and to whom men have committed much, of him they will ask the more." LUKE 12:48

Potential is...

...unexposed ability...reserved power...untapped strength...capped capabilities...unused success...dormant gifts...hidden talents...latent power.

...what you can do that you haven't yet done...where you can go that you haven't yet gone...who you can be that you haven't yet been...what you can imagine that you haven't yet imagined...how far you can reach that you haven't yet reached...what you can see that you haven't yet seen...what you can accomplish that you haven't yet accomplished.

> *"Most of the potential God gave you at birth still remains within you, unseen and unused."*

Thus, potential is the sum of who you are that you have yet to reveal. It's a deposit that waits to be released and maximized. You are capable of much more than you are presently thinking, imagining, doing, or being. That is your potential. Unless you continually try to reach higher, go farther, see over, and grasp something greater than you now know, you will never discover your full potential.

Every living thing that God created was blessed with potential. God also planted within you the ability to be much more than you are at any one moment. Like the apple seed, you possess hidden resources and capabilities. Most of the potential God gave you at birth still remains within you, unseen and unused. What I see when I meet you on any given day is not all you are.

Myles Munroe, *Releasing Your Potential*

$\mathcal{M}$y Gratitude

Loving what I have—what I am grateful for:

_____
_____
_____
_____
_____
_____
_____
_____
_____
_____
_____
_____
_____
_____
_____
_____
_____
_____
_____
_____
_____
_____
_____

"This is the day the Lord has made; we will rejoice and be glad in it."
PSALMS 118:24-(NKJV]

"I will seek that which was lost, and bring again that which was driven away, and will bind up that which was broken, and will strengthen that which was sick
And I will make them and the places round about my hill a blessing; and I will cause the shower to come down in due season; there shall be showers of blessing."

EZEKIAL 34: 16 & 26

When All Things Work Together

"And we know that all things work together for good to them that love God, to them that are called according to his purpose." ROMANS 8:28

Let me ask you this. If you mailed a gift to someone, how would you know if they received it? How would you know they liked it? How would you feel if they didn't even acknowledge that they had gotten it or that they knew you had sent it? What if you went by their house and saw it still in the box, or worse, in the garbage can waiting for pickup? Would you give them that same gift next year if you thought they didn't like it? And what if you ran into them and they told you they didn't even know you had sent them the gift because they hadn't bothered to read the card?

> *"If the truth were told, things always do go our way."*

Every good thing comes from God (see Jas. 1:17). It follows then that everything God gives is good and deserves to be acknowledged and appreciated. David said he would "bless the Lord at all times" (Ps. 34:1 - KJV), not just when things went the way he thought they ought to go. And if the truth were told, things always do go our way. Romans 8:28 tells us that all things work together for our good. Then Paul tells us in Philippians 4:4 to rejoice in the Lord always. And I should note here that Paul wrote the Book of Philippians from a prison cell where he was being persecuted and threatened with death and his religion was being mocked and scorned by fellow prisoners. Still, he said to rejoice, not once in that verse, but twice!

Discontentment—the refusal to celebrate change—can be detrimental to our relationship with God. You see, the celebration is not for God, it's for us. God is not going to be less God because we refuse to praise Him or thank Him for His blessings. But thanksgiving gets us through His gates and praise gets us into His courts.

_____

_____

_____

_____

_____

_____

_____

Dr. Wanda Turner, *Celebrating Change*

Grown Up Love

"For this is the message that you heard from the beginning, that we should love one another." 1 JOHN 3:11

Some people would be quick to tell you that love has no place in the business world. Unless, of course, we're talking about the love of money. The Bible, however, tells us in 1 Timothy 6:10 (NIV) that the love of money is the root of all kinds of evil. What do you suppose is in the hearts of executives who fill their pockets with gold at the expense of their employees and customers? It's certainly not love.

"Love is patient, and is kind; love does not envy; love does not boast itself, is not conceited, does not behave itself rudely, does not seek its own, is not easily provoked, thinks no evil; does not rejoice in iniquity, but rejoices in the truth; bears all things, believes all things, hopes all things, endures all things." 1 Cor 13:4-7.

> *"It has been said that love is a choice, and it takes a mature person to make that choice."*

I urge you to take a minute right now and ask yourself this important question: Who do I love? I'm sure you love your parents, your children, your spouse, your brothers and sisters, and your friends. Hopefully, loving those people comes naturally. But God expects us to demonstrate a much wider and broader circle of love. We are called to love everyone.

Ask yourself honestly if you love your neighbors—even the ones with the annoying dog that barks all night long? Do you love your co-workers—even the ones who loaf around and leave you to do most of the work? Do you love your bosses? Your teachers? Do you love the people you come into contact with in other parts of your life—the cashiers, the clerks, the waiters and waitresses?

It has been said that love is a choice, and it takes a mature person to make that choice. The truly mature person demonstrates a loving, caring attitude in everything they do and helps to make the world a better place. That's why the first habit we should strive to develop is an attitude of love.

_____

_____

_____

_____

_____

_____

Pat Williams, *American Scandal*

Brokenness

"In this you greatly rejoice, though now for a season, if need be, you are in sadness through many trials:" 1 PETER 1: 6

In the mid-1970's, a minister friend of mine went to Seoul, Korea. While there he decided to visit what would later become the world's largest church. When he arrived at the construction site, he saw nothing that even hinted of having the potential of what it is today. A cement slab with steel girders covered with bird dung was all that could be seen.

> *"It seems that the one whom God bruises, He uses. The ones who bless you the most are the ones who have bled the most."*

Construction on the mammoth auditorium had come to a grinding halt. The pastor of the church, Dr. Cho, was engaged in a fierce attack with the forces of darkness, and it looked as though satan would win.

As he walked across the cement, he noticed an elderly Korean man guarding the property. "It looks as though Dr. Cho's ministry has come to a screeching halt," remarked my friend. "Oh no," replied the guard. "God is breaking Dr. Cho. When God is through with him, he will rise higher and stronger."

In 1991 I had the privilege of attending this enormous church, which has reached a membership of more than 700,000. I was totally awestruck at what I observed there.

Read the biographies of the men and women chosen to be vanguards of revival, and you will detect a common thread. Whether physically or spiritually, they all endured some degree of suffering.

Morton Bustard, *The Impassioned Soul*

Do You Believe the Lie?

"But as it is written, "Eye has not seen, nor ear heard, neither have entered into the heart of man, the things which God has prepared for them that love him." 1 CORINTHIANS 2:9

Why do women feel they have to go after the men? Many women have believed a lie. They think, "I must get the best for myself because God may not give it to me." What do you think would have been the outcome of Ruth's life if she had chosen to believe this lie? Would she have returned home with Orpah and married one of the local guys? Would she have followed Naomi to a new land, but taken control of her own destiny in choosing a mate to care for herself and her mother-in-law?

> *"Only God has all things in view."*

God gives you the choice between His plans and yours. In the midst of her circumstances, Ruth could not have possibly seen that a man like Boaz would one day be her prince. Neither can you with your limited perspective see who or where your prince will be. Only God has all things in view. Don't look back one day and regret that you made your "life mate" choice from a limited perspective because you longed for the security of a relationship. God can and will give you His best if you wait for it.

_____
_____
_____
_____
_____
_____
_____
_____
_____
_____
_____
_____
_____

*N*ever Give Up

"Blessed are you, when men shall hate you, and when they shall separate you from their company, and shall reproach you, and persecute you, and shall say all manner of evil against you falsely, for the Son of man's sake." LUKE 6:22

As far back as he could remember, the young man had always wanted to be a writer. He spent almost every moment of his leisure time working on his craft, and the more he wrote, the more his passion for writing grew. Now, in his twenties, it was becoming apparent that he had chosen the wrong profession. He had received more than 120 rejections from various publishers. Their form letters said, "Thanks, but no thanks," and decorated the walls of his apartment. Not one of his short stories or novels had been accepted, but the young man continued to write and look for new publishers who might be interested.

> **"The rejection motivated me to keep going."**

On the 123rd try, someone finally said yes. A publisher was willing to take a chance on This Side of Paradise. That's when the writing career of F. Scott Fitzgerald finally got going. Fitzgerald is now universally regarded as one of the best American writers of the twentieth century. During the height of his popularity he talked about how he felt in the early days, when he was getting one rejection after another. "I didn't get discouraged," he said. "I got angry. The rejection motivated me to keep going."

If we both had the time and the pages to spare, I could tell you hundreds of stories about people like Fitzgerald, who persevered in the face of adversity and kept right on going until they finally finished—and won—the race. They demonstrated a spirit that could not be stopped or defeated, and they made the world a better place through their contributions.

Pat Williams, *American Scandal*

Called to the Mission Field

"For to one is given by the Spirit the word of wisdom; to another the word of knowledge by the same Spirit." I CORINTHIANS 12:8

"I'm called to the mission field," said the beautiful young woman. It was my first real encounter with the woman. As she spoke the words to me, I heard these words, "She's called to the mission field, but it's not what she thinks." I quietly kept this to myself until the following week when I felt compelled to share these words with her. She was taken aback by my motives, thinking I might simply be trying to gain her heart.

> *"I have sold all that I have to go to the mission field."*

Sometimes God speaks through others to move His purposes forward in an individual's life. He will speak through those willing to listen and speak. It is exciting to know God speaks to us and through us at times. Henry Blackaby, author of Experiencing God, believes God speaks by the Holy Spirit through the Bible, prayer, circumstances, and the Church (His Body) to reveal Himself, His purposes, and His ways.

After three days passed, the woman called me on the telephone and said, "I have sold all that I have to go to the mission field but have not been accepted as yet. I believe what you said is true. I've had a history of thinking the Lord was doing one thing in my life only to end up as another."

As the days progressed, God made it known these words were, in fact, true. She was called to the mission field of marriage and the marketplace with her husband, this writer.

_____

_____

_____

_____

_____

_____

_____

_____

_____

_____

Os Hillman, *Today God is First*

Get Started

"Which of you by worrying can add one cubit unto his stature?" MATTHEW 6:27

If there is something you want to do, but you're afraid to get started, take a lesson from the bamboo tree. Do you know how much the bamboo tree grows during the first year after it is planted? Zero. How about the second year? Zilch. For four years there is no visible evidence that anything has been planted. Anybody who didn't know better would say, "You wasted your time when you planted that thing. It's dead."

In reality, the bamboo plant is just getting ready for an incredible growth spurt in year five. How incredible? Ninety feet in thirty days. No, that's not a misprint. The plant grows three feet a day for an entire month. At the end of that time, it reaches as high as a nine-story building. It's really true that great things can and often do come from the smallest beginnings. As the old Chinese proverb says, "A journey of one thousand miles begins with a single step." But it's up to you and me to take that step. We have to start somewhere. And we have to start, period.

> *"Action is the antidote to despair."*

Singer Joan Baez said, "Action is the antidote to despair." In other words, it's counter-productive to sit around worrying about the condition of your life, your marriage, or the world today. Concern is only worthwhile if it motivates you to do something about the situation.

It's time to take the first step toward the life that we've always wanted to have, a life in which we use our God-given potential to the fullest, a life that pleases us because we know it is pleasing to God.

> The most difficult thing is the decision to act;
> the rest is merely tenacity. —Amelia Earhardt

Pat Williams, *American Scandal*

$\mathcal{F}$aith Makes Things Happen

"Therefore I say unto you, Whatsoever things you desire, when you pray, believe that you receive them, and you shall have them." MARK 11:24

Faith is the catalyst that makes things happen. It lifts you above the outward evidence of your life and empowers you to bring light out of darkness. Remember, you will receive whatever you believe.

If you expect trouble, you will get it. If you trust God and expect Him to work in the midst of your distressing circumstances, sooner or later you will see evidence of His presence.

Life without faith is foolish because life is not always what it seems. What you see or feel is not the whole story. Believe that things are going to work out. Reject the garbage that discourages you by taking your eyes off God—"You're never going to own a house. You can't even pay this rent. How're you going to afford a mortgage?"—and believe that you are going to make it. Make plans and, by faith, release your dreams by saying: "I know what I see, but I also know what I believe. I'm going to keep believing in my dreams, because all things are possible with God." Praise Him that you don't have to live by what you see. Believe in His promises and expect Him to move mountains for you (see Matthew 21:21). Refuse to believe his lies and be careful not to worry about the criticisms and objections of others. If God is the source of your dream, people cannot destroy it. You can accomplish what God wills.

> *"Remember, you will receive whatever you believe."*

So get back to God's Word and claim His promises. Make faith the daily foundation of your life and say, "God said, therefore I believe" until you start to see some differences. Above all, don't give up.

Before long you'll see the results of a life of faith. You'll get up in the morning expecting it to be a good day because there's nothing you and God can't handle together. That's living by faith. Nothing in this world can make you lose heart unless you allow it to.

Myles Munroe, *Releasing Your Potential*

Never, Never Quit

"But they that wait upon the Lord shall renew their strength; they shall mount up with wings as eagles; they shall run, and not be weary; they shall walk, and not faint." ISAIAH 40:31 (KJV)

I love stories about people who made it to the top in their professions despite being told by others that they just didn't have what it takes.

> *"If God is on your side, the bad guys don't stand a chance."*

When Wilma Rudolph fell ill with polio at the age of four, doctors told her parents she would be paralyzed for life. When she was twenty, she won three gold medals at the 1960 Olympics. Now a member of the Olympics Hall of Fame, Rudolph says her remarkable recovery came about primarily because of her mother, who massaged her legs and "encouraged me to gain movement in any way I could."

For months nothing happened. Then one day Wilma managed to wiggle her toes. It took years before she was walking with the aid of braces, but by the time she was twenty she was the fastest female runner in the world.

Remember, if you are in a correct relationship with God, He is on your side. You're always on the winning team if you're aligned with God. It doesn't matter if Saddam Hussein, Osama Bin Laden, and satan himself are coming against you, accompanied by every terrorist in the world and every demon from the depths of hell. If God is on your side, the bad guys don't stand a chance.

Most of the important things in the world have been accomplished by people who kept on trying when there seemed to be no hope at all.

—Dale Carnegie

$\mathcal{T}$ightly Tied Up

"And when he thus had spoken, he cried with a loud voice, 'Lazarus, come forth.' And he that was dead came forth, bound hand and foot with grave clothes: and his face was bound about with a cloth. Jesus said unto them, 'Loose him, and let him go.'" JOHN 11: 43-44

The scene is just out of Bethany village. There is a man lying dead in the cave. Here stands Jesus. There are the disciples, and Martha, and Mary, and the villagers, and a crowd from Jerusalem. The Master is speaking. His voice rings out clear and commanding—"Lazarus, come forth"—speaking to a dead man. And the simple record runs, "He that was dead"—life comes between those two lines of the record—"came forth, bound hand and foot with grave clothes, and his face was bound about with a napkin."

> "When Jesus, the Lord of life, gives life...He gives abundant life."

Will you please take a look at Lazarus as he steps from the tomb? Do you think his eyes are dull, or his cheeks hollow and pale? I think not! When Jesus, the Lord of life, gives life, either physical or spiritual, He gives abundant life. That face may have been a bit spare. There had been no food for at least four days and likely longer. But there is the flash of health in his eye and the ruddy hue of good blood in his cheeks. He has life. But look closer. He is bound hand and foot and face. He can neither walk nor speak.

Possibly some of us are in the same condition spiritually that Lazarus was in physically. We are tied up tight, hands and feet and face. Some in sin, some willing to compromise, some hushing that inner voice, something is wrong.

I have met some Christian people who reminded me forcibly of that scene. They are Christians. The Master has spoken life, and they have responded to His word. But they are so tied up with the grave clothes of the old life that there can be none of the power of free action in life or service. May I ask you very kindly, but very plainly, are you like that?

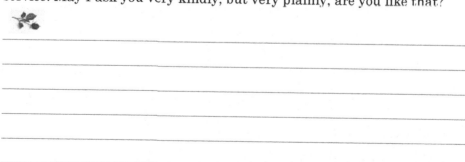

S. D. Gordon, *Quiet Talks on Power*

The Ultimate Franchise

"And he said unto them, 'How is it that you sought me? knew you not that I must be about my Father's business?'" LUKE 2:49

Earth is God's business. He has set up many franchises (churches) designed to send His representatives (Body of Christ) into the world to make known the best product ever given to mankind (Jesus). His branch managers (pastors) have been given the responsibility to teach and support those in the field. God's goal is to establish a franchise in every nation, state, and city. It is the ultimate business because when you introduce someone to His product (Jesus), you receive a reward from the home office (Heaven). God has promised that His representatives will have all the tools and customer support needed to accomplish their strategic plans.

> *"God has big plans for His franchise."*

Jesus knew that He was to be about His Father's business. He knew He was sent to earth not to enjoy the pleasure of lowly man, but to accomplish a task for which He alone was sent. When He had accomplished His mission, He was to entrust this mission to other representatives into whom He poured His life for three years. This field training allowed Jesus to mentor, model, befriend, and demonstrate firsthand the model for a successful business to be launched and sustained.

God has big plans for His franchise. He wants every human being to partake of His product; however, even God knows that not everyone will. Nevertheless, this does not thwart His efforts in seeking to make it known among His audience.

You have been called to be part of the ultimate franchise. How many new recruits have you been responsible for bringing into the franchise lately?

Os Hillman, *Today God is First*

$\mathcal{P}$ositive Self-Talk

"That you might walk worthy of the Lord unto all pleasing, being fruitful in every good work, and increasing in the knowledge of God;" COLOSSIANS 1:10

Do you remember the story of The Little Engine That Could? He kept repeating to himself, "I think I can! I think I can!" He kept repeating those words as he pulled a heavy load to the top of a steep hill. Finally he got to the point where he was saying, "I know I can! I know I can!" I know it's a children's story, but many of the stories we learned when we were kids are full of great truths based on universal experience. It's too bad that when people grow up, they forget so many of the truths they learned when they were children.

> *"Some people are harder on themselves than anyone else would be."*

Some people are harder on themselves than anyone else would be, like Groucho Marx, who said he wouldn't belong to any organization that was crummy enough to ask him to be a member. Or they feel like Woody Allen, who said, "My one regret in life is that I am not somebody else." That reminds me of the joke about the guy who asked his friend, "Why is it that everybody takes an instant dislike to me?"

"Because it saves time," his friend replied.

Or perhaps you've heard the one about the woman who whined, "The whole world is against me!"

"The whole world isn't against you," her friend comforted her. "Some people don't even know you yet."

The unfortunate thing is that if you go around beating yourself up, other people are going to start believing what you say about yourself—and they'll start beating you up too.

Please be nice to yourself! Say good things to yourself about who you are, and remind yourself that you have strengths and abilities nobody else has. Tell yourself over and over again that God loves you. If negative, self-deprecating thoughts begin to play in your brain, change the channel.

Pat Williams, *American Scandal*

Acceptance Without Measure

"Because you say, 'I am rich, and increased with wealth, and have need of nothing'; and do not know that you are wretched, and pitiful, and poor, and blind, and naked:" REVELATION 3:17

What we all need is the unique gift of acceptance. Most of us fear the bitter taste of rejection, but perhaps worse than rejection is the naked pain that attacks an exposed heart when a relationship is challenged by some struggle.

> *"I also admit that love is always a risk. Yet I still suggest that the risk is worth the reward!"*

Suppose I share my heart, my innermost thoughts, with someone who betrays me, and I am wounded again? The distress of betrayal can become a wall that insulates us, but it also isolates us from those around us. Yes, I must admit that there are good reasons for being protective and careful. I also admit that love is always a risk. Yet I still suggest that the risk is worth the reward! What a privilege to have savored the contemplations of idle moments with the tender eyes of someone whose glistening expression invites you like the glowing embers of a crackling fire.

Communication becomes needless between people who need no audible speech. Their speech is the quick glance and the soft pat on a shoulder. Their communication is a concerned glance when all is not well with you. If you have ever sunken down into the rich lather of a real covenant relationship, then you are wealthy.

This relationship is the wealth that causes street people to smile in the rain and laugh in the snow. They have no coats to warm them; their only flame is the friendship of someone who relates to the plight of daily living. In this regard, many wealthy people are impoverished. They have things, but they lack camaraderie. The greatest blessings are often void of expense, yet they provide memories that enrich the credibility of life's dreary existence.

*F*ailure Is Not Final

"Take, my brethren, the prophets, who have spoken in the name of the Lord, for an example of suffering affliction, and of patience. Behold, we count them blessed which endure." JAMES 5:10-11

David committed adultery with Bathsheba. When he learned that she was pregnant with his child, he conspired to have her husband killed (see 2 Sam.11). Living under the rule of a king who participated in this type of immoral behavior would not have been easy. David did not have to hire a string of attorneys to represent him before Congress to save him from impeachment. He did, however, have to pay his dues to God.

After repenting and suffering the consequences for the crime, David still merited a status given to no other: He is the only one in the Bible called a man after God's own heart (see 1 Sam. 13:14; Acts 13:22).

> *"When we mess up, we can get up if we refuse to give up."*

An adulterer who committed cold-blooded murder is not restricted from advancing in the Kingdom? That is the unparalleled beauty of contrition and repentance. When we mess up, we can get up if we refuse to give up.

Our pasts cannot stop us. Excuses will not exonerate us; nor can satan keep us from finding our place in the Kingdom. The ball lies in our court. Whether we will pursue our post or be pacified with the present is up to us.

God did not give up on David because David would not let go of God. He harnessed his desires and lusts and channeled them toward Heaven. Herein lay the secret of David's restoration.

"As the hart panteth after the water brooks, so panteth my soul after Thee, O God." (Psalm 42:1)

_____
_____
_____
_____
_____
_____
_____
_____

Morton Bustard, *The Impassioned Soul*

Three Kinds of Silence

"There remains therefore a rest to the people of God." HEBREWS 4:9

There are three kinds of silence: a silence of words, a silence of desires, and a silence of thoughts.

The first is perfect. The second is even more perfect and the third is the more perfect.

In the first, the silence of words, there is virtue that is acquired. In the second, the silence of desires, quietness is obtained; and in the third, the silence of thoughts...this is the goal: the internal recollection of all of your senses. To lay hold of the silence of thought is to arrive and abide at the center of your being, where Christ dwells.

> *"Rest is found only in this threefold silence."*

By not speaking, desiring, nor reasoning, we reach the central place of the inward man. It is there that God communicates Himself to our spirit; and there, in the inmost depths of our being, He teaches us Himself. He guides us to this place where He alone speaks His most secret and hidden heart. You must enter into this through all silence if you would hear the Divine Voice within you.

Forsaking the world will not accomplish this. Nor renouncing your desires. No, not even if you should renounce all things created!

What then?

Rest is found only in this threefold silence...only before an open door, where God may communicate Himself to you. It is in that place that He transforms you into Himself. –Michael Molinos, The Spiritual Guide

The Battlefield of Prayer

*"And this is the confidence that we have in him, that, if we ask anything
according to his will, he hears us: and if we know that he
hears us, whatsoever we ask, we know that we have the petitions
that we desired of him."* 1 JOHN 5:14-15

The greatest agency put into man's hands is prayer. Prayer is not persuading God. It does not influence God's purpose. It is not winning Him over to our side; never that. He is far more eager for what we are rightly eager for than we ever are. What there is of wrong and sin and suffering that pains you, pains Him far more. He knows more about it. He is more keenly sensitive to it than the most sensitive one of us. Whatever of hearts yearning there may be that moves you to prayer is from Him. God takes the initiative in all prayer. It starts with Him. True prayer moves in a circle. It begins in the heart of God, sweeps down into a human heart...so intersecting the earth which is the battlefield of prayer, and then it goes back again to its starting point, having accomplished its purpose on the downward swing.

> *"The door between God and one's own self must be kept ever open. The knob to be turned is on our side."*

A man's whole life is utterly dependent upon the giving hand of God. Everything we need comes from Him. Our friendships, ability to make money, health, strength in temptation, and in sorrow, guidance in difficult circumstances, and in all of life's movements; help of all sorts, financial, bodily, mental, spiritual—all come from God, and necessitate a constant touch with Him. There needs to be a constant stream of petition going up, many times wordless prayer. And there will be a constant return stream of answer and supply coming down. The door between God and one's own self must be kept ever open. The knob to be turned is on our side. He opened His side long ago, and propped it open, and threw the knob away. The whole of life hinges upon this continual intercourse with our wondrous God.

S. D. Gordon, *Quiet Talks on Prayer*

My God Shall Provide

"But my God shall supply all your need according to his riches in glory by Christ Jesus." PHILIPPIANS 4:19

Have you ever gone through a time of complete dependence on God for your material needs? Perhaps you lost a job and could not generate income on your own. Perhaps you got sick and could not work. There are circumstances in our lives that can put us in this place.

When God brought the people of Israel out of Egypt through the desolate desert, they had no ability to provide for themselves. God met their needs supernaturally each day by providing manna from Heaven. Each day they would awake to one day's portion of what they needed. This was a season in their lives to learn dependence and the faithfulness of God as provider. By and by, they entered the Promised Land. When they did, God's "supernatural provision" was no longer required.

> *"We must realize that the Lord is our provider; the job is only an instrument of His provision."*

For most of us, we derived our necessities of life through our work. Like the birds of the fields we are commanded to go out and gather what God has already provided. It is a process of participation in what God has already supplied. Sometimes it appears it is all up to us; sometimes it appears it is all up to God. In either case we must realize that the Lord is our provider; the job is only an instrument of His provision. He requires our involvement in either case.

Acknowledge the Lord as the provider of every need you have today. He is a faithful provider.

Os Hillman, *Today God is First*

Do What God Has Ordained

"... who has saved us, and called us with a holy calling, not according to our works, but according to his own purpose and grace, which was given us in Christ Jesus before the world began," 2 TIMOTHY 1:9

If you are only talented, you may feel comfortable taking your talents into a secular arena. Talent, like justice, is blind; it will seek all opportunities the same. But when you are cognizant of divine purpose, there are some things you will not do because they would defeat the purpose of God in your life! For instance, if it is your purpose to bless the Body of Christ in song or ministry, though you may be talented enough to aspire to some secular platform of excellence, if you are cognizant of your purpose, you will do what you are called to do. Being called according to purpose enables you to focus on the development of your talent as it relates to your purpose!

> *"Whenever we bring our efforts into alignment with His purpose, we automatically are blessed."*

Whenever we bring our efforts into alignment with His purpose, we automatically are blessed. Second Timothy 2:4-5 says, "No man that wars entangles himself with the affairs of this life; that he may please him who has chosen him to be a soldier.

And if a man also competes for masteries, yet is he not crowned, except he competes lawfully." In order to compete lawfully, our efforts must be tailored after the pattern of divine purpose. We often spend hours in prayer trying to convince God that He should bless what we are trying to accomplish. What we need to do is spend hours in prayer for God to reveal His purpose. When we do what God has ordained to be done, we are blessed because God's plan is already blessed.

Perhaps you have known times of frustration. Most of us at one time or another have found ourselves wrestling to birth an idea that was conceived in the womb of the human mind as opposed to the divine. For myself, I learned that God will not be manipulated. If He said it, that settles it. No amount of praying through parched lips and tear-stained eyes will cause God to avert what He knows is best for you.

T. D. Jakes, *365 Days to Healing, Blessings, and Freedom*

Run Away or Go In

"And they called the blind man, saying unto him, 'Be of good cheer, rise; he calls you.' And he, casting away his garmet, rose, and came to Jesus. And Jesus answered and said unto him, 'What will you that I should do unto you?'" LUKE 18:40-41A

And all the people saw the thunderings, and the lightnings, and the noise of the trumpet, and the mountain smoking: and when the people saw it, they moved, and stood afar off. (Exodus 20:18, 21-KJV)

> *"All God wanted them to do when He gave Moses the Ten Commandments was to clean up their act so He could do more than just see them from a distance."*

What a divine dichotomy! One ran in; the others ran away! God was calling the people to intimacy and they ran the other way! They told Moses, "...let not God speak to us, lest we die" (Ex. 20:19-KJV). They understood that only things that match the character of God as depicted in the Ten Commandments could stand to live in His presence. By running away, they were saying, "Look, we don't want to live up to that. Don't let God talk to us right now." All God wanted them to do when He gave Moses the Ten Commandments was to clean up their act so He could do more than just see them from a distance. He wanted to walk with them once again in the cool of the desert day. He wanted to sit with them and share His heart in intimate communion.

Nothing has changed, my friend. He wants to do the same thing now with you and me. Our proper response is, "Please, God, speak with us even if we have to die!"

The sad reality may be that most Christians in America don't have a real sense of the abiding presence of God because they refuse to clean up the clutter in their lives. And many of us who attempt to clear the clutter tend to get stuck in the logjam of legalism.

_____

_____

_____

_____

_____

_____

Tommy Tenney, *The God Chasers*

Survival Produces Peace

"When thou passest through the waters, I will be with thee, and through the rivers, they shall not overflow thee: when thou walkest through the fire, thou shalt not be burned; neither shall the flame kindle upon thee."
ISAIAH 43:2 (KJV)

Like a child who has fallen from his bicycle needs to find a place out of the view of his peers where he can honestly say, "Ouch! That hurt." We too need a private place of honesty. We need to be honest with ourselves. We need a place where we can sit down, reflect, and mourn. However, we must be careful not to mourn over the past longer than necessary. After the funeral, there is always a burial. The burial separates the survivor from the deceased, and it is as far as we can go. So you must come to a place of separation and decide to live on.

> *"...each adverse event leaves sweet nectar behind, which, in turn, can produce its own rich honey in the character of the survivor."*

"And the Lord said unto Samuel, How long wilt thou mourn for Saul, seeing I have rejected him from reigning over Israel? fill thine horn with oil, and go, I will send thee to Jesse the Bethlehemite: for I have provided Me a king among his sons." (1 Samuel 16:1· KJV)

In spite of the pain and distaste of adversity, it is impossible not to notice that each adverse event leaves sweet nectar behind, which, in turn, can produce its own rich honey in the character of the survivor. It is this bittersweet honey that allows us to enrich the lives of others through our experiences and testimonies. There is absolutely no substitute for the syrupy nectar of human experiences. It is these experiences that season the future relationships God has in store for us.

Unfortunately, many people leave their situation bitter and not better. Be careful to bring the richness of the experience to the hurting, not the unresolved bitterness. This kind of bitterness is a sign that the healing process in you is not over and, therefore, is not ready to be shared. When we have gone through the full cycle of survival, the situations and experiences in our lives will produce no pain, only peace.

T. D. Jakes, *365 Days to Healing, Blessings, and Freedom*

Life is But a Cup of Drink

"For I am now ready to be offered, and the time of my departure is at hand. I have fought a good fight, I have finished my course, I have kept the faith:"
2 TIMOTHY 4:6-7

Paul's perception of life, and the responsibility of each of us to maximize to its fullest potential, is expressed in this final message to his student, Timothy. Paul likened his life to the ceremonial drink offering administered by the priest in the Old Testament rituals of the temple, in which the priest filled a cup with wine and ceremonially poured it out at intervals in the service until the cup was completely empty. Using this example, Paul gives a very effective illustration of how our lives should be lived.

> *"True success is not a project but a journey."*

Your life is like a cup of drink served to the world by our great Creator. The drink is the awesome, untapped, valuable, destiny-filled treasure, gifts, and talents of potential buried within you. Every minute, day, month, and year is an interval of opportunity provided by God for the pouring out of another portion of yourself until you have exposed all His precious treasure that makes you unique. This is called maximum living.

True success is not a project but a journey. The spirit of achievement is guided by the notion that success is an installment plan on which we make daily payments until we maximize ourselves. This success begins where we understand and accept that life is a process of growing and developing. Thus, life is meant to be a never-ending education, a journey of discovery and adventure, an exploration into our God-given potential for His glory.

Myles Munroe, *Maximizing Your Potential*

*T*ravel Light

"Go your ways: behold, I send you forth as lambs among wolves." LUKE 10:3

Jesus had no delusions about the world—his initial pep talk to His disciples is not exactly encouraging: "I am sending you out like lambs into the midst of wolves." And it gets worse, Jesus is rather specific in his instructions—travel light—no ancient world equivalents of matching luggage, credit cards, travelers checks, cell phones, palm pilots, or SUV's crammed with 'stuff.' And depend on the local residents for hospitality—words which fly in the face of our cultural norms of acquiring, accumulating, and consuming as much as possible, depending on no-one.

His focus is the mission rather than comfort—the disciples, envoys of peace and wholeness, including healing, announcing the reign of God, and by their actions bringing its reality into the here and now. Jesus is not at all concerned with results. His commission—offer the good news. If it is accepted, share food, fellowship, and rejoicing. If not, proclaim and move on. To receivers or rejecters, the kingdom message is the same.

> *"His focus is the mission rather than comfort"*

Oddly enough, the report of their coming back does not seem to fit the sending. Bubbling with enthusiasm and pride, the seventy return, bursting with stories of miracles and powers and healings. Jesus cautions his eager disciples about overemphasizing their spiritual gifts, shifting focus to the heavenly book of life in which their names are written. As he rejoices with them, he reminds the disciples that the reason for rejoicing is not the great works done, rather it is God's declaration "This person belongs to me."

And with those words, we know we are as of the seventy—called by Jesus, sent out to find places that need healing, to prepare the way for his coming into the broken places so that people who are in despair can have hope—our mission, to speak of a way of relating to each other that is different, that is the way of love.

_____

_____

_____

_____

_____

Penelope Black, Holy Trinity Anglican Church, North Saanich, BC Canada

God's Destiny

"Hearken, my beloved brethren, Has not God chosen the poor of this world rich in faith, and heirs of the kingdom which he has promised to them that love him?" JAMES 2:5

Everyone faces a decisive choice in one way or another at different times in life. None of us are strangers to choices. Most of us ultimately realize that what choice we make determines which way our lives go and what happens to us. This is an inescapable fact of existence. Most of the time, it takes seeing the invisible to be able to choose the right way—God's destiny for your life. It certainly was that way for me.

I was drawn to the political arena and dreamed of becoming a lawyer and governor of Oklahoma someday. One summer I had been able to earn

> *"In my own crucible I learned the incalculable value of the right choice."*

enough money from helping political campaigns to buy my first car, a new Chevrolet Coupe—with cash! I was also able to shed my ill-fitting clothes for better suits, shirts, and shoes for appearing in the pulpit. When I went to preach, I no longer looked like I needed everything myself.

In churches with a poverty mentality, however, I was criticized for owning a new car. Not only were they poor people, but for the most part they had no ambition or hope to rise from their conditions by their faith. They actually equated their condition with living a righteous life. I felt that such a religious emphasis was unscriptural, thwarted legitimate ambition, held back progress, and condemned people to mediocrity and loss of hope. I came face-to-face with making the right or wrong decision at the most critical period of my young life in ministry.

We serve a mighty God. He's not weak or distant, but an awesome God, closer to us that our breath, and constantly revealing Himself to us when we are open to Him. We have a will and the God-given power of choice. In my own crucible I learned the incalculable value of the right choice.

Oral Roberts, *Still Doing the Impossible*

*T*he Supreme Talent Scout

"For none of us lives to himself, and no man dies to himself. For whether we live, we live unto the Lord; and whether we die, we die unto the Lord: whether we live therefore, or die, we are the Lord's." ROMANS 14:7-8

Major League outfielder Todd Hollandsworth says, "I understand that everything that happens to me—everything I go through—is orchestrated, is something that God already knows. He knows yesterday, today, and tomorrow. I'm a firm believer that every day is granted to us. He is just so loving and so gracious."

Most sports fans are familiar with the story of Rams' quarterback Kurt Warner, who was overlooked by talent scouts for years. He wound up playing in the Arena Football League, where he finally attracted enough attention that the Rams gave him a shot. All he did for the Rams was set all sorts of passing records en route to two Most Valuable Player awards and two Super Bowl appearances—one of which the Rams won.

> *"He knows yesterday, today, and tomorrow."*

Warner says now, "My story is about my faith in God and about how the Lord helped me get to this point. It wasn't being lucky or having all these bad breaks, and then finally getting a good break. It is about how the Lord used my whole situation and He built me up to where I could handle this. I could take hold of the success, and I could really take on responsibility for the position I had...the platform He gave me. I could use that to touch a lot of lives."

Pat Williams, *American Scandal*

Selfish Sanctity

"You ask, and receive not, because you ask wrongly, that you may consume it upon your passions." JAMES 4:3

"You have not because you ask not"—that explains many parched up lives and churches and unsolved problems: no pipelines run up to tap the reservoir, and give God an opening into the troubled territory. Then he pushes on to say—"Ye ask, and receive not"—ah! ...why?..."Because ye ask amiss to consume it upon your passion." That is to say, selfish praying; asking for something just because I want it; want it for myself.

> *"He never fails to work whenever he has a half chance..."*

Here is a wife praying that her husband might become a Christian. "He would go to church with me, and sit in the pew Sunday morning. I'd like that." Perhaps, she thinks, "He would be careful about swearing." She is thinking of herself; not of the loving grieved God against whom her husband is in rebellion. God might touch her husband's heart and say: "I want you to help Me win My poor world back." And the change would mean a reduced income, and a different social position. Oh! She had not meant that! Yes—what she wanted for herself!

To acknowledge that would be to see the mean contemptibility of it. Please notice that the reason for the prayer not being answered here is not an arbitrary reluctance upon God's part to do a desirable thing. He never fails to work whenever he has a half chance as far as it is possible to work. But the motive determines the propriety of such requests. Where the whole of one's life is for Him, these things may be asked for freely as His gracious Spirit within guides. He knows if the purpose of the heart is to please Him.

S. D. Gordon, *Quiet Talks on Prayer*

$\mathcal{A}$ren't You Ugly!

"For now we see through a mirror, dimly; but then face to face: now I know in part; but then shall I know even as also I am known." I CORINTHIANS 13:12

The deceiver distorted man's self-concept. He said to them: "Look at you. You are naked." So the man and woman felt bad about themselves and they put on clothes. They tried to cover up their bodies.

Ever since that day, we have become professional cover-ups. We don't like ourselves. We don't like our physical bodies. Yuk! I don't like how skinny I am—how fat I am—how my hair grows—how my eyes are— how my lips are. I don't like my black, brown, red, yellow or white skin. So we try to cover up what we don't like. It is strange how we work on things. If our hair is curly, we straighten it. If our skin is too pale, we get a tan. We don't like what we are. Nobody is satisfied with themselves. We all walk around saying, "Why do you want to be like me? I want to be like you."

> "We have become professional cover-ups"

This attitude is from the devil. We can't just be ourselves because satan has destroyed our appreciation of what God made. Our potential has been distorted so that we don't want to be black or tall or fat. We don't want to have curly hair or fat lips or small eyes. We have accepted satan's ploy to destroy our esteem for the beautiful creation God made us to be.

_____

_____

_____

_____

_____

_____

_____

_____

_____

_____

_____

Myles Munroe, *Understanding Your Potential*

Patience For Winter To Pass

"And let us not be weary in well doing: for in due season we shall reap, if we do not lose heart." GALATIANS 6:9

We will always have seasons of struggles and testing. There are times when everything we attempt to do will seem to go wrong. Regardless of our prayers and consecration, adversity will come. We can't pray away God's seasons. The Lord has a purpose in not allowing us to be fruitful all the time...When God sends the chilly winds of winter to blow on our circumstances, we must still trust Him. In spite of our dislike for the blinding winds and the icy grip of winter seasons, there is a purpose for these temporary inconveniences.

> *"When God sends the chilly winds of winter to blow on our circumstances, we must still trust Him."*

The apostle Paul calls such times "light affliction, which is but for a moment" (2 Corinthians. 4:17). I say, "This too shall pass!" Some things you are not meant to change, but to survive. So if you can't alter it, then outlive it! Be like a tree. In the frosty arms of winter the forest silently refurbishes its strength, preparing for its next season of fruitfulness. Its branches rocking in the winds, the sap and substance of the tree go underground. It is not good-bye, though; in the spring it will push its way up into the budding of a new experience. Temporary setbacks create opportunities for fresh commitment and renewal. If you were to record your accomplishments, you would notice that they were seasonal. There are seasons of sunshine as well as rain. Pleasure comes, then pain, and vice versa. Each stage has its own purpose.

One of the greatest struggles I have encountered is the temptation to make permanent decisions based on temporary circumstances. Temporary circumstances do not always require action. I have found that prayer brings us into patience. Patience results from trust.

Prayer is the seasoning of good judgment. Without it, our decisions will not be palatable.

_____

_____

_____

_____

_____

T. D. Jakes, *365 Days to Healing, Blessings, and Freedom*

Wise Choices

"And let us consider one another to arouse one another unto love and to good works:" **HEBREWS 10:24**

Do you think your ideals and standards are too high? Do you feel the pressure to compromise and settle for the generic version of life? Ruth lived in an era that was exactly like modern America. Judges 21:25 (NKJV) describes the era in which she lived: "In those days there was no king in Israel; everyone did what was right in his own eyes." We too live in a culture where it seems that no one fears God and people just "do their own thing."

You, like Ruth, will be greatly affected by your choices. Ruth's wise choices allowed her to break a godless family cycle and begin a new cycle that the Word of God triumphantly records. God has not changed—and neither have men. The high standards in God's Word are not irrelevant, but completely applicable to finding God's best for your life. Choices, guided by your convictions rather than by chance, determine your destiny.

> *"Choices, guided by your convictions rather than by chance, determine your destiny."*

You cannot make good choices without proper, biblical convictions. Don't carelessly leave your dating/relating standards to chance. Too much depends on your decisions in this area.

Debbie Jones & Jackie Kendall, *Lady in Waiting—Meditations of The Heart*

The Maximum of Mediocrity

"For to their ability, I bear witness, yes, and beyond their ability they were willing of themselves;" 2 CORINTHIANS 8:3

What does it mean to maximize? What is maximum? The word maximum may be defined as "supreme, greatest, highest, and ultimate." It is synonymous with such concepts as pinnacle, preeminence, culmination, apex, peak, and summit. It implies the highest degree possible. Just a brief look at these concepts immediately convicts us of the many opportunities we have abused and forfeited because we have failed or have refused to give our all.

> *"Simply put, mediocrity is living below our known, true potential."*

How tragic that most of the nearly six billion people on this planet will settle for an average life limited only by their unwillingness to extend themselves to the summit of their own selves. Anything less than maximum is mediocrity. In other words, mediocrity may be defined as the region of our lies bounded on the north by compromise, on the south by indecision, on the east by past thinking, and on the west by a lack of vision. Mediocrity is the spirit of the average, the anthem of the norm, and the heartbeat of the ordinary.

This failure to do our best, to go beyond the expectations of others, to express ourselves fully, to live up to our true potential, to extend ourselves to the limit of our abilities, to give it all we have, to satisfy our own convictions, is called mediocrity. Simply put, mediocrity is living below our known, true potential. It is accepting the norm, pleasing the status quo, and doing what we can get by with. Therefore, to maximize is to express, expose, experience, and exercise all the hidden, God-given abilities, talents, gifts, and potential through God's vision breathed in our souls to fulfill His purpose for our lives on earth.

Myles Munroe, *Maximizing Your Potential*

The Shortest Way to God

"Therefore if you bring your gift to the altar, and there remember that your brother has anything against you; leave there your gift before the altar, and go your way; first be reconciled to your brother, and then come and offer your gift." MATTHEW 5:23-24

A thing spoken of as hindering prayer is an unforgiving spirit. You have noticed that Jesus speaks much about prayer and also speaks much about forgiveness. But have you noticed how, over and over again He couples these two—prayer and forgiveness? I used to wonder why. I do not so much now. Nearly everywhere evidence keeps slipping in of the sore spots. One may try to keep his lips closed on certain subjects, but it seems about impossible to keep the ears entirely shut. And continually the evidence keeps sifting in revealing the thin skin, raw flesh, wounds never healed over, and some jaggedly open, almost everywhere one goes.

> *"The shortest way to God for that man is not the way to the altar, but around by that man's house."*

Run through Matthew alone a moment. Here is the fifth chapter: "If you bring your gift to the altar"—that is approaching God; what we call prayer—"and there remember that your brother has anything against you...leave there your gift and go your way; first be reconciled ..." Here comes a man with a lamb to offer. He approaches solemnly, reverently, towards the altar of that man, with whom he has had difficulty. And instantly he feels the grip tightening on the offering, and his teeth shutting closer at the quick memory. Jesus says, "If that be so lay your lamb right down." What! Go abruptly away! Why! How the folks around the temple will talk! "Lay the lamb right down, and go thy way." The shortest way to God for that man is not the way to the altar, but around by that man's house. "First, be reconciled"—keep your perspective straight—follow the right order—"first be reconciled"—not second, "then come and offer your gift."

S. D. Gordon, *Quiet Talks on Prayer*

Make Plans, Set Goals

"I press toward the goal for the prize of the high calling of God in Christ Jesus." PHILIPPIANS 3:14

God wants us to become people who have plans. He says, "Use your imagination. I won't give you a thought if you can't do it. If you think it, I'm ready to do it." Plans are documented imaginations. If you can document an imagination, you've developed a plan for action.

Progress requires a plan of action. Ideas must be put down if they are to influence the way you live. Many of us plan our meals for the next week, but we have nothing planned for our lives. The food we eat just goes away—it doesn't touch the future.

> *"Progress requires a plan of action"*

Stop. Set your course. Imagine into your future as far as you can. Chart what you are going to do for the next five months—twelve months—two years. Start imagining what you want to be—what you want to accomplish—where you want to go—who you want to influence. Do something and then put your plan in a convenient location so you can check your progress, seeing how close you are to your next goal.

You will be amazed how that will make you work every day. It will encourage you to move. You will begin to see God's power at work within you, and that will motivate you even more. Don't worry how you are going to meet all your goals. God says, "You make the plan and I will give the answer how it will be accomplished."

God created you to change the world. He carefully designed a plan for your life that allows you to share in His work of creation. Because you were made in God's image, you share His potential to be and do much more than is visible now. Everything you see was originally a thought in the mind of God-an invisible idea that God worked into sight. Make a plan. Give yourself something to be motivated toward. As you dream, think, imagine and plan who you want to be, you will begin to see why God created you and the work He has designed you to do. You are destined by God to reveal His glory-His very nature.

_____

_____

_____

_____

_____

Myles Munroe, *Understanding Your Potential*

$\mathcal{M}$y Gratitude

Loving what I have—what I am grateful for:

_____

_____

_____

_____

_____

_____

_____

_____

_____

_____

_____

_____

_____

_____

_____

_____

_____

_____

_____

_____

_____

_____

_____

_____

_____

_____

_____

_____

"Therefore be not anxious for tomorrow: for tomorrow shall take care for the things of itself. Sufficient unto the day is the evil thereof."
MATTHEW 6:31

$\mathcal{F}$aithfulness to Convict

"And when he is come, he will expose the world of sin, and of righteousness, and of judgment." JOHN 16:8

I had recently come back from a mountaintop experience. As I attempted to get back into my routine, I found a great cloud of oppression come over me. Each day I attempted to press though it, but with no success. Fear, anxiety, doubt, and unbelief were setting in. I knew I was fretting over my future. I had been in a long period of transition in my business life and was tired of the place of waiting. Yet I didn't understand the oppression. It was definitely spiritual warfare.

> *"Imagine God using my own words to convict me of sin!"*

That night I was reading a book regarding our calling from God. The author made mention that we can become envious of others when we get into a place where we are dissatisfied. Suddenly, I realized I was guilty of envying where other businesspeople were in their lives. I was "subconsciously" angry that the calling God had placed on my life had such adversity. I had to repent.

As if this were not enough, the next day the Holy Spirit confirmed my assessment in the most unusual way. That morning I turned on my computer to read my own Marketplace Meditation that is sent to my computer. The message was on "Envying Others" and included the same Scripture reference as the author's in the book. Imagine God using my own words to convict me of sin! The nerve of Him! To make matters worse, at lunchtime I tuned into the local Christian radio station to hear an interview with the same author as he cited the very passage I had read the day before. I was shocked to realize how the Holy Spirit could be so precise in His ability to convict and give proof of His activity in my life.

Do you question if the Holy Spirit is active in your life? The Lord has promised that the Holy Spirit will convict us of sin when we move away from Him. It is His responsibility as our guide.

Not Now

"I waited patiently for the Lord; and He inclined unto me, and heard my cry. He brought me up also out of an horrible pit, out of the miry clay, and set my feet upon a rock, and established my steps. And He has put a new song in my mouth 'praise to our God.'" PSALM 40:1-3 (NJKV)

We come into this world fully cognizant of the fact that we have a limited amount of time. We don't live here for very long before we are confronted with the cold realities of death. Yet what disturbs me most is not the quantity of life, but the quality of life. Simply stated, when death comes to push me through its window from time into eternity, I want to feel as though I accomplished something worthwhile. I want to feel that my life made some positive statement.

> *"God's answer is not always yes or no; sometimes He says, "Not now!"*

It would be terrible to look back over your life and see that the many times you thought your request was denied was actually only delayed. Life will always present broken places, places of struggle and conflict. If you have a divine purpose and life has put you on hold, hang on! Stay on the line until life gets back to you. If you believe as I do, then it's worth the wait to receive your answer from the Lord.

The real test of faith is in facing the silence of being on hold. Those are the suspended times of indecision. Have you ever faced those times when your life seemed stagnant? Have you felt you were on the verge of something phenomenal, that you were waiting for that particular breakthrough that seemed to be taunting you by making you wait? All of us have faced days that seemed as though God had forgotten us. These are the moments that feel like eternity. These silent coaches take your patience into strenuous calisthenics. Patience gets a workout when God's answer is no answer. In other words, God's answer is not always yes or no; sometimes He says, "Not now!"

The Motive Check

"Consider the lilies of the field, how they grow; they toil not, neither do they spin: and yet I say unto you, That even Solomon in all his glory was not arrayed like one of these." MATTHEW 6:28B-29

Before you go to another activity to spend time with the available guys, as you check your hair and makeup and teeth, give yourself a thorough "heart flossing." A woman with selfish motivation mentally plots the next maneuver to capture the attention of the man of her dreams. Ask the Lord to reveal any impure motive that resides in your heart. This is not to say that you cannot do nice things for a man; it is simply a warning to check your motives. Before you bake one more thing for a brother or purchase one more book or meaningful card, be very careful to check your motive and honestly respond to whatever the Lord shows you. You can save yourself many tears and much frustration if you are just willing to do a regular "motive check" on your heart.

> *"You can save yourself many tears and much frustration if you are just willing to do a regular "motive check" on your heart."*

Manipulation and maneuvering can be deadly. If you maneuver to get a man, you will have to maneuver to keep him! This is not implying that there is no work involved in a good relationship, but there is a huge difference between working and maneuvering. You recognize the difference between the two by discerning your motive.

You Can Do Everything God Asks

"Let us therefore, as many as be mature, be thus minded: and if in anything you be otherwise minded, God shall reveal even this unto you."
PHILIPPIANS 3:15

God is good. He has built into you the potential to produce everything He calls for. When God says, "Love your enemies," Don't start listing reasons why you can't. The ability to love is built in-it's there-no excuses. God wouldn't ask for it if it wasn't available. He wired you to produce everything He demands.

God also wired everything else to produce what He demands from it. God looks at a piece of fruit and says, "In you there is a tree. There is a seed in you, and that seed is a tree. It's there, and I demand what I put in." So God says, "Plant that seed and a tree has to come out; I put a tree in that seed. Before you were given the fruit, I made the seed with the tree." That's the way God thinks. Hallelujah!

> *"Whenever God gives you a responsibility, He also gives you the ability to meet that responsibility."*

Whenever God gives you a responsibility, He also gives you the ability to meet that responsibility. In other words, whatever God calls for, He provides for. If God tells you to do something, He knows you can do it. So don't you dare tell God that you can't. Just because He told you to assume that responsibility means He knows you can do it. The problem isn't that you can't, it's just that you won't.

Whether you use the ability God has deposited within you is totally up to you. How well you assume the responsibilities God gives you is not so much a question of how much you do, but rather how much of the available power you use. What you are doing is not near what your ability is. What you have accomplished is a joke when compared with what you could accomplish-you are not *working* enough with the power of God

A Matter of Trust

"His master said unto him, 'Well done, good and faithful servant; you have been faithful over a few things, I will make you ruler over many things."
MATTHEW 25:21

I have no doubt most, or all of us here today, trust Him. Let me ask you very softly now: Can He trust you?

While we might all shrink from saying "yes" to that, there is a very real sense in which we may say "yes," namely in the purpose of the life.

> *"God judges man not by his achievements, but by his purposes."*

Every life is controlled by some purpose. What is yours? To please Him? If so, He knows it. It is a great comfort to remember that God judges man not by his achievements, but by his purposes; not by what I am, actually but by what I would be, in the yearning of my inmost heart, the dominant purpose of my life. God will fairly flood your life with all the power he can trust you to use wholly for him.

Commercial practice furnishes a simple but striking illustration here. A man is employed by a business house as clerk. His ability and honesty come to be tested in many ways constantly. He is promoted gradually, his responsibility increased. He is trusted with the combination to the inner box in the vault. Because it has been proven by actual test that he will use everything only for the best interest of his house, and not selfishly.

Here the whole thing moves up to an infinitely higher level, but the principle does not change. If I will come into a relationship implied in these words—it shall be the one controlling desire and purpose of my life to do the things that please Him—then those promises of Jesus with their wonderful sweep, their limitless sweep are mine to use as I will.

S. D. Gordon, *Quiet Talks on Prayer*

I'm Not Dead Yet

"...knowing this, that the testing of your faith works perseverance." JAMES 1:3

Sometimes Christians become frustrated and withdraw from activity on the basis of personal struggles. They think it's all over, but God says not so! The best is yet to come. The Lord doesn't like pity parties, and those who have them are shocked to find that although He is invited, He seldom attends. Many morbid mourners will come to sit with you as you weep over your dear departed dreams. But if you want the Lord to come, you mustn't tell Him that you aren't planning to get up.

> *"I would rather nearly drown and have to be saved than play it safe and never experience the miraculous."*

If you ever get around people who have accomplished much, they will tell you that those accomplishments didn't come without price. Generally that cost is much more expensive than you normally want to pay. Still, the cost of total transformation means different things to different people. When you arrive at your destination, don't be surprised that some people will assume everything you achieved came without price. The real price of success lies within the need to persevere. The trophy is never given to someone who does not complete the task. Setbacks are just setups for God to show what He is able to do. Funerals are for people who have accepted the thought that everything is over. Don't do that; instead tell the enemy, "I am not dead yet."

The whole theme of Christianity is one of rising again. There are obstacles that can trip you as you escalate toward productivity. But it doesn't matter what tripped you; it matters that you rise up. People who never experience these things generally are people who don't do anything. There is a certain safety in being dormant. Nothing is won, but nothing is lost. I would rather walk on the water with Jesus. I would rather nearly drown and have to be saved than play it safe and never experience the miraculous.

What Can You Do?

"I can do all things through Christ which strengthens me." PHILIPPIANS 4:13

For about two years now my little boy has been coming to me when he's trying to do something and saying, "I can't do this." I always respond to him by saying, "There is nothing named 'can't'."

When he comes back to me and says, "I don't know how to do it," I always reply, "There's always a way to do everything."

Several days ago my son and I were out in the yard playing bat and ball. I was throwing the ball to him and he kept on missing with the bat. Finally he became really upset and said, "I can't do that," to which I replied, "There's nothing named 'can't'." Slowly he repeated after me, "There's nothing named 'can't'." Then I said, "Hold the bat," and I threw the ball. He hit the ball and then said, "There's nothing named 'can't'."

> *"The people who change the world are the people who have taken impossible out of their dictionaries."*

Several days later when I stopped by home to drop off my daughter, my son came running and wanted to play basketball. When I said that I had to go back to the office to do some work, he insisted that he wanted to play ball with me then. When I again replied that I had to go to the office, he said, "There's nothing named 'can't'."

Do you see the point? If he begins to think that way at four years of age, this world is in for a winner. Too often we fail in our efforts because we have been brought up believing that we cannot do some things. The people who change the world are people who have taken impossible out of their dictionaries. The men and women who make changes in history are those who come against the odds and tell the odds that it's impossible for the odds to stop them.

Myles Munroe, *Understanding Your Potential*

August 8

Seventy Times Seven

"Then Peter came to him, and said, "Lord, how often shall my brother sin against me, and I forgive him? until seven times?" Jesus said unto him, "I say not unto you, Until seven times: but, Until seventy times seven."
MATTHEW 18:21

In this sixth chapter of Matthew, God gives the form of prayer which we commonly call the Lord's prayer. It contains seven petitions. At the close He stops to emphasize just one of the seven. You remember which one; the one about forgiveness. In the eighteenth chapter Jesus is talking alone with the disciples about prayer.

Peter seems to remember the previous remarks about forgiveness in connection with prayer; and he asks a question. It is never difficult to think of Peter asking a question or making a few remarks. He says, "Master how many times must I forgive a man? Seven times!" Apparently Peter thinks he is growing in grace. He can actually think now of forgiving a man seven times in succession. But the Master in effect says, "Peter, you haven't caught the idea. Forgiveness is not a question of mathematics, not a matter of keeping tab on somebody; not seven times but seventy times seven." And Peter's eyes bulge open with an incredulous stare—"four hundred and ninety times!...one man!...straightway!!" Apparently the Master is thinking, that he will lose count or get tired of counting and conclude that forgiveness is preferable—or else, by practice, breathe in the spirit of forgiveness—the thing He meant.

> *"Forgiveness is not a question of mathematics, not a matter of keeping tab on somebody; not seven times but seventy times seven."*

S. D. Gordon, *Quiet Talks on Prayer*

*T*he Principle of Capacity

"... we speak the wisdom of God in a mystery, even the hidden wisdom, which God ordained before the world unto our glory: which none of the rulers of this world knew: for had they known it, they would not have crucified the Lord of glory." 1 CORINTHIANS 2:7-8

The implication of these verses is that no human has the right or the ability to fully determine or measure the capacity of the potential you possess. The apostle Paul, in a letter to the church at Corinth, spoke of the hidden secret wisdom of our destiny that is invested in each of us by our Creator God.

> *"...your true capacity is not limited...by the opinion of others"*

The true capacity of a product is determined not by the user but the manufacturer. The automobile was built with the capacity to travel at 180 mph; therefore its full potential was determined by the manufacturer. The true potential of the car was not affected by my opinion of its ability or by my previous experience with driving. Whether or not I used the full capacity of the car's engine did not reduce its potential capacity.

The same principle applies to your life. God created you like He did everything else, with the capacity to fulfill your purpose. Therefore, your true capacity is not limited, reduced, or altered by the opinion of others or your previous experience. You are capable of attaining the total aptitude given to you by your Creator to fulfill His purpose for your life. Therefore, the key to maximizing your full potential is to discover the purpose or reason for your life and commit to its fulfillment at all cost.

The Purpose of Calamity

"And that we may be delivered from unreasonable and wicked men: for not all men have faith. But the Lord is faithful, who shall establish you, and keep you from evil." 2 THESSALONIANS 3:2-3

There is a deep-seated need in all of us to sense purpose—even out of calamity. Out of this thirst for meaning is born the simplistic yet crucial prayer, "Why?"

Many times, we want to know and understand. It is part of our superior creative ability. It separates us from lower forms of life that tend to accept events as they come. There is within us this insatiable need to understand. No matter how painful the quest, we will still search through the rubbish of broken dreams, broken promises, and twisted childhood issues looking for clues.

> *"The struggle truly begins not when men surround us, but rather when they forsake us."*

We ambitiously pursue these clues because we believe there is a reward for the discovery. This emotional autopsy often takes us through the bowels of human attitudes and dysfunctional behavior. We don't have to necessarily erase the cause of our pain; we mainly just want to find some reason or justification for the pain and discomfort.

"And Jacob was left alone; and there wrestled a man with him until the breaking of the day." Genesis 32:24 (KJV)

Like Jacob, all of us know what it means to be left alone. Whether through death, desertion, or even disagreement, we have all been left alone at times. We are sometimes disillusioned when we find out how easily people will leave us. Generally they leave us when we think that we need them.

This may be difficult, but it is all part of God's "scholastic-achievement program" for strong believers. He is determined to strip us of our strong tendency to be dependent on others, thereby teaching us self-reliance and God-reliance. Thus the struggle truly begins not when men surround us, but rather when they forsake us. It is then that we begin to discover our own identity and self-worth!

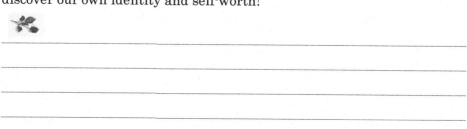

T. D. Jakes, *365 Days to Healing, Blessings, and Freedom*

The Key to Your Potential

"I am the true vine, and my Father is the vinedresser. Every branch in me that bears no fruit he takes away: and every branch that bears fruit, he prunes it, that it may bring forth more fruit." JOHN 15:1-2

The secret to a happy and productive life is remaining attached to your Source.

A grape vine is an interesting plant. The vine, which is the thick wooden part running from the ground up the pole, is the only part of the plant that contains life ability. None of the life is in the branches; all of it is in the vine. There is no life in the little green things you see on the side with the grapes hanging on them. They are getting their life from the vine. They have no root in themselves.

> *"Whatever God speaks comes out of what He spoke to."*

Each small branch has to depend on the life flowing up and down the great branch, the vine, to give it life. Thus the branches cannot live without the vine. The relationship of the vine and its branches is reflected throughout God's creation. Life is not possible when a thing is separated from its source.

When God wanted plants He spoke to the soil, and out of the soil came what God spoke. The principle is simple. Whatever God wants He speaks to what He wants it made out of. Whatever God speaks comes out of what He spoke to.

When God wanted animals, He spoke to the ground. When God wanted plants He spoke to dirt. Because God wanted man to come out of Himself, He spoke to Himself when He created man.

When God wanted man, He spoke to Himself. Therefore man is what God spoke to. Man is spirit because man came out of the spirit realm.

_____

_____

_____

_____

_____

_____

_____

_____

_____

_____

Myles Munroe, *Understanding Your Potential*

*T*rue North

"How do you think? if a man has a hundred sheep, and one of them be gone astray, does he not leave the ninety and nine, and go into the mountains, and seek that which is gone astray?" MATTHEW 18:12

Modern technology has produced a device known as the GPS (global positioning system). This is the device that was used in the Gulf War to guide smart bombs to Saddam Hussein's bunker. After the war, they were made available to the public, and now they can be purchased at the nearest department store for less than $200. Hunters and fishermen use the GPS to avoid getting lost in the woods. Pilots whose cockpits are outfitted with expensive navigation technology many times rely on this tiny device due to its incredible accuracy.

> *"It is imperative that we have something in our life that we place momentous value on, something so dear that the greatest arbitrator cannot persuade us into relinquishing it."*

I cannot help but ask this question: In man's quest to invent machinery to provide direction, why does he ignore ancient landmarks that have proven themselves throughout the ages? The one thing that will never change is the Word of God.

It is imperative that we have something in our life that we place momentous value on, something so dear that the greatest arbitrator cannot persuade us into relinquishing it.

Love, honor, respect, and integrity are virtues rather than gifts one is born with. If we come into possession of these great attributes, we will have earned them, not with dollars, but by establishing principles to live by and sticking to them regardless of how we might benefit otherwise.

Morton Bustard, *The Impassioned Soul*

Don't Outgrow Your Foundation

"I will liken him unto a wise man, which dug deep, and laid the foundation on a rock: which built his house upon a rock: and the rain descended…and could not shake it; and the winds blew, and beat upon that house, and it did not fall: for it was founded upon a rock." MATTHEW 7:24B-25

Once I was praying for the Lord to move mightily in my ministry. I had asked, fasted, and prayed. I had probably begged a little and foamed at the mouth too, but none of it hurried the plan of God in my life. After many days of absolute silence, He finally sent me a little answer. The Lord answered my prayer by saying, "You are concerned about building a ministry, but I am concerned about building a man." He concluded by mentioning this warning, which has echoed in my ears all of my life. He said, "Woe unto the man whose ministry becomes bigger than he is!" Since then I have concerned myself with praying for the minister and not for the ministry. I realized that if the house outgrows the foundation, gradually the foundation will crack, the walls will collapse, and great will be the fall of it!

> *"If the house outgrows the foundation, gradually the foundation will crack, the walls will collapse, and great will be the fall of it!"*

No matter what you are trying to build, whether it is a business, a ministry, or a relationship, give it time to grow. Some of the best friendships start out gradually. I am still amazed at who I am becoming as I put my life daily into His hands. He is changing me. He's not finished. There is so much more that needs to be done.

Humility is a necessity when you know that every accomplishment had to be the result of the wise Master Builder who knows when to do what. He knew when I needed friends. He knew when I needed to sit silently in the night, wrap my arms around my limitations, and whisper a soft request for help into the abyss of my pain. He is the One who rolls back the clouds on the storms and orders the rain to stop.

_____
_____
_____
_____
_____
_____

T. D. Jakes, *365 Days to Healing, Blessings, and Freedom*

With Us In The Fire

"If we live in the Spirit, let us also walk in the Spirit." GALATIANS 5:25

It has been suggested that if you walk in the Spirit, you won't have to contend with the fire. Real faith doesn't mean you won't go through the fire. Real faith simply means that when you pass through the fire, He will be with you. The presence of the Lord can turn a burning inferno into a walk in the park! The Bible says a fourth person was in the fire, and so the three Hebrews were able to walk around unharmed in it (see Dan. 3).

King Nebuchadnezzar was astonished when he saw them overcome what had destroyed other men. I cannot guarantee that you will not face terrifying situations if you believe God. I can declare that if you face them with Christ's presence, the effects of the circumstance will be drastically altered. It is quite popular to suggest that faith prohibits trouble. But when I read about these young Hebrew men, I realize that if you believe God, you can walk in what other men burn in. Seldom will anyone fully appreciate the fire you have walked through, but be assured that God knows the fiery path to accomplishment. He can heal the blistered feet of the traveler.

> *"The presence of the Lord can turn a burning inferno into a walk in the park!"*

When John was on the isle of Patmos, he was limited to a cave but free in his spirit (see Rev. 1). John's predicament on Patmos proves that negative circumstances reveal Christ, not veil Him. While in the dank, dismal, dark caves of persecution, surrounded by the sounds of other abused prisoners, John caught a vision. In his newfound image of Christ, he describes the crisp clarity of a revelation given in the midst of chaos. A crisis can clear your perceptions as you behold His face, looking for answers that will not be found in the confines of the situation.

Shortcuts Don't Work

"Fight the good fight of faith, lay hold on eternal life, to which you are also called, and have professed a good profession before many witnesses."
1 TIMOTHY 6:12

Ben Johnson is an athlete from Canada who set many world records. In 1987 he set the world record in the one hundred yard dash at 9.83 seconds. In 1988 he broke his own record, winning the race in 9.79. But it is difficult to be correct in calling that a world record because the last record set was not the record of Ben Johnson.

It was the record of a steroid pill. That record belongs to Ben Johnson plus the chemicals.

We will never know Ben Johnson's potential as far as running the one hundred yard dash is concerned. Could he have run one

| *"Shortcuts negate potential"* |

hundred yards in 9.79 seconds without the chemical? Possibly, but we will never know because Ben Johnson negated his potential by trying a shortcut. There was no reason for his shortcut. He had a world record. He had his name in history, and it was a good name. How sad to destroy a good name by a little bit of chemical.

I picked up a magazine on an airplane in which there was an advertisement that said, "Would you like a doctorate degree? Call us." I often read that advertisement and wonder how many have called them. If I did not realize that you cannot get something for nothing, I probably would have called them. There are people out there with doctorate degrees, or with doctorate letters in front of their names, who will never know their potential. They didn't allow themselves the chance to see what they could really do. They have the degrees, but they didn't fulfill the requirements.

There are no shortcuts to developing your potential. You will never know what you might have achieved if you use a crutch to get there.

_____

_____

_____

_____

_____

_____

_____

Myles Munroe, *Understanding Your Potential*

*I*nterstal Destinies

"And he said unto me, 'My grace is sufficient for you: for my strength is made perfect in weakness.'" 2 CORINTHIANS 12:9A

Only when we are weary from trying to unlock our own resources do we come to the Lord and allow Him to release in us the power to become whatever we need to be. Actually, isn't that what we want to know—our purpose? Then we can use the power to become who we really are. Life has chiseled many of us into mere fragments of who we were meant to be. To all who receive Him, Christ gives the power to slip out of who they were forced into being so they can transform into the individual they each were created to be.

> *"He gives us the power to become who we are eternally and internally."*

What Christians so often refer to as grace truly is God's divine enablement to accomplish predestined purpose. When the Lord says to Paul, "My grace is sufficient for you..." (2 Corinthians 12:9), He is simply stating that His power is not intimidated by your circumstances. You are empowered by God to reach and accomplish goals that transcend human limitations! Problems are not really problems to a person who has the grace to serve in a particular area.

How many times have people walked up to me and said, "I don't see how you can stand this or that." If God has given us the grace to operate in a certain situation, those things do not affect us as they would someone else who does not have the grace to function in that area. Therefore, it is important that we not imitate other people. Assuming that we may be equally talented, we still may not be equally graced. Remember, God always empowers whomever He employs. Ultimately, we must realize that the excellency of our gifts are of God and not of us. He doesn't need nearly as much of our contributions as we think He does. So it is God who works out the internal destinies of men. He gives us the power to become who we are eternally and internally.

*T*riumphant Defeats

"This is now the third time that Jesus showed himself to his disciples, after that he was risen from the dead." JOHN 21:14

So often defeat is what is required before victory can be won. Jesus said that unless the seed dies and goes into the ground it cannot bring forth fruit (see John 12:24). The death of a vision is often required before the fulfillment can really take place. Have you failed at something in your life? Have you seen the vision fulfilled you thought you were given? The vision may yet happen.

> *"So often defeat is what is required before victory can be won."*

The disciples thought they suffered their greatest defeat when Jesus died on the cross. However, this defeat became the greatest victory on earth. Christ's death gave liberty. Forgiveness came to all men. New life came forth—new strength for the disciples. Resurrection and new life came as a result of a "defeat."

"There are triumphant defeats that rival victories."
—Montaigne, French philosopher

The Search for True Friendship

"A man that hath friends must shew himself friendly: and there is a friend that sticketh closer than a brother." **PROVERBS 18:24 (KJV)**

Friendship is the last remaining sign of our fleeting childhood dreams. It is the final symptom of our youth that lingers around the shadows of our adult mind. It reminds us of the sweet taste of a chosen love. Different from family love, which is not chosen but accepted, this love develops like moss on the slippery edges of a creek. It emerges without warning. There is no date to remember. It just gradually grows until one day an acquaintance has graduated into a friend. Love is the graduation diploma, whether discussed or hinted.

> *"The truth is that real relationship is hard work."*

It is real and powerful, sweet and bitter. It is fanciful, idealistic, and iridescent enough to shine in the chilly night of an aloof world that has somehow lost the ability to interpret or appreciate the value of a friend. Only occasionally in the course of a lifetime do we meet the kind of friend that is more than an acquaintance. This kind of kindred spirit feels as warm and fitting as an old house shoe, with its personalized contours impressed upon soft fabric for the benefit of weary feet.

The tragedy is that we all yearn for, but seldom acquire, true trust and covenant. The truth is that real relationship is hard work. Let no man deceive you; contouring the heart to beat with another requires extensive whittling to trim away the self-centeredness with which many of us have enveloped ourselves. It is like riding the bus. If you are going to have company riding with you, you must be willing to scoot over and rearrange to accommodate another person and the many parcels that he brings. Your actions in doing this expresses the importance of the other person.

Every relationship undergoes adjustments. The reason one relationship becomes more valuable than others is found in its ability to survive circumstances and endure realignments. There must be a strong adhesive that can withstand the pressure and not be weakened by outside forces.

God's Love Language

"But without faith it is impossible to please him." HEBREWS 11:6

On May 7, 1992, I finished reading my Bible and recorded the thought: "I delight God." It was such an awesome concept to consider the delight that I am capable of bringing to God. When I think about delighting God and loving on Him, it is almost more than I can bear!

One year later, May 10, 1993, I journaled the following: "I have been thinking about Gary Chapman's teaching on the five love languages." As I thought about the different ways of showing love to others, suddenly I felt as though Jesus was sitting down right beside me on the couch. I heard Him say, "Jackie, what do you think My love language is?" At first, I was caught off guard by the question, and then I began to ponder it: What fills God's love tank?

> *"What fills God's love tank?"*

You may think this question is ridiculous, but I really allowed myself to consider what God's love language is. I ran through Gary Chapman's list: touch, meaningful communication, acts of service, quality time, and gifts. I could see how all of them—except maybe touch—could fill God's love tank.

Then the light went on in my heart, and I said to Jesus, "Your love language is faith/trust, isn't it?" The Lord reminded me of a scripture in Hebrews that validated my answer. The verse talks about the impossibility of ever totally satisfying the Lord without faith. Every challenging situation I face is an opportunity to love on the Lord. Every crisis I face that demands deep faith is a great time for loving on the Lord. As Philip Yancey says, "God doesn't want to be analyzed; He wants to be trusted." This is another way of saying, "He just wants to be loved by you."

The next time you face a trial, crisis, disappointment, broken dream, or heartbreak, remember that you are facing not only a chance to exercise your faith, but also an opportunity to "love on the Lord."

Jackie Kendall, *Say Goodbye to Shame*

Wholeness From the Sender

"If you then, being evil, know how to give good gifts unto your children, how much more shall your Father which is in heaven give good things to them that ask him?" MATTHEW 7:11

Jesus healed ten lepers (Luke 17:11-19) and only one returned to Him. When he came to Jesus, he fell down at His feet and worshiped Him. Then Jesus asked a question. It's seldom that Jesus, the omniscient One, would ask anything—but this time He had a question. I shall never forget the pointedness of His question. He asked the one who returned, "Where are the nine?"

Perhaps you are the one in ten who has the discernment to know that this blessing is nothing without the One who caused it all to happen. Most people are so concerned about their immediate needs that they fail to take the powerful experience that comes from a continued relationship with God! This is for the person who goes back to the Sender of gifts with the power of praise. Ten men were healed, but to the one who returned Jesus added the

> *"Healing can be found anywhere, but wholeness is achieved only when you go back to the Sender."*

privilege of being whole. Many will climb the corporate ladder. Some will claim the accolades of this world. But soon all will realize that success, even with all its glamour, cannot heal a parched soul that needs the refreshment of a change of peace. Nothing can bring wholeness like the presence of a God who lingers on the road where He first blessed you to see if there is anything in you that would return you from the temporal to embrace the eternal.

Remember, healing can be found anywhere, but wholeness is achieved only when you go back to the Sender with all of your heart and thank Him for the miracle of a second chance. Whatever you do, don't forget your roots. When you can't go anywhere else, my friend, remember you can go home!

How Boldly Can We Pray?

"And they which went before warned him, that he should hold his peace: but he cried so much the more, 'Son of David, have mercy on me.'" MARK 10:48

In Luke chapter 11 Jesus teaches His disciples how to pray. While rereading this familiar passage, I almost missed a most precious nugget: Luke 11:5-8. In these verses Jesus tells a story of a very inconvenient request from a friend at midnight. The friend grants the request not because of friendship, but because of the petitioner's persistence, i.e., boldness.

> *"When was the last time you or I prayed with "unabashed audacity" and "shameless boldness"?"*

I decided to look up persistence/boldness. Hold onto your hats! The Greek word anaiden, for persistence/boldness, means "unabashed audacity," "shameless boldness," "brazen persistence displayed," "in the pursuit of something," "an insistence characterized by rudeness."

Wow, when was the last time you or I prayed with "unabashed audacity" and "shameless boldness"? As I pondered this question, the Lord reminded me of the prayer life of my first mentor. As Mamie Hinch prayed with such "shameless boldness," I would wonder if my confidence in God would ever be strong enough for me to pray with such glorious audacity.

I am fired up that Jesus reminds me today that "shameless boldness" is a critical aspect of prevailing prayer power. May we pray with holy audacity and shameless boldness, because prayer can do whatever God can do.

Jackie Kendall, *Say Goodbye to Shame*

Living in a Suspended Mode

"While we look not at things which are seen, but at the things which are not seen: for the things which are seen are temporal; but the things which are not seen are eternal." 2 CORINTHIANS 4:18

I am told that Mozart, one of the great composers of all time, sat late at night writing what was to be a masterpiece of symphonic excellence. He decided to stop and go to bed. Stumbling upstairs to his room, he changed with all the agility of a sluggish child who merely wants to go immediately to bed.

Strangely, once he was in bed, he found sleep evasive and he tossed and turned into the night. His work continued churning around in the chambers of his mind. You see, he had ended the symphony with an augmented chord. An augmented chord gives the feeling of waiting on something else to be heard. It is a feeling of being suspended over a cliff. Finally, when this composer could stand it no longer, he rose, tossed

> *"People can never rest while living in a suspended mode."*

his wool plaid robe across his willowy shoulders, and stumbled down the steps. He went through all that to write one note. Yet how important that note was. It gave a sense of ending to the piece, and so was worth getting out of bed to write. People can never rest while living in a suspended mode. This composer then placed the quill back on his desk, blew out the lantern once more, and triumphantly retraced his way up the stairs and back to bed.

Now this great patriarch of symphonic excellence slipped into the bed with a feeling of satisfaction. He fluffed beneath his head the pillow that had once felt like a rock and just before the whistling wind outside his window ushered him into the sleep that only the peaceful can enjoy, he sighed faintly. Then his body gave way to the gentle caress of fatigue and he entered through the portal of tranquility with the slightest hint of a smile hanging around the corners of his mouth. For him, the struggle was over.

---

*I*f God Is For Me, Who Can Be Against Me?

*"What shall we then say to these things? If God be for us,
who can be against us?"* ROMANS 8:31

Have you ever been criticized so harshly that the pain knocked the breath right out of you? I lived in a household where this was a part of the daily schedule! One day a godly woman said to me, "Whenever you are criticized, consider the source and that will help you monitor your reaction." I thought a long time about the expression, "consider the source," and I became so excited about this fact: God, who knows me through and through, still chose me for Himself.

> *"Excuse me, do you know with whom you are speaking?"*

God's foreknowledge did not keep Him from choosing a sinner like me. Without foreknowledge, people make some serious mistakes—but God, who is all-knowing, never makes mistakes and is never caught off guard. This all-knowing God did not choose against me, but for me.

Whenever I am criticized, I first ask the Lord to show me any aspect of the criticism that may be truth, so I can repent and let Jesus transform that blind spot in my life. When the criticism contradicts something that Jesus says about me, I choose to value Jesus' opinion rather than people's opinions. Whatever people say about me, I accept but lay the comments alongside Jesus' biographical sketch of me—that is where I live, rest, and have confidence.

The next time someone speaks to you in a harsh and critical manner, just pause and think: Excuse me, do you know with whom you are speaking? That thought always puts a smile on my face, which puzzles the one who would slay me verbally.

_____

_____

_____

_____

_____

_____

_____

_____

Jackie Kendall, *Say Goodbye to Shame*

*T*he Finish Line Ahead

"Therefore seeing we also are surrounded with so great a cloud of witnesses, let us lay aside every weight, and the sin which does so easily entangle us, and let us run with perseverance the race that is set before us," HEBREWS 12:1

There must be something beyond the acquisition of a goal. If there isn't, then this book is nothing more than a motivational message, something which the secular field is already adept at. Many people spend all their lives trying to attain a goal. When they finally achieve it, they still secretly feel empty and unfulfilled. This will happen even in the pursuit of godly goals and successes if we don't reach beyond the mere accomplishment of an ambitious pursuit. In short, success doesn't save! Why then does God put the desire to attain in the hearts of His men and women if He knows that at the end is, as Solomon so aptly put it, "Vanity of vanities...all is vanity" (Eccles. 12:8-KJV)? Could it be that we who have achieved something of effectiveness must then reach a turn in the road and begin to worship God beyond the goal!

> *"No runner would run a race and then receive the broken ribbon as the symbol of his success."*

A runner trains himself to achieve a goal. That goal ultimately is to break the ribbon, the mark of success. After he has broken the ribbon, if there is no prize beyond the goal, then the race seems in vain. No runner would run a race and then receive the broken ribbon as the symbol of his success. At the end of the race is a prize unrelated to the race itself—a trophy that can be given only to people who have reached the pinnacle of accomplishment. What we must understand in the back of our minds as we ascend toward God's purpose is it blesses God when we attain what we were created to attain. It is His eternal purpose that we pursue.

However, we can be blessed only by the God behind the purpose. If we build a great cathedral for the Lord and fail to touch the God whom the cathedral is for, what good is the building aside from God?

T. D. Jakes, *365 Days to Healing, Blessings, and Freedom*

*T*he Secret of the Alabaster Box

"There came a woman having an alabaster jar of very precious ointment, and she broke open the jar, and poured it on his head, as he sat at the table."
MARK 14:3

In the days of Jesus, when a young woman reached the age of availability for marriage, her family would purchase an alabaster box for her and fill it with precious ointment. The size of the box and the value of the ointment would parallel her family's wealth. This alabaster box would be part of her dowry. When the young man came to ask for her in marriage, she would respond by taking the alabaster box and breaking it at his feet. This gesture of anointing his feet showed him honor.

One day when Jesus was eating in the house of Simon the leper, a woman came in and broke her alabaster box and poured the valuable ointment on Jesus' head; this woman found Jesus worthy of such sacrifice and honor. In fact, Jesus memorialized her gesture in Matthew 26:13: "Truly I say unto you, Wheresoever this gospel shall be preached throughout the whole world, this also that she has done shall be spoken of for a memorial of her." Can you imagine how angry people were that Jesus memorialized a "sinner"? Way to go, King Jesus!

> *"What is in your alabaster box?"*

This broken alabaster box is full of great meaning. The woman not only anointed Jesus for his approaching burial, but she also gave her all to a heavenly Bridegroom. Yes, she was a sinner. But this sinner had her dreams, and she wisely broke her alabaster box in the presence of the only One who can make a woman's dream come true.

What is in your alabaster box? Is it full of dreams begun as a little girl while you heard, and even "watched," fairy tales about enchanted couples who lived happily every after? Have you already broken your box at the feet of a young man who has not fulfilled your dreams and has even broken some of your dreams? Or have you been holding on tightly to your alabaster box of dreams, forever searching for a man worthy of the contents of your box? Whether your alabaster box is broken or sealed tightly shut, I encourage you to bring your box and place it at the feet of Jesus.

Jackie Kendall, *Say Goodbye to Shame*

The Honor of Faith

"I lead in the way of righteousness, in the midst of the paths of judgment. That I may cause those that love me to inherit substance, and I will fill their treasures." PROVERBS 8:20 (KJV)

Hebrews chapter 11 is a faith "hall of fame." It lists great people of God who believed Him and accomplished great exploits. Abraham is given tremendous attention in this chapter. He is revered by millions as the father of faith. He is the first man in history to believe God to the point where it was counted as righteousness. He was saved by faith. Jesus said that the infirm woman was a daughter of Abraham. She was worthy. She had merit because she was Abraham's descendant and had faith.

> *"God does not honor morality. He honors faith."*

There are two contrasting women mentioned in the faith "hall of fame." Sarah, Abraham's wife, is listed. Rahab, the Jericho prostitute, is listed as well. A married woman and a whore made it to the hall of fame. A good clean godly woman and a whore made it into the book. I understand how Sarah was included, but how in the world did this prostitute get to be honored? She was listed because God does not honor morality. He honors faith. That was the one thing they had in common; nothing else.

The Bible doesn't talk about Rahab having a husband. She had the whole city. Sarah stayed in the tent and knit socks. She moved wherever her husband went and took care of him. There was no similarity in their lifestyles, just in their faith. God saw something in Sarah that He also saw in Rahab. Do not accept the excuse that because you have lived like a Rahab you can't have the faith experience.

_____

_____

_____

_____

_____

_____

_____

_____

_____

_____

Look Up, Not Down

"And when they had sent away the multitude, they took him even as he was in the ship...and, behold, there arose a great tempest in the sea, and the waves beat into the ship..." MARK 4:36A-37

If you could catch a glimpse of what awaits you at the top of the mountain, you would labor with all that is within you to scale the summit. An important key to a successful climb is to never look down. Instead, fasten your gaze upon the goal.

There are several things in common with each time the disciples got into a ship and set sail (see Mk. 4–5):

> *"If you find yourself in rough waters, take consolation in the fact that you have been selected for the storm."*

The multitudes were sent away.

They were confronted with storms.

No one was lost at sea.

Great miracles happened when they arrived on the other shore.

If you find yourself in rough waters, take consolation in the fact that you have been selected for the storm. Others will enjoy the loaves and fishes, but then they will be sent away (see Mark 4). An invitation has been extended to you. Jesus knows there is a storm brewing, and He wants you in it. It is not His motive to terrify you at sea; He has peace that passes human logic, and He wants to impart it to you (see John 14:27; Phil. 4:7).

Decide that you will make it. The belly of the boat may be full of water and the timbers snapping like twigs, but you're going to make it. The memories of the storm will pale in comparison to the joy that welcomes you on the other side. Before long the tumultuous waves and howling winds will be at your back and sweet victory just ahead.

_____

_____

_____

_____

_____

_____

Morton Bustard, *The Impassioned Soul*

God is Following Up

"And if any man thinks that he knows anything, he knows nothing yet as he ought to know. But if any man loves God, the same is known of him."
1 CORINTHIANS 8:2-3

Man was made to live in close touch with God. That is his native air. Out of that air his lungs are badly affected. This other air is too heavy. It's malarial, and full of gases and germy dust. In it he chokes and gasps. Yet he knows not why. He gropes about in the night made by his own shut eyes. He doesn't seem to know enough to open them. And sometimes he will not open them. For the hinge of the eyelid is in the will. And having shut the light out, he gets tangled up in his ideas as to what is light. He puts darkness for light, and light for darkness.

> *"For the hinge of the eyelid is in the will"*

Once man knew God well; close up. And that means loved, gladly, freely. But one day a bad choice was made. The world turned down the wrong lane, and has been going that way pell-mell ever since. Yet so close is the wrong lane to the right that a single step will change lanes. Though many results of being in the wrong lane will not be changed by the change of lanes. It takes time to rest up the feet made sore by the roughness of the wrong lane. And some of the scars, where men have measured their length, seem to stay.

The result of that wrong turning has been pitiable. Separation from God, so far as man could make separation. There is no separation on God's part. He has never changed. He remains in the world, but because of man's turning his face away, He remains as a stranger, unrecognized. He remains just where man left Him. And anyone going back to that point in the road will find Him standing waiting with an eager light glistening in His eyes. No! That's not accurate. He is a bit nearer than ever He was . . . He is following us.

S. D. Gordon, *Quiet Talks About Jesus*

$\mathcal{P}$urifying the Soul

"But the wisdom that is from above is first pure, then peaceable, gentle, and easy to be submissive, full of mercy and good fruits, without partiality, and without hypocrisy." JAMES 3:17

God wishes to make your soul pure. He purifies it by His Wisdom just as a refiner purifies metal in the furnace. Fire is the only thing which can purify gold.

Again, the fire that consumes us utterly is His highest wisdom.

This fire gradually consumes all that is earthly; it takes out all foreign matter and separates these things from the gold.

The fire seems to know that the earthly mixture cannot be changed into gold. The fire must melt and dissolve this dross by force so that it can rid the gold of every alien particle. Over and over again, the gold must be cast into the furnace until it has lost every trace of pollution. Oh, how many times the gold is plunged back into the fire—far, far more times than seem necessary. Yet you can be sure the Forger sees impurities no one else can see. The gold must return to the fire again and again until positive proof has been established that it can be no further purified.

> *"Fire is the only thing which can purify gold."*

There comes a time, at last, when the goldsmith can find no more mixture that adulterates the gold. When the fire has perfected purity—or should I say simplicity—the fire no longer touches it. If the gold remained in the furnace for an eon, its spotlessness would not be improved upon nor its substance diminished!

Now the gold is fit for the most exquisite workmanship. In the future, if the gold should get dirty and seem to lose its beauty, it is nothing more than an accidental impurity which touches only the surface.

Rare would be the man who would reject a pure, golden vessel because its surface had some external dirt on it, preferring some cheap metal only because its surface had been polished.

Gene Edwards, *100 Days in the Secret Place*

*I*t's Not a Pride Thing; It's a Hunger Thing

"Therefore are they before the throne of God, and serve him day and night in his temple: and he that sits on the throne shall dwell among them. They shall hunger no more, neither thirst anymore," REVELATION 7:15-16A

You can get so caught up in being "religious" that you never become spiritual. It doesn't matter how much you pray. (Pardon me for saying this, but you can be lost, not even knowing God, and still have a prayer life.) I don't care how much you know about the Bible, or what you know about Him. I'm asking you, "Do you know Him?"

I'm afraid that we have satiated our hunger for Him by reading old love letters from Him to the churches in the Epistles of the New Testament. These are good, holy, and necessary, but we never have intimacy with Him. We have stifled our hunger for His presence by doing things for Him.

> *"When you pursue God with all your heart, soul, and body, He will turn to meet you and you will come out of it ruined for the world."*

A husband and wife can do things for each other while never really loving each other. They can go through childbirth classes together, have kids, and share a mortgage, but never enjoy the high level of intimacy that God ordained and designed for a marriage (and I'm not just talking about sexual things). Too often we live on a lower plane than what God intended for us, so when He unexpectedly shows up in His power, we are shocked. Most of us are simply not prepared to see "His train fill the temple".

Our problem is that we have never really been hungry. We have allowed things of this realm to satisfy our lives and satiate our hunger. We have come to God week after week, year after year, just to have Him fill in the little empty spaces. I tell you that God is tired of being "second place" to everything else in our lives.

When you pursue God with all your heart, soul, and body, He will turn to meet you and you will come out of it ruined for the world. I pray that you get so hungry for God that you don't care about anything else. I think I see a flickering flame. He will "fan" that.

_____

_____

_____

_____

_____

_____

Tommy Tenney, *The God Chasers*

The Lifeblood of Faith

"For of him, and through him, and to him, are all things: to whom be glory for ever." ROMANS 11:36

God's will includes His plan for a world, and for each life in the world. Both concern us. He would first work in us, that He may work through us in His passionate outreach for a world. His will includes every bit of one's life; and therefore obedience must also include every bit. A run out in a single direction may serve as a suggestion of many others.

> *"Faith has three elements: knowledge, belief and trust."*

The law of my body, which obeyed brings or continues health is God's will, as much as that which concerns moral action. Our bodies are holy because God lives in them. Overwork, insufficient sleep, that imprudent diet and eating which seems the rule rather than the exception, carelessness of bodily protection in rain or storm or drafts or otherwise—these are sins against God's will for the body, and no one who is disobedient here can ever be a channel of power up to the measure of God's longing for us.

Whatever disturbs an active abiding trust in God must be driven out of doors, and kept out. Doubt chills the air below normal. Anxiety overheats the air. A calm looking up into God's face with an unquestioning faith in Him under every sort of circumstance—this is trust. Faith has three elements: knowledge, belief and trust. Knowledge is acquaintance with certain facts. Belief is accepting these facts as true. Trust is risking something that is very precious. Trust is the lifeblood of faith.

S. D. Gordon, *Quiet Talks on Power*

$\mathcal{M}$y Gratitude

Loving what I have—what I am grateful for:

_____
_____
_____
_____
_____
_____
_____
_____
_____
_____
_____
_____
_____
_____
_____
_____
_____
_____
_____
_____
_____
_____
_____
_____
_____
_____

"I will praise thee; for I am fearfully and wonderfully made:"
PSALMS 139:14a (KJV)

The Fallacy of Full-Time Christian Work

"And whatsoever you do, do it heartily, as to the Lord, and not unto men; knowing that of the Lord you shall receive the reward of the inheritance: for you serve the Lord Christ." COLOSSIANS 3:23-24

"I didn't know you were in full-time Christian work," said my close friend as we were driving. "I didn't realize that," she went on. I responded, "Every person who has followed the will of God in their life is in full-time Christian work." God calls some to the mission field, others to be accountants, and others to be advertising executives, and still others to be construction workers. God never made a distinction between sacred and secular. In fact, the Hebrew word "avodah" is the root word having the same meaning of "work" and "workship." God sees our work as workship.

> *"Wherever you are called, serve the Lord in that place."*

We have incorrectly elevated the role of the Christian worker to be more holy and committed than the person who is serving in a more secular environment. Yet the call to the secular marketplace is as important as any other calling. God has to have His people in every sphere of life. Otherwise, many would never come to know Him because they would be separated from society.

I learned this lesson personally when I sought to go into "full-time" service as a pastor in my late 20s, only to have God thrust me back into the business world unwillingly. This turned out to be the best thing He could have done for me, because it was never His will for me to be a pastor. He knew I was more suited for the marketplace.

We are all in missions. Some are called to foreign lands. Some are called to the jungles of the marketplace. Wherever you are called, serve the Lord in that place. Let Him demonstrate His power through your life so that others might experience Him through you today and see your vocation as worship to His glory.

_____

_____

_____

_____

_____

_____

_____

_____

Os Hillman, *Today God is First*

Maximizing Fellowship With God

"I can of my own self do nothing: as I hear, I judge: and my judgment is just; because I seek not my own will, but the will of the Father which has sent me." JOHN 5:30

As single, you have a wonderful opportunity to use your time to maximize your fellowship with God. When you love someone, you give them your heart, the center of your being. God asks for no less. He desires a totally devoted heart. Deuteronomy 6:5 (KJV)says that you are to love Him with all your heart (deepest devotion), your soul (what you think and what you feel), and your might (your strength and energy).

Many women today are devoted, all right! They have devoted themselves to developing a love relationship, but not with the Lord. They erroneously seek for love in sensations and promises. The world's version of love is something they want to "fall into." Meanwhile, "true love" escapes them. True love can only be found in undistracted devotion to Jesus Christ.

> *"True love can only be found in undistracted devotion to Jesus Christ."*

To love Him like this, you must know Him intimately. It is a personal, intimate knowledge. Do you have a devotion to God that causes people to marvel at how intimately you know Him? Do you know God in a way that causes Him to be an intimate, personal part of your being as you may desire a husband to one day be?

Debbie Jones & Jackie Kendall, *Lady in Waiting—Meditations of The Heart*

Cultivate Your Potential

"So the servants of the landowner came and said unto him, 'Sir, did not you sow good seed in your field? from where then has it weeds?'" MATTHEW 13:27

Your potential will not be released until you take your thoughts, plans, and imaginations and put them into action. You must work to mine your hidden potential.

Many times we are initially excited by the glimpses God gives us of the potential He planted within us. Perhaps you are tapping some of the wealth God stored in you for the world's benefit, but your progress is slowing or even stopping. The following standards are keys to encouraging your garden to maturity as you liberate all the potential that God deposited in you.

> *"You must work to mine your hidden potential."*

Experienced gardeners know that weeds often grow faster than vegetables. If a gardener goes away for several weeks, he will return to stunted and sickly vegetable plants that yield little or no fruit. Or even worse, he may find that he has no vegetable plants at all because the weeds smothered and choked the tender shoots. Cultivation is necessary for a healthy and productive garden.

The same is true of your potential. You need to cultivate your life carefully to remove the influences and the stimulants that seek to stunt your potential or kill it completely. Seek those persons who are positive and encouraging. Remove yourself from those activities and situations that might encourage you to return to your former way of life. Cling to your Source and allow Him to cleanse you of those things that would deter you from maximizing your potential. Much emerging potential dies for want of cultivation. The careful and consistent nurturing of your potential will enable you to meet the full responsibilities that God planned for your life.

Myles Munroe, *Releasing Your Potential*

The Source of All Supply

"In him was life; and the life was the light of men." JOHN 1:4

I had never noticed in my Bible and my other study materials that from the beginning God had made Himself the source of all life and the all-continuous supply of life.

He is the Creator, the Father of us all—and the One who so loved us that "...He gave His only begotten Son, that whosoever believeth in Him should not perish, but have everlasting life." (John. 3:16-KJV)

The light shone through—Abram was unlike those of that era who worshiped idols of their own making and placed them on the highest hills. He saw God who is most high—highest of all. He saw that God owned both Heaven and earth equally. Satan did not own one inch of ground or drop of water—all was the property of the Most High God.

> *"...from the beginning God had made Himself the source of all life and the all-continuous supply of life."*

As Abram had faced these four conquering enemy armies and with "a few defeated the many" he saw God as the One who delivered him from all of his enemies. We today who are of faith are Abraham's children...our faith comes from him. And we who are "in Christ" are Abraham's seed. In other words, faith runs in a direct line to use from 35 hundred years ago in Abraham's time when he first discovered God as His source.

Today we take the counterpart of the old covenant and bring it into the new covenant of our Savior, Jesus Christ of Nazareth.

God owns the earth and its fullness (see Psalm 24:1)... and all the silver and gold in the earth (see Hagar 2:8) ...and all things come from Him (see John 1:3).

Why Is Waiting So Hard?

"And we know that all things work together for good to them that love God, to them who are the called according to his purpose." ROMANS 8: 28

If God is faithful, why is it so easy to lose patience? Why is it so hard to wait? Why is it easier to settle for less than God's best? Fear is a huge hindrance to waiting.

God has always desired to bless His people, but He will not force them to do what is best. In His Word He has often warned us to wait, to be careful, and to trust Him. His heart of love begs us to listen and obey so He may bless us and the dear ones who will one day look to and follow us. The words He gave to the children of Israel in Deuteronomy 30:15-20 show the love and concern He has for the choices you make.

> *"If you have seen patterns in your life that show a lack of patience, commit yourself right now to waiting for God's best."*

"...So choose life in order that you may live, you and your descendants, by loving the Lord your God, by obeying His voice, and by holding fast to Him." (Deuteronomy 30:19-20-NAS)

You must choose to wait patiently for God's best. If you have seen patterns in your life that show a lack of patience, commit yourself right now to waiting for God's best.

Just as a father has compassion on his children, so the Lord has compassion on those who fear Him. For He Himself knows our frame; He is mindful that we are but dust (Psalm 103:13-14-NAS).

_____

_____

_____

_____

_____

_____

_____

_____

_____

*F*inding Favor

"Out of the mouth of babies and nursing infants you have perfected praise."
MATTHEW 21:16B

I wish you could see my youngest daughter's room. There are entire toy stores that don't carry as much variety as what is contained in that relatively small space!

Many of these "treasures" are acquired while we're traveling together. We can hardly pass a store anymore that one of my girls doesn't want to visit—and once inside, we can hardly leave without one of them finding a little something that they just can't live without! It isn't fair, really; I'm helpless against their advances. All they need to do is look up at me with their big, puppy dog eyes and say, "Pleeeeeeeeeeeeeeeease!"

> *"God longs for those moments with His kids too!"*

Within reason...I usually give in. And for a few golden moments all is well in the world. But these moments are fleeting! Soon the smiles fade into wistful longings again as the next desirable object comes into view. And I'm left literally holding the bag as they examine their next prospective purchase!

My most precious moments with my children aren't when they're excited and thanking me for getting them some new toy. The moments I crave the most are when they drop their toys, forget about their "wish list," and climb up into my lap for no reason in particular—just to love me and be with me. In those moments, nothing else matters.

God longs for those moments with His kids too!

_____

_____

_____

_____

_____

_____

_____

_____

_____

Tommy Tenney, *The Daily Chase*

Give Up the Past

"Therefore if any man be in Christ, he is a new creation: old things are passed away; behold, all things are become new." 2 CORINTHIANS 5:17

It was a difficult season. It was as if satan had deliberately stirred up every serene and settled circumstance of my life and God was commanding me to navigate the turbid waters using faith as my vessel, oar, and compass. So I rowed, with great difficulty at first. I sometimes lost my focus when I considered the unfairness or the uncertainty of my situation. But in our seasons of greatest peril, God shows up with the most miraculous provision.

> *"In our seasons of greatest peril, God shows up with the most miraculous provision."*

All God needed was my willing heart. That day He got it and together we began the journey to understanding how to recognize, discern, embrace, and eventually celebrate change.

The first gift on this path to celebrating change came quickly. The peace that I fought so hard to hold on to in the past, washed over me and rushed through me, settling my heart, clearing my mind, and calming my senses. I was still tired. But when I surrendered my will to God—when I determined that day to learn how to celebrate change and not just tolerate it—He made me a promise. He said He would not leave me or forsake me.

It was not the first time He had said that. It was not the first time I had believed Him for it. But it was the first time that I knew with certainty that all the changes in my life were good changes.

Celebrating change is an act of our will. My surrender was a signal to God and the world that I was ready. Then God set out to make me able. He put me on the path to becoming one who would be capable of celebrating change. And the first step on that path was making peace with the truth that change had arrived.

Dr. Wanda Turner, *Celebrating Change*

Whatever Happened to the Bread?

"But woe unto you, scribes and Pharisees, hypocrites! for you shut up the kingdom of heaven against men: for you neither go in yourselves, neither allow them that are entering to go in." MATTHEW 23:13

The sign is still up. We still take people into our churches and show them the ovens where we used to bake bread. The ovens are all still in place and everything is there, but all you can find is crumbs from last year's visitation . . . There is another problem God is concerned with, and Jesus revealed it when He rebuked the religious leaders of His day: "But woe unto you, scribes and Pharisees, hypocrites! for you shut up the kingdom of heaven against men: for you neither go in yourselves, neither allow them that are entering to go in" (Mt. 23:13).

> *"I want God to break out somewhere in my lifetime so that in the future my children can say, 'I was there. I know; it's true.'"*

It is bad enough when you refuse to go in yourself, but God gets extra agitated when you stand at the door and refuse to let anybody else in either! Through our ignorance of spiritual matters and our lack of hunger, we have figuratively "stood at the door" by the way we have done things, and have barred the lost and hungry from entering in. Our constant claims of hot bread backed only by stale crumbs on a frayed carpet of man's tradition have left countless generations hungry, homeless, and with nowhere else to go but Moab. And so they grow weary with the cruel taskmaster who takes his tax in their marriages, children, and lives.

I am tired of reading about God's visitations of yesteryear. I want God to break out somewhere in my lifetime so that in the future my children can say, "I was there. I know; it's true." God has no grandchildren. Each generation must experience His presence. Recitation was never meant to take the place of visitation.

Tommy Tenney, *The God Chasers*

Doors Open, Doors Close

"These things says he that is holy, 'he that is true, he that has the key of David, he that opens, and no man shuts; and shuts, and no man opens."
REVELATION 3:7

The letter to the Philadelphia church, the church of brotherly love, basically ends with the words, "I am the One who closes doors." The art to surviving painful moments is living in the "yes" zone. We need to learn to respond to God with a yes when the doors are open, and a yes when they are closed. Our prayer must be:

> *"We need to learn to respond to God with a yes when the doors are open, and a yes when they are closed."*

I trust Your decisions, Lord; and I know that if this relationship is good for me, You will allow it to continue. I know that if the door is closed, then it is also for my good. So I say "yes" to You as I go into this relationship. I appreciate brotherly love, and I still say "yes" if You close the door.

This is the epitome of a trust that is seldom achieved, but is to be greatly sought after. In so doing, you will be able to savor the gift of companionship without the fear of reprisal!

If God allows a relationship to continue, and some negative, painful betrayals come from it, you must realize that He will only allow what ultimately works for your good. Sometimes such a betrayal ushers you into the next level of consecration, a level you could never reach on your own. For that we give thanks! What a privilege to live in the assurance that God is in control of you, and of everyone whom He allows to get behind "the shield" of His purposes for your life! Any good parent tries to ensure that his or her children are surrounded by positive influences. The unique thing about God's parenting is that He sometimes uses a negative to bring about a positive.

_____

_____

_____

_____

_____

_____

_____

Dominate, Rule, and Subdue

"All things are lawful unto me, but all things are not expedient: all things are lawful for me, but I will not be brought under the power of any."
I CORINTHIANS 6:12

God's perspective on our potential also says that we have the power to dominate and subdue the earth.

Now what does it mean to be a dominator of the earth? It means that the earth should not rule or control us. If you are addicted to cigarettes, you are being controlled by a leaf. If you are ruled by alcohol, you are being controlled by grain. Leaves and grain are the earth. God created you to dominate the earth, not the earth to dominate you. If you are being controlled by any habit, you are submitting to the very things God commands you to dominate.

> *"You have the power to beat whatever habit is ruling you. It's there whether you use it or not."*

The Apostle Paul confirms God's intent for man when he writes:

I therefore so run, not as uncertainly; so I fight, not as one that beats the air: but I keep control of my body, and bring it into subjection: lest that by any means, when I have preached to others, I myself should be disqualified. (1 Corinthians 9:27)

He's telling you to use your head. There are things in the earth that will rule you if you allow them to take control of your physical body.

God's given you the potential to dominate the earth. You have the power to beat whatever habit is ruling you. It's there whether you use it or not. Your ability to release the full purpose for which God created you is dependent on your decision to use the potential God gave you to control those things that seek to entrap and subdue you. It's up to you whether you exercise the power God built into you.

The Keys That Jingled in God's Hand

"And I will give unto you the keys of the kingdom of heaven: and whatsoever you shall bind on earth shall be bound in heaven: and whatsoever you shall loose on earth shall be loosed in heaven." MATTHEW 16:19

The thing God promised is going to happen, and a flood of God's glory is going to come. It is going to start somewhere with someone, but where? Who will find the ancient keys that jingled in the hands of God when He told Peter, "Here are the keys to the Kingdom. Whatever you open on earth will be opened in Heaven"? (See Matthew 16:19). Who will hear a knock at the other side and slip that ancient key into that door to open the gate of Heaven? Wherever it happens, whoever opens that door, the result will be an unstoppable, immeasurable flood of the glory of God. If the glory of God is going to cover the earth, it has to start somewhere. Why not here? Why not you?

> *"Who will find the ancient keys that jingled in the hands of God ...?"*

There are some Kingdom keys lying around, and somebody has to find them and prop the door open. God said, "I sought for a man among them who would make a wall, and stand in the gap before Me on behalf of the land, that I should not destroy it; but I found no one" (Ezek. 22:30 NKJV). We need to strip away our overly religious ways of looking at things to really understand what God is saying. Where and what is this "gap" that God wants us to fill?

God never intended for us to use our favorite hymns or worship songs to mark our divine encounters or to hold open the gates of Heaven. A sermon won't do it; nor will a sparkling personality or a powerful healing ministry do it. God has a better idea. Prop open that gate with your own life! Become a doorkeeper and open the door to let the light of Heaven shine.

Tommy Tenney, *The Daily Chase*

Turn Lose and Change!

"But we all, with unveiled faces beholding as in a mirror the glory of the Lord, are changed into the same image from glory to glory, even as by the Spirit of the Lord." 2 CORINTHIANS 3:18

When we face changes in our lives, they appear monumental to us. And it's so easy to get caught up in and consumed by how much of our effort, emotions and ego go into dealing with the sifting and shaking that goes on in our little consciousness, let alone how other people's changes affect us.

Change is so much more than "here today, different tomorrow." It's not just a night's weeping endured until morning. It goes way past the renewing of our minds and spiritual fruit-bearing. Change is God's way of preparing us for what He has prepared for us. And that is so much more than what we can see, taste, think, buy, give, wish for, speak, or even have faith for. And it never, ever ends. We serve an infinite God, who was long before every yesterday and will be long after the last tomorrow lives. And our very lives are in Him! Change is not just about what goes on in my life, our lives, or on this earth. Change is a never-ending journey into the heart of God!

> *"Change is God's way of preparing us for what He has prepared for us."*

Take your mind off of the mundane things of this earth. Let it travel, unfettered past the end of time itself to a place where there is no day, no night, no time, no sorrow, no care, no sickness, and no fear or dread. A place where no hands have toiled, but there is no lack. A place where life everlasting, joy unspeakable, perfect peace, perpetual praise, and worship in spirit and truth are the only items on your list of things to do every day, forever and ever. And every moment only makes it more so. My Lord! Change brings us to exceeding abundance and beyond to where no eye has seen, nor ear heard, nor heart imagined. This is the promise of change. And change is the very reason we pray to God.

Dr. Wanda Turner, *Celebrating Change*

There's Got to Be More

"All things were made by him; and without him was not anything made that was made." JOHN 1:3

I don't know about you, my friend, but there's a driving passion in my heart that whispers to me that there's more than what I already know, more than what I already have. It makes me jealous of John, who wrote Revelation. It makes me envious of people who get glimpses out of this world into that world and see things that I only dream about. I know there's more.

> *"He is the composite of everything, both the glue that holds the pieces of the universe together and the pieces themselves!"*

One reason people flow out the back doors of our churches as fast as they come in through the front door is because they have more of a "man encounter" with our programs than a "God encounter" with the unforgettable majesty and power of the Almighty God.

This speaks strongly of the difference between the omnipresence of God and the manifest presence of God. The phrase, "omnipresence of God," refers to the fact that He is everywhere all the time. The Gospel of John touches on this quality of God when it says, "...and without him was not anything made that was made" (John. 1:3b). God is everywhere in everything. He is the composite of everything, both the glue that holds the pieces of the universe together and the pieces themselves!

You may be thinking, Wait a minute. God is always here. He's omnipresent. That's true, but why did He say, "If My people, which are called by My name, shall humble themselves, and pray, and seek My face..."? (2 Chronicles 7:14.) If they are already His people, what other level of "Him" are they to "seek"? Seek His face! Why? It is because His favor flows wherever His face is directed. You can be God's child and not have His favor, much as an earthly child would be in disfavor but not be disowned. The only thing that is going to turn the focus and favor of God toward us is our hunger. We must repent, reach for His face, and pray, "God, look at us, and we'll look to You."

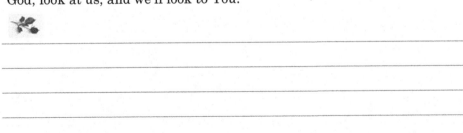

Tommy Tenney, *The God Chasers*

Life on Hold

"...he has sent me to heal the brokenhearted, to proclaim deliverance to the captives, and recovery of sight to the blind, to set at liberty them that are oppressed..." LUKE 4:18

Some singles see the lack of a mate as God denying them something for a more "noble purpose"—a cross to bear! Our selfish nature tends to focus on what we do not have rather than on what we do have—free time—that can be used for others and ourselves. Is your life on hold until you have someone to hold?

Have you experienced a crushing emotional blow? Psalm 34:18 (NIV) says, "The Lord is near to the brokenhearted, and saves those who are crushed in spirit." [A] broken hearted woman had put her life on hold after her husband divorced her. Such a response is understandable, but this now single woman decided to take her broken heart, her empty arms, and her loneliness and give them to Jesus. In exchange, Jesus taught her how to resist feeling sorry for herself and

> *"Is your life on hold until you have someone to hold?"*

how to stop living in the arena of bitterness. After she made the choice of recklessly abandoning herself to Jesus as Lord, she was free to serve Him. This once brokenhearted single woman has been transformed into a fearless servant of the Lord.

Have you also put your life on hold? Do you have an excuse for not serving Jesus?

Debbie Jones & Jackie Kendall, *Lady in Waiting—Meditations of The Heart*

You Can Do Anything

"Jesus said unto him, 'If you can believe, all things are possible to him that believes.'"   MARK 9:23

God has also given human beings the capacity to imagine and plan and believe anything into reality. That's an awesome potential. The Bible reveals this power in the story of the building of the tower of Babel:

> *"Consistent with man's ability to make plans and bring them to completion is his power to believe impossibilities into possibilities."*

The Lord said, "If as one people speaking the same language they have begun to do this, then nothing they plan to do will be impossible for them." (Genesis 11:6 – NIV).

In other words, God says, "If I don't interfere, man will be able to do anything he thinks about and plans."

God did interfere in the building of that tower, but He didn't stop the people from thinking. He stopped them from understanding one another. You have the potential to think, to imagine, to plan, and to put your plan into action. Anything you carry through from thought to action is within your power to accomplish.

Consistent with man's ability to make plans and bring them to completion is his power to believe impossibilities into possibilities. Jesus said to the father of a demon-possessed boy:

"...all things are possible to him that believes." (Mark 9:23)

This ability is an extension of man's potential to operate like God.

_____

_____

_____

_____

_____

_____

_____

_____

Myles Munroe, *Releasing Your Potential*

Love Notes From the Heart

"And I went unto the angel, and said unto him, 'Give me the little scroll.' And he said unto me, 'Take it, and eat it up; and it shall make your belly bitter, but it shall be in your mouth sweet as honey.'" REVELATION 10:9

Too many of us have become "milk babies" who want to sit on padded pews in an air-conditioned and climate-controlled building where someone else will pre-digest what God has to say and then regurgitate it back to us in a half-digested form. (We're afraid of getting "spiritual indigestion" from messages we think are "too rough" to handle.) Tender tummies are unused to tough truth!

> *"Tender tummies are unused to tough truth!"*

The solution is hunger and desperation for God Himself without intermediaries. We need to pray, "God, I'm tired of everybody else hearing from You! Where is the lock on my prayer closet? I'm going to lock myself away until I hear from You for myself!"

We make a great deal out of reading the Word and that is important. But we need to remember that the early Church didn't have access to what we call the New Testament for many years. They didn't even have the Old Testament Scriptures because those expensive scrolls were locked up in synagogues. The only Scriptures they had were the verses from the law, the Psalms, and the prophets that had been passed down orally from grandfathers and grandmothers—and that only if they were Jewish believers. So what did they have? They walked and talked with Him in such a rich level of intimacy that it wasn't necessary for them to pour over dusty love letters that were written long ago. They had God's love notes freshly written on their hearts.

God is tired of having long distance relationships with His people. He was tired of it thousands of years ago in Moses' day, and He is tired of it today. He really wants to have intimate, close encounters with you and me. He wants to invade our homes with His abiding presence in a way that will make every visitor begin to weep with wonder and worship the moment they enter.

Who Are Your Kidding?

"If you abide in me, and my words abide in you, you shall ask what you will, and it shall be done unto you." JOHN 15:7

We can't deal with fear by lying about it. We may as well deal with lung cancer by smoking a pack of cigarettes a day! That sounds ridiculous to you, doesn't it? But if God did not give you a spirit of fear, who do you think gave it to you? So you deal with something you got from the father of lies by lying? Come on, now.

> *"He never tells you to do anything He hasn't already given you the power to do."*

Brother, you know in your heart that God has shown you your wife. But you're so afraid of losing your "Mack status," you're not going to move forward with her. Instead, you tell her, "things are good the way they are, baby," or "If it ain't broke, don't fix it." But let me tell you right here, man of God, if you don't embrace this change, you may not be able to embrace your destiny, and God will find her another Adam to complete.

Sister, you can keep that weight on if you want to. And you can tell all your friends that you are a "big, beautiful, proud woman of God." And you can cry yourself to sleep at night, because you don't want to be that big, but you don't believe you can change. But God has told you to be a good steward over that body He has gifted you with. He has told you to change your eating habits and stop making food your idol and your weight a dubious badge of honor. And He never tells you to do anything He hasn't already given you the power to do. So don't hide your fear. Tell Him about it. Then give it to Him. But don't hold onto it.

Dr. Wanda Turner, *Celebrating Change*

Live in the Present Moment

"Listen now, you that say, 'Today or tomorrow we will go into such a city, and continue there a year, and buy and sell, and get gain': whereas you know not what shall be tomorrow. For what is your life? It is even a vapor, that appears for a little time, and then vanishes away." JAMES 4:13-14

I think it's fine to be proud of the things you've accomplished. But it's not fine to go around with your nose in the air, thinking you're better than everyone else because of something you did yesterday. A person who is truly humble knows that what's really important is how they are acting now, at this very moment.

Because the humble person lives realistically in the present moment, they will not waste someone else's time. They will do their best to be on time for appointments. They won't show up late for meetings. They understand that, because life is measured out in seconds and minutes, everyone's time is of equal importance.

> *"The only time to do what must be done is now."*

Another reason why humble people live in the present moment is that they understand that life is fleeting. The only time to do what must be done is now. This present moment is the only guarantee any of us has.

Fame does things to people. So does power. And most of what it does is not good. It causes people to believe the flattering things others say about them and to think they deserve to be treated like gods and goddesses instead of ordinary human beings—which is what we all are.

Great people have little use for fame or notoriety.
They are consumed with productivity; not image.
They do not feel the need to project their self-worth to anyone.
They are content when the moment calls for them to be little,
ordinary, or common...as long as the goal is achieved.—John Maxwell

Pat Williams, *American Scandal*

*H*othouse Christian

"But everyone that hears these sayings of mine, and does not do them, shall be likened unto a foolish man, that without a foundation built his house upon the sand: and the rain descended, and the floods came; against which the stream did beat violently; and the winds blew, and beat upon that house; and immediately it fell: and great was the fall of it; and the ruin of that house was great." LUKE 6:49

Most Christians in North America are "hothouse Christians" who bloom as long as they are kept in a protected and carefully controlled environment far from fear, distress, or persecution. "God forbid that it should 'cost' us something to speak the name of Jesus." But time and again, we have seen that if you take hothouse Christians out of their protected environment and put them into the real world where the wind of adversity blows and the rain of sorrow falls; if they have to endure the hot sun and the drought it brings, then they discover that they never developed a root system in the hothouse. So they wither and say, "I'm just not cut out for this!"

> *"Most Christians in North America are "hothouse Christians" who bloom as long as they are kept in a protected and carefully controlled environment far from fear, distress, or persecution."*

If it takes the "perfection of environment" to prove the presence of God in your life, then my guess is that the persecuted Christians just don't have God. How can they? They don't have Bible seminars; they don't have choirs or the latest worship music. They don't have air conditioning, ushers, nurseries, electronic paging systems, carpeted sanctuaries, or staff counselors.

True church growth, wherever it may be, in freedom or persecution, comes because of only one thing. It springs forth from an intimate knowledge of the living God.

Tommy Tenney, *The God Chasers*

*F*orgive the Unforgiven

"Let all bitterness, and wrath, and anger, and clamor, and evil speaking, be put away from you, with all malice: and be kind one to another, tenderhearted, forgiving one another, even as God for Christ's sake has forgiven you." EPHESIANS 4:31-32

That word unforgiving! What a group of relatives it has, near and far! Jealousy, envy, bitterness, the cutting word, the polished shaft of sarcasm with the pointed tip, the green eye, the acid saliva—what kinsfolk these are!

"Oh, well," someone says, "you do not know how hard is it to forgive." You think not! I know this much—that some persons and some things you cannot forgive of yourself. But I am glad to say that I know this too that if one allows the Spirit of Jesus to sway the heart He will make you love persons you cannot like. No natural affinity or drawing together through disposition, but a real yearning love in the heart. Jesus' love, when allowed to come in as freely as He means, fills your heart with pity for the man who has wounded you. An infinite, tender pity that he has sunk so low as to be capable of such actions.

> *"If one allows the Spirit of Jesus to sway the heart He will make you love persons you cannot like."*

If prayer be partnership in the highest sense, then the same spirit must animate both partners, the human and the divine, if the largest results are to come.

May we not well pray: Search me, oh God, and know my heart and help me know it; try me and know my innermost undermost thoughts and purposes and ambitions, and help me know them; and see what way there be in me that is a grief to Thee; and then lead me—and here the prayer may be a purpose as well as a prayer—lead me out of that way unto Thy way, the way everlasting. For Jesus' sake; yea for men's sake, too.

S. D. Gordon, *Quiet Talks on Prayer*

One of the Twelve

"...and that he died for all, that they which live should not henceforth live unto themselves, but unto him which died for them, and rose again."
2 CORINTHIANS 5:15

It is believed that there were about 5,000 believers during the time of Christ. Among those believers, it was thought there were three types. The largest number of believers were those who came to Jesus for salvation.

> *"If you had to say which group best represented your life, which one would you fall into...?"*

They served Him little beyond coming to Him to receive salvation. A much smaller number, say 500, actually followed Him and served Him. Then, there were the disciples. These were those who identified with Jesus. They lived the life that Jesus lived. Each of these ultimately died in difficult circumstances. They experienced the hardships, the miracles, and the fellowship with God in human form.

If you had to say which group best represented your life, which one would you fall into–the 5,000 who simply believed, the 500 who followed and sought to implement what they were learning from the Savior, or the 12 who identified completely with the life and mission of the Savior? Jesus has called each of us to identify with Him completely. "...hereby we know that we are in him. He that says he abides in him ought himself also so to walk, even as he walked" (I John. 2:5b-6 TSB).

Pray that God will allow you to walk as Jesus did. Experience His power and love in your life today so that others will see the hope that lies in you.

_____

_____

_____

_____

_____

_____

_____

_____

Os Hillman, *Today God is First*

Pearl of Great Price

"Again, the kingdom of heaven is like a merchant, seeking beautiful pearls: who, when he had found one pearl of great price, went and sold all that he had, and bought it." MATTHEW 13:45

One of life's most costly and beautiful objects is born out of pain and irritation—the pearl. A tiny piece of sand slips into an oyster's shell and begins to rub against the soft tissue, causing irritation. In response to the irritation, the oyster produces a hard substance. This substance eventually develops into one of the world's most beautiful jewels—a lovely luminous pearl. In fact, the greater the irritation, the more valuable the pearl!

> *"The greater the irritation, the more valuable the pearl!"*

Many single women view themselves as ugly oyster shells lying on the beaches of life, beset with the trials and problems that come with not being married. To make matters worse, they compare their crusty exterior to all the beautiful seashells around them and wonder how any man could ever give his attention to them.

If you are one of these women, be encouraged. Don't view the trials of singleness as irritating grains of sand to be discarded as quickly as possible. Realize that God has them there to create something beautiful in you.

God is using the sands of singleness to make you perfect and complete. He's developing pearls of character in your life.

Nothing Is Instant

"And others fell on good ground, and did yield fruit that sprang up and increased; and brought forth fruit, some a hundredfold, some sixtyfold, some thirtyfold." MARK 4:8

Nothing in life is instant. People think miracles are instant, but they really are not. They are just a process that has been sped up. Nothing God created is instant, because God does not operate in the instant. He is a God of the potential principle. Everything begins as potential.

He did not create a ready-made human race—the earth was not given an instant population. God made one person, not a million people. He started with one seed. Then from that one He created another. Then He said to those seeds, "Bless you (that means, 'You have My permission'). Be fruitful and multiply and replenish the earth."

> *"God knows the potential principle because He introduced it"*

In Adam, God gave the earth a seed with the potential of one...one hundred...one thousand...one million. The five billion people on the earth today were in that one man's loins. God knew that in Adam and Eve there were enough people to fill the earth. That's the way God works. He knows the potential principle because He introduced it. It is Him.

Potential is always present, waiting to be exposed. It demands that you never settle for what you have accomplished. One of the greatest enemies of your potential is success.

Never accept success as a lifestyle—it is but a phase. Never accept an accomplishment as the end—it is but a mark in the process. Because you are God's offspring, there are many selves within you that lie dormant, untapped and unused. Your primary problem is that you do not think like God does.

There are many selves within you that lie dormant, untapped and unused. God is always looking for what is not yet visible.

_____

_____

_____

_____

_____

_____

Myles Munroe, *Understanding Your Potential*

The Path of Most Resistance

". . . and be clothed with humility: for 'God resists the proud, and gives grace to the humble.'"   1 PETER 5:5

First Peter 5:5 tells us to be "clothed with humility: for God resists the proud, and gives grace to the humble." Which would you rather have? When God offers you change that's hard to swallow, take a deep breath and swallow it. If you don't, your choice to resist will come back to swallow you. Peter says that God gives grace to the humble. The humble are those who understand that He is the God who sits high and looks low. To them, He is gracious. To that one who is willing to embrace change and defer to the intelligence, wisdom, and foresight of an omniscient God, grace is given. And God's grace is sufficient in all things. Peter goes on to say in the next verse that if you humble yourself under God's mighty hand, He will exalt you "in due time."   So here are your choices when it comes to making changes you don't like. Change now, receive grace, and be exalted later. Or, don't change now and get clobbered; then receive the grace of being made low. Pick one.

> *"Change now, receive grace, and be exalted later."*

Finally, we choose complacency over change because we are genuinely satisfied with our lives the way they are. It's a subtle difference between this type of complacency and the last. With the former, we reject change because we don't like the change. Here, we ignore the charge to change because we don't want to abandon what we already have. We don't really care what God is offering; we're not buying. We are satisfied, even comfortable, with the status quo. There are two problems with apathy. First, as with pride, we presume to put ourselves on the level of decision-maker with God. The second and more ominous issue is that God has ceased to be the center and focus of our lives. The truth is that all sin is an act of choosing yourself over God. But apathy has the nerve to tell Him so to His face.

_____

_____

_____

_____

_____

_____

Dr. Wanda Turner, *Celebrating Change*

Choked Channels

"Finally, be you all of one mind, having compassion one of another, love as brethren, be tenderhearted, be courteous: not rendering evil for evil, or insult for insult: but on the contrary blessing; knowing that you are for this called, that you may inherit a blessing." 1 PETER 3:8-9

The Master's plan—and what a genius of a plan it is—is this, that the world should be won, not by the preachers—though we must have these men of God for teaching and leadership—but by everyone who knows the story of Jesus telling someone, and telling not only with his lips earnestly and tactfully, but even more, telling with his life. That is the Master's plan of campaign for this world. And it makes a great difference to Him and to the world outside whether you and I are living the story of His love and power among men or not.

> *"The Master is thinking about you, studying your life, longing to carry out His plan if He could only get permission."*

And when here and there they meet one whose acts are dominated by a pure, high spirit, whose faces reflect a sweet radiance amid all circumstances, and whose lives send out a rare fragrance of gladness and kindliness and controlling peace, they are quick to recognize that, to them, intangible something that makes such people different.

There is a third one watching us today with intense interest. The Lord Jesus! Sitting with the scar-marks of earth on face and form, looking eagerly down upon us who stand for Him in the world that crucified Him—He knows. I imagine Him saying, "There is that one down there whom I died for, who bears My name; if I had the control of that life what power I would gladly breathe in and out of it, but—he is so absorbed in other things." The Master is thinking about you, studying your life, longing to carry out His plan if He could only get permission.

_____

_____

_____

_____

_____

_____

_____

S. D. Gordon, *Quiet Talks on Power*

Business as Usual

"And she brought forth her firstborn son, and wrapped him in swaddling clothes, and laid him in a manger; because there was no room for them in the inn." LUKE 2:7

Imagine if the God of the universe decided to visit planet Earth as a new baby and you were given the opportunity to host His first night...in your hotel! Think of the future promotional possibilities "God stayed here His first night!" you could sell tickets to see the room where He was born. What an opportunity to make history as a small-business owner!

God had need of a business owner's establishment one night 2,000 years ago. But there was no room for God in this business that night. There was no room for the unexpected miracle, no awareness of what was taking place in the heavenlies, no sign that God might be reaching out to this businessperson to be used like no other in all of history.

> *"But there was no room for God in this business that night"*

Every day God has need of some businessman or woman's business. He wants to demonstrate miracles in their business. But there is on room in their business for Jesus. He is not asked to participate.

That night God slept in a stable. That night a business opportunity from Heaven was missed. It was business as usual.

May we all have spiritual eyes and ears to know then our Master is needing what He has entrusted to us for His purpose.

Os Hillman, *Today God is First*

Take the Radical Route

"Fear not, little flock; for it is your Father's good pleasure to give you the kingdom." LUKE 12: 32

Does it seem too unrealistic for a woman of the 90's to set her sights on a knight in shining armor? A single friend (a modern Ruth) wrote a letter in which she admitted that her high ideals often made her feel like the "Long Ranger." She said, "So often I meet women who don't want to go to the deeper, more radical route of separation from our culture in seeking after God's standards." Do we lower our standards because we seem out of step with all our peers? Does the woman in Proverbs 31 seem obsolete? Maybe for the "cosmopolitan" woman she is obsolete, but not for the Lady of Conviction. God has the best in hand for those who seek Him.

> *"A Bozo is a counterfeit of a Boaz."*

What is a Bozo? A Bozo is a guy whose outward appearance is a façade. It is hard to discern who he really is because of the "makeup and costume" he wears. What he appears to be physically, socially, and even spiritually is just a performance. A Bozo is a counterfeit of a Boaz.

Ruth's choice to wait for God's best resulted in her union with a Boaz. Ruth not only married a man who was a "pillar of strength" (Boaz), but she also was blessed by the privilege of bearing a son (Obed) who would be part of the lineage of Jesus Christ. Ruth's wise choices resulted in her experiencing God's overwhelming goodness.

A Living Sermon

*"And the King shall answer and say unto them, 'Truly I say unto you,
Inasmuch as you have done it unto one of the least of these my brethren, you
have done it unto me.'"* MATTHEW 25:40

There is a story about the late Dr. Albert Schweitzer that illustrates
the importance of living in the present moment. Many years ago dozens of
dignitaries and members of the media had gathered at a train station in
Chicago to await Dr. Schweitzer's arrival. Schweitzer,
who had dedicated his life to bringing life-saving
medical help to the poorest of the poor in Africa, had
just won the Nobel Prize. Excitement was in the air as
the train squealed slowly to a stop, the doors opened,
and the good doctor stepped out onto the platform.

> *"I'd rather
> see a
> sermon
> than hear
> one any
> day."*

He was instantly recognizable—tall (six-foot, four
inches), with bushy hair and a large mustache. Dozens
of flashbulbs exploded as government officials pressed forward.
Schweitzer started to respond, but then his attention was captured by
something going on behind them.

"Will you excuse me for just a moment?" he asked—and then strode
right on through the assembled crowd. As everyone followed along behind
him, Schweitzer hurried to the side of a frail elderly woman who was
struggling with two suitcases that were much too heavy for her. Sweeping
the suitcases up in his large hands, he escorted the lady on to her train.
After politely wishing her a safe journey, he returned to the platform and
apologized for keeping everyone waiting. Newspapers later quoted one of
the government officials as saying, "That's the first time I've ever seen a
sermon walking."

You know, I'd rather see a sermon than hear one any day. And I'd
much rather be a sermon than preach one. How about you?

Pat Williams, *American Scandal*

An Audience of One

"And be not conformed to this world: but be you transformed by the renewing of your mind, that you may test what is that good, and acceptable, and perfect, will of God." ROMANS 12:2

What audience do you play to? Each day you are seen by many who will make a judgment about the way you handle yourself among different audiences. Politicians have learned to play to their audiences, customizing messages for the needs of their particular groups. Musicians have learned to play to their audiences. Businesspeople play to the audiences who will buy their product.

> *"Today, be aware of which audience you are playing to."*

Christ has called us to play to one audience—the audience of Himself. When you seek to please any other audience in your life, you become susceptible to situational ethics and motivations based on the need for the moment. Your audience becomes a pawn in your hands because you know what they want. Is that wrong? Sometimes it is, sometimes it isn't.

Pure obedience to pleasing God in our lives will often meet the needs of those around us. It is God's will that you and I love our spouses, provide good services to our customers, and look to the interests of others before ourselves. This will result in meeting many needs of the audiences in our lives.

However, there are other times when our audiences are asked for something contrary to God's will. Politicians are often forced to appease their audiences, even though it may go against God's laws. When we are asked to go with the flow, we discover which audience is most important in our lives. Is it the audience of One—or the audience of many?

Today, be aware of which audience you are playing to. Ask yourself why you are taking a particular action. Is it to please the audience of One? Or is to please the audience of others who might negatively impact you should you not play their tune?

*P*atience For the Holding Pattern

"For when God made a promise to Abraham, because he could swear by no greater, he swore by himself, saying, "Surely blessing I will bless you, and multiplying I will multiply you." And so, after he had patiently endured, he obtained the promise." HEBREWS 6:13-15

It is God's timing that we must learn. He synchronizes His answers to accomplish His purpose. Recently, while traveling on a major American airline, we were told that the plane could not land at its scheduled time. Evidently the air traffic controller instructed that we should wait in the air. What a strange place to have to wait—in the air! I have often felt like that aircraft suspended in the air when God says, "Wait!" Then the captain spoke into the PA system. He said, "We are going to assume a holding pattern until further instructions come from the tower." After some time, a few, rather intoxicated passengers began to question the traffic controller's decision. Perhaps we were all concerned. It's just that some had their concern lubricated with several stiff shots of rum!

> *"Do you have enough faith to assume a holding pattern and wait for the fulfillment of the promise?"*

The anxious looks and acidic remarks that came from the crowd subsided as the stewardess quickly eased people's fears. She informed several worried passengers that the planes always carry enough fuel to withstand the demands of these kinds of delays. There was a calm assurance on the faces of the attendants. I would have to attribute it to the fact that they had prepared for a delay. I began to wonder if we as the children of God shouldn't be better prepared for those times in our lives when God speaks from His throne, "Assume a holding pattern until further notice." The question is not always, "Do you have enough faith to receive?" Sometimes it is this: "Do you have enough faith to assume a holding pattern and wait for the fulfillment of the promise?"

_____

_____

_____

_____

_____

_____

_____

_____

T. D. Jakes, *365 Days to Healing, Blessings, and Freedom*

*M*y Gratitude

Loving what I have—what I am grateful for

_____

_____

_____

_____

_____

_____

_____

_____

_____

_____

_____

_____

_____

_____

_____

_____

_____

_____

_____

_____

_____

_____

*"Sing unto the Lord with thanksgiving; sing praise upon the harp
unto our God."* PSALMS 147:7-(KJV)

*T*he Razor's Edge

"And whatsoever we ask, we receive of him, because we keep his commandments, and do those things that are pleasing in his sight."
1 JOHN 3:22

The relationship that underlies prayer has an absorbing purpose. Its controlling purpose is to please God. That sentence may sound simple enough. But do you know there is no sentence I might utter that has a keener, a more freshly honed razor edge to it than that. That the purpose which controls my action in every matter be this: to please Him. If you have not done so, take it for a day, a week, and use it as a touchstone regarding thought, word, and action. Take it into matters personal, home, business, social, fraternal. It does not mean to ask, "Is this right? Is this wrong?" Not that. Not the driving of a keen line between wrong and right. There are a great many things that can be proven to be not wrong, but that are not best, that are not His preference.

> *"Prayer is not extracting favors from a reluctant God."*

It will send a businessman running his eye along the shelves and counter of his store. "The controlling purpose to please Jesus...Hmmm, I guess maybe that stuff there ought to come out. Oh, it is not wrong; I can prove that. My Christian brother merchants handle it here, and over the country; but to please Him: a good clean sixty percent profit too, cash money, but to please Him"—and the stuff must go down and out.

It will make one think of his personal habits, his business methods, and social intercourse, the organizations he belongs to, with the quiet question cutting its razor-way into each.

Prayer is not extracting favors from a reluctant God. The true basis of prayer is sympathy, oneness of purpose. God above and a man down here, in such sympathetic touch that God can think His thoughts over in this man's mind, and have His desires repeated upon the earth as this man's prayer.

S. D. Gordon, *Quiet Talks on Prayer*

A Shoe Salesman

"And Jesus looking upon them said, 'With men it is impossible, but not with God: for the things which are impossible with men are possible with God. For with God all things are possible.'" MATTHEW 19:26

Dwight L. Moody was a poorly educated, unordained shoe salesman who felt God's call to preach the gospel. Early one morning he and some friends gathered in a hay field for a season of prayer, confession, and consecration. His friend Henry Varley said, "The world has yet to see what God can do with and for and through and in a man who is fully and wholly consecrated to Him." Moody was deeply moved by these words. He later went to a meeting where Charles Spurgeon was speaking. In that meeting Moody recalled the words spoken by his friend, "The world is yet to see!... with and for and through and in!...A man!"

> *"...with and for and through and in!"*

Varley meant any man! Varley didn't say he had to be educated, or brilliant, or anything else. Just a man! Well, by the Holy spirit in him, he'd be one of those men. Then suddenly, in that high gallery, he saw something he'd never realized before. It was not Mr. Spurgeon, after all, who was doing that work; it was God. And if God could use Mr. Spurgeon, why should He not use the rest of us, and why should we not all just lay ourselves at the Master's feet and say to Him, "Send me! Use me!"

D.L. Moody was an ordinary man who sought to be fully and wholly committed to Christ. God did extraordinary things through this ordinary man. Moody became one of the great evangelists of modern times. He founded a Bible college, Moody Bible Institute in Chicago, that sends out men and women trained in service for God.

Are you an ordinary man or woman in whom God wants to do extraordinary things? God desires that for every child of His. Ask God to do extraordinary things in your life. Begin today to trust Him to accomplish great things for His Kingdom through you.

ƒulfillment

"Every good gift and every perfect gift is from above, and comes down from the Father of lights, with whom is no variation, neither shadow of turning."
JAMES 1:17

Have you assumed that your ultimate fulfillment would be found in marriage? Have you privately entertained the notion that the only satisfied women are married women? Have you been expecting your career to satisfy you until you are married? If you have answered "yes" to any of these questions, then you have a prospect of disillusionment looming in the future. "...A woman becomes a woman when she becomes what God wants her to be."* This priceless truth can help keep your perspective clear in relation to true fulfillment in life. Too many Christian women think that the inner longings of their heart relate only to love, marriage, and motherhood.

> *"Fulfillment for a Christian woman begins with the Lordship of Christ in every area of her life."*

Look a little closer and see if that longing isn't ultimately for Jesus. Gary Chapman once remarked, "I feel very strongly that marriage is not a higher calling than the single state. Happy indeed are those people, married or single, who have discovered that happiness is not found in marriage but in a right relationship with God."

Fulfillment for a Christian woman begins with the Lordship of Christ in every area of her life.

*Kenneth G. Smith, *Learning to Be a Woman* (Downers Grove, Illinois: InterVarsity Press, 1972)

Twisted Values

"But we have this treasure in earthen vessels, that the excellence of the power may be of God, and not of us." 2 CORINTHIANS 4:7

Our ignorance of God's will and His ways has twisted our world. We devalue what God values and elevate what is insignificant to Him. He sees the tremendous ability we have and we look at the earth houses that contain that treasure. He created us to show forth His power, but we are more interested in success by the world's standards. He affirms out ability to tap into His wisdom, but we make decisions based on the information we receive from our physical senses and our education.

Our poverty of knowledge is revealed by our inability to fulfill God's potential on our own. We live aimlessly without purpose, flitting from one thing to another and never accomplishing anything. Such life is a waste of time. Without a sense of purpose we are like stillborn babies.

> *"God rejects those who reject His knowledge."*

God rejects those who reject His knowledge. In other words He says, "We can't do business. You haven't used the tools I gave you, so I can't help you. You cant even talk intelligently with Me." Ignorance affects how God answers our prayers because we ask for things we don't need or shouldn't want. To ask rightly we must understand how we operate, how the devil operates, how the world operates, and how God operates. Asking God to do something for us before we understand these aspects of our situation is wasting our time and God's. He must reject everything we request because our prayers and His ways, will, and desires for us do not line up.

Your potential will be wasted if you do not allow god to cleanse your sight and redirect your values. Then you can escape this purposeless existence. This occurs as you become aware of the world's standards and compare them carefully with God's. You may be surprised by what you find.

_____

_____

_____

_____

_____

_____

Myles Munroe, *Maximizing Your Potential*

$\mathcal{H}$e Knows Your Calling

"After these things the Lord appointed seventy others also, and sent them two and two before his face into every city and place, where he himself would come." LUKE 10:1

I heard recently the concluding words of an address in which the speaker pronounced triumphantly, "and we are prepared to use any means necessary to achieve our ends."

Any means necessary? I found myself wondering if, as a society, we have become a people fixated on our own desires, our language one of self and want—our "eyes on the "ends" in a way that suggests we may not be too particular about the "means"—want, deserve, need, faster, more, mine—integral to "any means necessary." Paul speaks to the Galatians about acting towards one another in a spirit of gentleness, not by any means necessary, like threats, ostracizing, manipulation, or violence—counseling the church that you reap whatever you sow.

> *"God alone knows our every need, our every gift, woven within the womb."*

The account of Jesus' sending out of the 70 into the neighboring towns and villages in an aggressive outreach program. The 70 willing messengers are ambassadors. How they were chosen, how many were women, what parts of the country or strata of society they came from, we have absolutely no idea. They are chosen, commissioned, and sent out to prepare the way—to go about their evangelistic task with an urgency that we as a church no longer seem to feel.

For the farmer, harvest time is the most urgent season of the year. Most of us can survive failure on an ordinary day, but failure in the "harvest" season is disastrous. Given the urgency of the situation, Jesus told the 70 to go, but only after a call for prayer that leaves no illusion as to who is in charge of the harvest and the sending. He does not say, "would any of you mind doing this," he commands them to pray and to go—a powerful reminder that God does not call for our expertise, or opinion, but for our faith. God alone knows our every need, our every gift, woven within the womb.

Penelope Black, Holy Trinity Anglican Church, North Saanich, BC Canada

*T*he Invisible Became Visible

"Through faith we understand that the worlds were framed by the word of God, so that things which are seen were not made of things which do appear."
HEBREWS 11:3

In the beginning, God was pregnant with the universe and all things were made by Him. But how did these things come out of Him? How was the universe formed? All things were formed at God's command. He spat them out—poof! From the invisible came the visible. Things that are seen came from things that were unseen.

> *"All things were formed at God's command."*

God always had everything in Him, but we couldn't see it. All we now see was once in an invisible state. Everything that man has ever seen first existed in an invisible state. (Please note that invisible does not mean nonexistent.)

In the beginning there was only God. At creation the entire unseen universe became visible. Everything that has been created was made by the word of God. Although it already existed, God spoke so that what was invisible could become visible. You would never have known it existed, except God spat it out in faith.

By faith God spat out what was in Him. Everything in Him started to come forth. What we now see was birthed by God from what was invisibly within Him. Whatever you see came from the unseen—nothing exists that was not at some time in God. Thus, faith is not the evidence of things that do not exist. It is the evidence of things that are not yet seen. Everything we see has always been. It became visible when God spoke it into being. God is the source of life.

Myles Munroe, *Understanding Your Potential*

ℋe Sees the Clutter

"Jesus saw Nathanael coming to him, and said of him, 'Behold an Israelite indeed, in whom is no deceit!' Nathanael said unto him, 'How do you know me?'" JOHN 1:47-48

When we clean our homes we tend to focus our efforts first on what people will see rather than on what they will not see. Only the most ardent of housekeepers spends as much time scrubbing the basement steps as she does the foyer or the living room. We emphasize what will be inspected.

Can you imagine how much clutter we allow to fester in our minds, simply because no one sits in our heads sipping tea and examining the thoughts and imaginations of our hearts? If no one knows what we think, why shouldn't we allow our minds to collect scum and clutter without any regard to cleaning and renewing the mind? There are several reasons not to do that, but I will give only three.

> *"God sits in the living quarters of the minds of men and beholds their thoughts."*

First, a certain Someone does know what we think. Second, we need to continually purge our thoughts because we become what we think. Third, we need to renew our minds daily in God's presence, for I believe that as we hear the thoughts of God, His thinking becomes increasingly contagious.

God sits in the living quarters of the minds of men and beholds their thoughts. He knows our thoughts afar off (Ps. 139:2). If we are serious about entertaining His presence, we cannot lie to Him—He sees us from the inside out. We must be honest and admit to Him: This is what I am being tempted with. I cannot hide from You. All my thoughts are played on the screen before You. I want to clean up this mess so You can replace it with a greater revelation and a stronger direction for my life. I praise You for loving me, in spite of all You know about me. Forgive me for condemning and judging anybody else. I know that if it were not for Your mercy, I would be guilty of the very things for which I have disdained others.

T. D. Jakes, *365 Days to Healing, Blessings, and Freedom*

*I*f God Has It, You Have It

"But the fruit of the Spirit is love, joy, peace, patience, gentleness, goodness, faithfulness, meekness, self-control: against such there is no law."
GALATIANS 5:22-23

Each of these fruits of the Spirit is an attribute of God. God unconditionally says, "They are you." God knows you have love. He knows you have joy-it doesn't matter what you are going through. God knows you have joy down there inside you, because Christ is joy.

Peace. How do you explain that? I used to think the Prince of Peace. "Hello, Prince." I always thought: "Others have the peace. Give me some, Jesus." But that's not what the Bible teaches. The Bible says you have peace. When you are unhappy and everything is going wrong, God says, "Have peace." He doesn't say, "I'll give you some peace," because He can't give you what you already have. Peace is not a gift; It's a fruit. Joy is not a gift; it's a fruit. If God has it, you have it.

> *"Love isn't a decision you make, because you already have it."*

In the beginning there was only God. All that is and all that was, was in God-everything. We came out of God. Thus, everything that is in God, is in us: love ... joy ... peace ... patience ... kindness ... goodness ... faithfulness ... gentleness ... self control. These are in God and in us.

"Love? I can't like *that* person."

"You're lying to me," God says, "What do you mean you can't love? Your spirit connected to My Spirit can do all things. Since I love, you can too."

It's not that you *can't* love; you just don't *want* to love. Love isn't a decision you make, because you already have it. That's why you *can* love your enemies.

These things are already in you, and God is saying, "Go for it!" You don't have to pray for these things. They are already in you.

_____
_____
_____
_____
_____
_____
_____

Myles Munroe, *Understanding Your Potential*

Symphonies of Enlightenment

"Then said Jesus unto the twelve, 'Will you also go away?'
Then Simon Peter answered him, 'Lord, to whom shall we go? you have the
words of eternal life.'" JOHN 6:67-68

We need to renew our minds daily in God's presence, for I believe that as we hear the thoughts of God, His thinking becomes increasingly contagious. It is so important that we have a relationship with Him. His Word becomes a lifeline thrown to a man who would otherwise drown in the swirling whirlpool of his own thoughts. Peter was so addicted to hearing Jesus speak that when other men walked away, Peter said, "Lord, to whom shall we go? you have the words of eternal life" (John 6:68).

Peter recognized his need to keep hearing the Word of God. Many years before Peter, Job said that he esteemed God's Word more than his necessary food (Job 23:12). As for me, God is my counselor. He talks with me about my deepest, darkest issues; He comforts the raging tide of my fears and inhibitions. What would we be if He would wax silent and cease to guide us through this perilous maze of mental mania? It is His soft words that turn away the wrath of our nagging memories. If He speaks to me, His words become symphonies of enlightenment falling like soft rain on a tin roof. They give rest and peace.

> *"As we hear the thoughts of God, His thinking becomes increasingly contagious."*

For as the rain cometh down, and the snow from heaven, and returneth not thither, but watereth the earth, and maketh it bring forth and bud, that it may give seed to the sower, and bread to the eater: so shall my word be that goeth forth out of my mouth: it shall not return unto me void, but it shall accomplish that which I please, and it shall prosper in the thing whereto I sent it. For ye shall go out with joy, and be led forth with peace: the mountains and the hills shall break forth before you into singing, and all the trees of the field shall clap their hands. Instead of the thorn shall come up the fir tree, and instead of the brier shall come up the myrtle tree: and it shall be to the Lord for a name, for an everlasting sign that shall not be cut off. (Isaiah 55:10-13 · KJV)

_____

_____

_____

_____

Born to Expose His Nature

*"And Jesus said unto them, Because of your unbelief: for truly I say unto you,
If you have faith as a grain of mustard seed, you shall say unto this
mountain, 'Move from here to yonder place;' and it shall move;"*
MATTHEW 17:20

God designed you to live out the careful plans He prepared for you.
You are made in God's image. The plan He wrote for you is perfect and
right. No detail or part is missing. You have the potential to live out all
that God has planned for your life—but only if you accept Jesus Christ as
your Savior and Lord. That's the first step toward
understanding why you were born.

> *"He knows there is more to you than we can see because He placed part of Himself in you."*

Not only did God carefully plan for the details of
your life, He also determined how your life would fit
into His total plan for man. Part of the answer to the
why of our birth is revealed in God's desire that we
should show forth His glory. The glory of God is the
excess of His nature. It's all the potential of our
omnipotent God that has not yet been revealed. He's
full of so much more than we can think or imagine and
He's waiting to use us to realize that potential.
Throughout the Bible, God tells us to make His name
great in the earth.

God created you to bring glory to His name. His predestined plan for
your life was designed to bring Him glory. He knows there is more to you
than we can see because He placed part of Himself in you. His plan for
your life is part of His creative work—through you God wants to continue
the birth of His potential. Because you share God's omnipotent nature,
Jesus said you can do even greater things than He did, if you only believe.

$\mathcal{R}$ock-Rooted Purpose

"Whosoever will come after me, let him deny himself, and take up his cross daily, and follow me." MATTHEW 16: 24

To him whose heart burns for power in prayer, I urge a careful review of these words. "If any man would come after Me" means a rock-rooted purpose; the jaw locked; the tendrils of the purpose going down around and under the gray granite of a man's will, and tying themselves there; and knotting the ties; sailor knots, that you cannot undo.

"Come after Me" means all the power of Jesus' life, and has the other side, too. It means the wilderness, the intense temptation. It may mean the obscure village of Nazareth for you. It may mean the first Judean year for you—lack of appreciation. It may mean for you that last six moths—the desertion of those hitherto friendly. It will mean without a doubt a Gethsemane. Everybody who comes along after Jesus has a Gethsemane in his life. It will never mean as much to you as it meant to Him. But then, it will mean everything to you. And it will mean too having a Calvary in your life in a very real sense, though different from what that meant to Him. And if that sounds hard and severe to you let me quickly say that it is an easy way for the man who is willing.

> *"The presence of Jesus in the life overlaps every cutting thing."*

If a man will go through Matthew 16:24, and habitually live there he may ask what he wills, and that thing will come to pass. The reason, without question, why many people do not have power in prayer is simply because they are unwilling—I am just talking very plainly—they are unwilling to bare their breasts to the keen-edged knife in these words of Jesus. And on the other side, if a man will quietly, resolutely follow the Master's leading—nothing extreme—nothing fanatical, or morbid, just a quiet going where the inner Voice plainly leads day by day, he will be startled to find what an utterly new meaning prayer will come to have for him.

_____

_____

_____

_____

_____

S. D. Gordon, *Quiet Talks on Prayer*

The Old Eden Language of Love

"He that has an ear, let him hear what the Spirit says unto the churches; to him that overcomes will I give to eat of the tree of life, which is in the midst of the paradise of God." REVELATION 2:7

Jesus is God spelling Himself out in language that man can understand. God and man used to talk together freely. But one day man went away from God. And then he went farther away. He left home. He left his native land, Eden, where he lived with God. He emigrated from God. And through going away he lost his mother tongue.

> *"He is the A and the Z, and all between, of the Old Eden language of love."*

A language always changes away from its native land. Through going away from his native land man lost his native speech. Through not hearing God speak he forgot the sounds of the words. His ears grew dull and then deaf. Through lack of use he lost the power of speaking the old words. His tongue grew thick. It lost its cunning. And so gradually almost all the old meanings were lost.

God has always been eager to get to talking with man again. Nobody yet seems to have spelled Him out fully, though they're all trying: All on the spelling bench. That is, all that have heard. Great numbers haven't heard about Him yet.

Of course he had to use a language that man could understand. Jesus is God spelling Himself out so man can understand. He is the A and the Z, and all between, of the Old Eden language of love.

Some of the great nouns of the Eden tongue—the God tongue—He spelled out big. He spelled out purity, the natural life of Eden; and obedience, the rhythmic harmony of Eden; and peace, the sweet music of Eden; and power, the mastery and dominion of Eden; and love, the throbbing heart of Eden. It was in biggest, brightest letters that love was spelled out. He used the biggest capitals ever known, and traced each in a deep dripping red, with a new spelling—s·a·c·r·i·f·i·c·e.

$\mathcal{A}$ Broken Dream In The Making

"Listen now, you that say, 'Today or tomorrow we will go into such a city, and continue there a year, and buy and sell, and get gain'; For you ought to say, 'If the Lord is willing, we shall live, and do this, or that.'" JAMES 4:13, 15

I am a planner, a dreamer, and a list maker—I get as much fun from planning and anticipating an event as from the actual event! But the downside of this grand adventure comes when the event never materializes after all my dreaming and planning. When I was a young Christian, I would always preface my dreams and plans with the biblical expression, "If the Lord wills..." Using that phrase in front of my plans always reminded me that I needed to yield my plans, as well as my hopes and dreams, to God.

A couple of years into my Christian walk, after hearing me use the phrase, "If the Lord wills," an older Christian said, "You do not need to use that phrase to try to sound spiritual." Now, I never thought of the phrase

> *"Lord Willing"*

as a way of sounding spiritual. I used that phrase to remind myself who is ultimately in charge of my life's blueprints. Fearing others would think that I was using a "Christianese" expression, I stopped saying, "If the Lord wills" or "Lord willing."

When I grew older and (thank God) wiser, I realized that the phrase, "Lord willing," is not only a wonderful reminder for the one who uses these two words, but also for the one who hears them. Why did the Holy Spirit tell us to preface our blueprints and dreams with the expression, "If the Lord wills"? I think one of the reasons is to remind us to give our blueprints and dreams to the Lord for His authorization on a continual basis. but one thing I know for sure:

"Every expectation, every plan every dream not yielded to God, is a potential broken dream in the making."

I am still a planner, dreamer, and list maker but I am using the phrase "If the Lord wills" more than ever these days.

Jackie Kendall, *Say Goodbye to Shame*

*O*ne People, One Church

"Woe unto you, scribes and Pharisees, hypocrites! for you journey sea and land to make one convert, and when he is made, you make him twofold more the child of hell than yourselves." MATTHEW 23:15

Too often, our stance as Christians has been aloof, exclusive or sanctimonious. How frequently our contemporary church utters woes and pronounces judgment on those who are marginalized, addresses social and political problems by warning people that if they don't smarten up, God will get them—the them that we never see ourselves as connected to. And when we do feel connected, they become the problem to which we, in all our self-righteousness, have the solution.

> *"God's peace is the unconditional love of Jesus, the Lamb of God who wanders, uninvited, into the wilderness of our lives and brings God's peace right to our doorstep."*

How often is our focus on wooing church hoppers from each other, our faith placed in the wizardry of multi-media technology to attract newcomers, our proclamation about the growth in numbers—grandstanding, at which St Paul pokes pointedly, claiming that his opponents consider converts as trophies to be waved rather than souls to be cared for.

Jesus' commission challenges the comfort of our cultured, sophisticated, enlightened modern lives, saying "come to the table," a message we will not hear if we remain steadfast in our self-centered ways, acting like the wolves amongst whom we are commanded to go.

God's peace is the unconditional love of Jesus, the Lamb of God who wanders, uninvited, into the wilderness of our lives and brings God's peace right to our doorstep. The Lamb who commands us today: pray, go, encounter, love—embrace those who stand alone and apart, saying come to the table, rejoice, the kingdom of God is among us.

_____
_____
_____
_____
_____
_____

Penelope Black, Holy Trinity Anglican Church, North Saanich, BC Canada

*B*end But Don't Break

"For I say, through the grace given unto me, to every man that is among you, not to think of himself more highly than he ought to think; but to think soberly, according as God has dealt to every man the measure of faith."
ROMANS 12:3

Don't take yourself too seriously. Don't think that you should somehow be protected from the misfortunes that befall other people.
- Robert Louis Stevenson

> *"Humble people are able to laugh at themselves."*

Another way of stating this is that humble people are able to laugh at themselves. They don't take themselves too seriously. They understand that, no matter how important you may think you are, sooner or later you'll get the props knocked out from under you.

Tonight Show host Jay Leno, one of the nicest people in television, tries to answer as many letters as possible, and sometimes calls people who have written him.

On one such occasion, when he asked for Susan, the voice on the other end said she wasn't home and asked "Who's this?"

"This is Jay Leno."

"Well, this is her mother, what do you want?"

"She wrote me a letter," Leno replied.

There was a deep sigh on the other end of the line.

"Yeah, well, she writes to every crackpot on TV."

As author Paul Powell wrote, "Blessed is he who has learned to laugh at himself, for he shall never cease to be entertained."

Pat Williams, *American Scandal*

God Works On the Left Side

"Behold, I go forward, but He is not there; and backward, but I cannot percive Him: on the left hand, where He doth work, but I cannot behold Him; He hideth Himself on the right hand, that I cannot see Him." JOB 23: 8-9 (KJV)

Great growth doesn't come into your life through mountaintop experiences. Great growth comes through the valleys and low places where you feel limited and vulnerable. The time God is really moving in your life may seem to be the lowest moment you have ever experienced. God is working on you, your faith and your character, when the blessing is delayed. The blessing is the reward that comes after you learn obedience through the things you suffered while waiting for it!

> *"The blessing is the reward that comes after you learn obedience through the things you suffered while waiting for it!"*

I am not finished with the left hand—nor do I want to be finished. The prerequisite of the mountain is the valley. If there is no valley, there is no mountain. After you've been through this process a few times, you begin to realize that the valley is only a sign that with a few more steps, you'll be at the mountain again! Thus if the left hand is where He works, and it is; if the left hand is where He teaches us, and it is; then at the end of every class is a promotion. So just hold on!

It is difficult to perceive God's workings on the left hand. God makes definite moves on the right hand, but when He works on the left, you may think He has forgotten you! If you've been living on the left side, you've been through a period that didn't seem to have the slightest stirring. It seemed as if everything you wanted to see God move upon, stayed still. "Has He gone on vacation? Has He forgotten His promise?" you've asked. The answer is no! God hasn't forgotten. You simply need to understand that sometimes He moves openly. I call them right-hand blessings. But sometimes He moves silently, tiptoeing around in the invisible, working in the shadows. You can't see Him, for He is working on the left side!

_____

_____

_____

_____

_____

_____

T. D. Jakes, *365 Days to Healing, Blessings, and Freedom*

Humble and Exalted

"Humble yourselves in the sight of the Lord, and he shall lift you up."
JAMES 4:10

There's a reason why so many of Jesus' contemporaries did not recognize Him as the Messiah. They expected the Messiah to enjoy the company of princes and kings. Instead, He spent his time healing lepers and telling the poor about God's love. They expected Him to come with a flourish of trumpets and a blaze of glory, but He came riding on a long-eared, braying donkey.

Jesus was humble, but He wasn't a wimp. He knew who He was and was sure of His authority. He drove moneylenders out of the temple. He got right in the Pharisees' faces when it was necessary. He was a powerful person, but He was humble. Jesus told us that the man or woman who wants to be the leader of all must strive to be the servant of all, and He wasn't being ironic. He was telling it the way it is. Humility—real humility—is not weakness. Being humble does not mean you are a wimp. It simply means that you have a proper view of yourself. Humility starts with an understanding that all of your abilities, strengths, and positive attributes are a gift from God.

> *"Pride builds walls between people; humility builds bridges."*

On the other hand, Proverbs 16:18 (NIV) tells us that "pride goes before destruction," and it's true. I love what author Rick Warren says about humility: "Self-importance, smugness, and stubborn pride destroy fellowship faster than anything else. Pride builds walls between people; humility builds bridges. Humility is the oil that soothes and smoothes relationships. That's why the Bible says, 'and be clothed with humility' (1 Peter 5:5). The proper dress for fellowship is a humble attitude. The rest of that verse says, 'for "God resists the proud, and gives grace to the humble."' This is the other reason we need to be humble: Pride blocks God's grace in our lives, which we must have in order to grow, change, heal, and help others."

_____

_____

_____

_____

_____

_____

_____

Pat Williams, *American Scandal*

$\mathcal{A}$ Dog's Life

"For you have not received the spirit of bondage again to fear; but you have received the Spirit of adoption, whereby we cry, 'Abba, Father.'" ROMANS 8:15

Step with me into the opulent dining hall of the royal palace. The golden candelabras emit a soft light, revealing a banquet fit for a king. Pleasant aromas ascend from the table, drifting gently through the air, suggesting how delectable the meal will taste. Notice the glimmering cutlery and golden chalices arranged meticulously at each setting. One cannot avoid seeing the exquisite artistry lining the walls, telling of past victories.

> *"We had nothing to offer the Father, but He took us as we were. It wasn't what we could do for Him, but what He could do for us."*

Seated at the table are Amnon, Tamar, Solomon, and Absalom. At the head of the table sits King David. But not an ounce of food is being consumed; it is not proper to begin eating when a chair remains empty.

As the waiting continues, the sound of shuffling feet is heard approaching the dining hall. Mephibosheth slowly drags his crippled feet along the plush carpet. His handicap is a constant reminder of the grace extended to him by the king.

For nearly 20 years he lived in Lodebar, which in Hebrew means a barren place, a place without pasture. He was five years old when he suffered a fall, and he has been a cripple ever since. If King David were to follow that pattern set with his predecessors, Mephibosheth would have been executed. But instead of death David chooses life for Mephibosheth, and the lame boy moved into the big house.

Although he can be of no service to David, he gets to live here just the same. The others at the table were born to David; Mephibosheth is adopted. The story reminds us of ourselves. We had nothing to offer the Father, but He took us as we were. It wasn't what we could do for Him, but what He could do for us (2 Sam. 9; Romans 8:15.).

Morton Bustard, *The Impassioned Soul*

Contented With Crumbs in the Carpet

"The kingdom of heaven is likened unto a man which sowed good seed in his field: but while men slept, his enemy came and sowed weeds among the wheat, and went his way." MATTHEW 13:24-25

There is much more of God available than we have ever known or imagined, but we have become so satisfied with where we are and what we have that we don't press in for God's best. Yes, God is moving among us and working in our lives, but we have been content to comb the carpet for crumbs as opposed to having the abundant loaves of hot bread God has prepared for us in the ovens of Heaven!

We ignore God's summons while carefully counting our stale crumbs of yesteryear's bread. Meanwhile millions of people outside our church walls are starving for life. They are sick and overstuffed with our man-made programs for self-help and self-advancement. They are starving for Him, not stories about Him. They want the food, but all we have to give them is a tattered menu vacuum-sealed in plastic to protect the fading images of what once was from the grasping fingers of the desperately hungry. This is why we see highly educated men and women wearing crystals around their necks in the hopes of getting in touch with something beyond themselves and their sad existence.

> *"People don't sense God's presence in our gatherings because it's just not there sufficiently enough to register on our gauges."*

People don't sense God's presence in our gatherings because it's just not there sufficiently enough to register on our gauges. This, in turn, creates another problem. When people get just a little touch of God mixed with a lot of something that is not God, it inoculates them against the real thing. Once they've been "inoculated" by a crumb of God's presence, then when we say, "God really is here"; they say, "No, I've been there, done that. I bought that T-shirt, and I didn't find Him; it really didn't work for me." The problem is that God was there all right, but not enough of Him!

Tommy Tenney, *The God Chasers*

The All-Inclusive Passion

"For I am persuaded, that neither death, nor life, nor angels, nor principalities, nor powers, nor things present, nor things to come, nor height, nor depth, nor any other creature, shall be able to separate us from the love of God, which is in Christ Jesus our Lord." ROMANS 8:38-39

That marvelous tender passion—the love of God—heightless, depthless, shoreless, shall flood our hearts, making us as gentle and tenderhearted and self-sacrificing and gracious as He. The all-inclusive result is love. Every phase of life will become a phase of love.

> *"Enthusiasm is love burning. Hope is love expecting."*

Peace is love resting. Bible study is love reading its lover's letters. Prayer is love keeping tryst. Conflict with sin is love jealously fighting for its Lover. Hatred of sin is love shrinking from that which separates from its lover. Sympathy is love tenderly feeling. Enthusiasm is love burning. Hope is love expecting. Patience is love waiting. Faithfulness is love sticking fast. Humility is love taking its true place. Modesty is love keeping out of sight. Soul-winning is love pleading.

Love is revolutionary. It radically changes us, and revolutionizes our spirit toward all others.

Love is democratic. It ruthlessly levels all class distinctions.

Love is intensely practical. It is always hunting something to do.

S. D. Gordon, *Quiet Talks on Power*

The Root of Bitterness

"... looking diligently lest any man fail of the grace of God; lest any root of bitterness springing up trouble you, and thereby many be defiled;"
HEBREWS 12:15

The enemy of our souls has a very specific strategy to destroy relationships. Whether these relationships are in business, marriage, or friendships, his strategy is the same. A conflict arises, judgments are made, and feelings are hurt. What happens next is the defining point of whether the enemy gains a foothold, or the grace of God covers the wrong.

When a root of bitterness is allowed to be planted and grown, it not only affects that person, but it also affects all others who are involved. It is like a cancer.

> *"Choose grace instead of bitterness"*

Breaking satan's foothold requires at least one person to press into God's grace. It cannot happen when either party "feels" like it, for none of us will ever feel like forgiving. None of us feel like talking when we have been hurt. Our natural response is to withdraw or lash out at the offending party. It is only obedience that allows God's grace to cover the wrongs incurred. This grace prevents the parties from becoming victims who will seek compensation for their pain.

The next time you are hurt by someone, realize the gravity of the crossroads where you find yourself. Choose grace instead of bitterness. Then you will be free to move past the hurt, and a root of bitterness will not be given opportunity to grow.

Os Hillman, *Today God is First*

*T*alented For a Purpose

"Even so you, Inasmuch as you are zealous of spiritual gifts, seek that you may excel to the edification of the church." 1 CORINTHIANS 14:12

You would be surprised to know how many people there are who never focus on a goal. They do several things haphazardly without examining how forceful they can be when they totally commit themselves to a cause. The difference between the masterful and the mediocre is often a focused effort. On the other hand, mediocrity is masterful to persons of limited resources and abilities. So in reality, true success is relative to ability. What is a miraculous occurrence for one person can be nothing of consequence to another. A person's goal must be set on the basis of his ability to cultivate talents and his agility in provoking a change. I often wonder how far my best work is in front of me. I am convinced that I have not fully developed my giftings.

> *"People who are effective at only one thing have little to decide."*

But, I am committed to the cause of being. "Being what?" you ask. I am committed to being all that I was intended and predestined to be for the Lord, for my family, and for myself. How about you—have you decided to roll up your sleeves and go to work? Remember, effort is the bridge between mediocrity and masterful accomplishment!

Multiple talents can also be a source of confusion. People who are effective at only one thing have little to decide. At this point let me distinguish between talent and purpose. You may have within you a multiplicity of talent. But if the Holy Spirit gives no direction in that area, it will not be effective. Are you called to the area in which you feel talented? On the other hand, consider this verse: "And we know that all things work together for good to them that love God, to them who are the called according to His purpose" (Rom. 8:28). So then you are called according to His purpose and not your talents.

_____

_____

_____

_____

_____

_____

_____

T. D. Jakes, *365 Days to Healing, Blessings, and Freedom*

The Umpire Has the Final Word

"For all that is in the world, the lust of the flesh, and the lust of the eyes, and the pride of life, is not of the Father, but is of the world. And the world passes away, and the lust thereof: but he that does the will of God abides for ever."
1 JOHN 2:16-17

Your lack of contentment is because of pride. Pride can be described as an excessively high opinion of what one deserves. When a single's life is not moving in the direction she wants (husband, career children, house, etc.), the arguing often begins. With whom is the single woman arguing? It is none other than the umpire, the arbitrator: Jesus. "And let the peace of Christ rule [arbitrate, umpire] in your hearts..." (Col. 3:15 - ASV).

> "Why would a woman argue with such an all-wise Umpire?"

The struggle with the Umpire is not limited to the single woman up to bat! Every woman who has descended from Eve must learn to trust the call of her heavenly Umpire. The trouble from the beginning was a woman not listening to the Umpire, but reaching for a life on "her terms." Why would a woman argue with such an all-wise Umpire? "Pride only breeds quarrels" (Proverbs 13:10a NIV).

Exchange your pride for Jesus' strength so you may accept whatever assignment the Umpire has for you from this moment forward. Dating is not a reward or a prize for living for Jesus. A Friday night without a date is often a night of "being spared" by an all-wise Umpire.

Debbie Jones & Jackie Kendall, *Lady in Waiting—Meditations of The Heart*

Watered With Tears

"For the Lamb which is in the midst of the throne shall shepherd them, and shall lead them unto living fountains of waters: and God shall wipe away all tears from their eyes." REVELATION 7:17

Greatness has a tremendous thirst. This thirst is quenched in the tear-stained struggle toward destiny. One thing I learned about life is neither fellowship nor friendship can lower the price of personal sacrifice. What I mean is, no one can water your dreams but you.

No matter how many people hold your hand, you still must shed your own tears. Others can cry with you, but they can't cry for you! That's the bad news. The good news is there will be a harvest at the end of your tears!

> *"Ask God to give you the patience you need to become empowered to perform."*

On the other hand, you must know when you have shed enough tears. It is important that you don't get stuck in a state of lamentation. In short, don't overwater the promise! A certain amount of tears is necessary during the time of sowing. But when you have come into harvest, don't let the devil keep you weeping. Tears are for the sower, but joy is for the harvester. Harvest your field with joy. You've paid your dues and shed your tears—now reap your benefits. It's your turn. Reap in knee-slapping, teeth-baring, hand-clapping, foot-stomping joy!

Everything has a season and a purpose (see Eccles. 3:1.). You need to understand that God is just and that He appropriates opportunities to advance according to His purpose. I don't know whether this is true for everyone, but usually obscurity precedes notoriety. The first Psalm teaches that the blessed man meditates on the Word while he waits. It says that you bring forth fruit in your own season. It is good to recognize your season and prepare for it before it comes. But the fruit will not grow prior to its right season. Don't demand fruit when it is not in season. Even restaurant menus have a notation that says certain items can be served only when their fruit is in season.

T. D. Jakes, *365 Days to Healing, Blessings, and Freedom*

You Can Do Greater Works

"Truly, truly, I say unto you, He that believes on me, the works that I do shall he do also; and greater works than these shall he do; because I go unto my Father. And whatsoever you shall ask in my name, that will I do, that the Father may be glorified in the Son. If you shall ask anything in my name, I will do it." JOHN 14:12-14

During His last days on earth, Jesus spent much time with His disciples teaching them, praying for them, and encouraging them to live in His power. As He spoke of His return to the Father, Jesus assured His disciples that they would continue the work He had begun because they would receive the same power they had witnessed in His ministry (see Acts 1:8.).

We usually measure those works in terms of the height of the water we will walk on or the number of people we will feed from a few groceries. That is, we interpret Jesus' words to mean that we will do more works, when that was not His intent. Jesus was one man in one body with the Spirit of God living inside Him. His ministry consisted of that which He could accomplish as one person, in a specific geographic

> *"Therefore, the greater works did not refer to greater in quality, but in quantity and dimension."*

area, at a certain point in history. After Jesus' death and His return to the Father, the Spirit of God was freed to fill millions of people, not just one. The book of Acts tells the story of the Spirit's outpouring on the early Church.

When Jesus foretold that His disciples would do greater works than He had done, He was talking about the baptism of the Holy Spirit and the power that outpouring would bring into their lives. Therefore, the greater works did not refer to greater in quality, but in quantity and dimension. These works were no longer limited to one body or one geographical location, but became worldwide. What potential!

Myles Munroe, *Releasing Your Potential*

Reprogram Yourself

"It shall come to pass, that before they call, I will answer; and while they are yet speaking, I will hear." ISAIAH 65:24 (KJV)

I am always so awed by the miracle of a resurrected spirit. To earthly eyes, tears are little more than punctuation for the statement of sorrow. But spiritual eyes discern the process of restoration, the rushing of angels and of God Himself to the aid of the one lost, hurt, afraid, or dying. It is one of those odd and incredible paradoxes of the Kingdom that the smoldering wish of the spirit is not extinguished, but ignited when we release the flood of our tears.

Often we are challenged to prioritize our lives during difficult times or circumstances that seem insurmountable. We are required to interrupt cycles of grief, pain, and anger to get our lives together. Alongside the troubles that confront us, the Word of God confronts us more aggressively and reminds us that God is faithful to do whatever He has promised. Isaiah 49:14-16 illustrates a wonderful promise from God to each of us. Israel said, "The Lord has forsaken us and forgotten us." But the Lord told Isaiah to say to Israel, "Can a woman forget her nursing child? She may, but I will not forget you. Behold, I have inscribed you upon the palms of My hands."

> *"We can start the party in the midst of our peril."*

It matters not how desperate we are for relief. Help is always on the way and on time because God does not forget us. That's why we can "count it all joy" when we fall into various temptations (see James. 1:2). In other words, we can start the party in the midst of our peril because we know victory is on the way. Think differently, reconsider your behavior, and reprogram yourself to keep a good attitude, having faith in God and His Word.

Dr. Wanda Turner, *Celebrating Change*

*T*he Courage to Get Involved

"for I was hungry, and you gave me food: I was thirsty, and you gave me drink: I was a stranger, and you took me in:" MATTHEW 25:35

"I don't want to get involved." Have you ever heard someone say that? Have you ever said it yourself? That's understandable, because there are plenty of reasons not to get involved, especially in this dangerous time.

Edmund Burke said, "The only thing necessary for the triumph of evil is for good men to do nothing." Moreover, God calls us to be involved in life. He tells us to "Bear one another's Burdens" (Galatians 6:2). We can't do that if we don't have the courage to become involved with each other. He also tells us to meet the needs of those who are hungry and thirsty, to clothe the naked, to be hospitable to strangers, to look after the sick, and to visit those who are in prison. You certainly can't do any of these things if you don't have the courage to get involved.

> *"Courage is fear that has said its prayers"*

How can we be the light of the world or salt of the earth if we're holed up at home watching television? You may say, "That may be true, but how do you get the courage you need to get involved in life?"

The first way is to pray, for as someone has said, "Courage is fear that has said its prayers." The second way is to understand that, as Ambrose Redmoon said, "Courage is not the absence of fear, but rather, the judgment that something is more important than fear." Ralph Waldo Emerson put the same thought in a slightly different way: "Do the thing you fear, and the death of fear is certain." Believe me—you can make a tremendous difference in this world, if you are willing to do it.

For all the law is fulfilled in one word, even in this: "You shall love your neighbor as yourself." (Galatians 5:13)

October 28

Courage is Contagious

"Notwithstanding the Lord stood with me, and strengthened me; that by me the preaching might be fully known, and that all the Gentiles might hear: and I was delivered out of the mouth of the lion." 2 TIMOTHY 4:17

I heard about a college philosophy class in which the professor referred to himself as a "convinced atheist." He often mocked and ridiculed faith in God and was especially venomous toward anyone who believed in Jesus Christ. Most of his students sat in silence while he raved on. There was one young woman in the class—Audrey—who spoke up about her faith, but she seemed to be a lone voice crying in the wilderness.

> *"When a brave man takes a stand, the spines of others are stiffened."*

One day, after a particularly heated exchange, the professor wanted to show Audrey just how ridiculous her faith was. He obviously felt that none of his other students would be "superstitious" enough to believe in God. He said sarcastically, "I'd like to find out how many of you share Audrey's point of view. If you believe in God, I want you to stand up right now."

Audrey stood up, but nobody else moved.

"Go ahead," the professor sneered. "Don't be shy. Stand up." He glanced around the room. "Well," he said smugly, "it looks like you're outnumbered."

At that moment, a young man on the other side of the room stood up.

"Well, Adam, this is a surprise," the professor said. "I never would have thought..." Before he could finish his sentence, two more students stood up. Then another...and another...until half the students were standing to express their faith.

You see, courage is contagious!

I mentioned earlier in this chapter that James was the first of the Apostles to be executed. According to legend, the man who was responsible for James' arrest was so impressed by the apostle's courage that he became a Christian during the trial. He made a public profession of his faith and wound up being executed alongside the man he had arrested.

_____

_____

_____

_____

_____

Pat Williams, *American Scandal*

Behavior Patterns

"Submit yourselves therefore to God. Resist the devil, and he will flee from you. Draw near to God, and he will draw near to you. Cleanse your hands, you sinners; and purify your hearts, you double-minded." JAMES 4:7-8

Part of reckless abandonment is realizing how much our culture has affected our behavior patterns. You want to be Christlike, but your life style is a reflection of Vogue magazine or Cosmopolitan rather a new creation in Christ.

Ruth had to forsake the familiar and comfortable in order to receive God's best for her life. When Ruth told Naomi, "your people shall be my people," she understood that she would not be able to grow closer to the God of Israel if she remained among the Moabites (her own people). Ironically, God called Moab His washbasin (see Ps. 60:8; 108:9). One rinses dirt off in a washbasin. Ruth chose to leave the washbasin and head for Bethlehem which means the "house of bread."*

> *"Part of reckless abandonment is realizing how much our culture affected our behavior patterns."*

One single was persecuted, not by non-Christians but by Christians, because she chose to spend her summer studying at a Bible Institute rather than playing in the sunshine with her friends. They actually accused her of thinking she was better than them because she planned to study the Bible intensively for eight weeks.

Even today there exist "Moabites" who will undermine your growth if you spend too much time with them. Realizing that one's friends drive you either toward or away from God, you may need to find a "new people" who will encourage your growth and not hinder it.

*Scofield Bible (New York: Oxford University Press, 1967)

ℱorget the "High Entertainment" Index

"Repent therefore of this your wickedness, and pray God, if perhaps the thought of your heart may be forgiven you." ACTS 8:22

The things that God likes and the things that we like are almost always two different things. God would rather have moments with a few who really love Him than for everybody to come and be entertained. Yet we are hosting a party for God in which we trade presents with each other while totally ignoring Him! Maybe it's not very pleasing to us, and maybe we think it doesn't do anything for us or seem pleasing in our eyes, but it sure does something for God.

> *"He's looking for people who are hot after His heart."*

You need to forget who's around you and abandon the "normal protocol." God is in the business of re-defining what we call "church" anyway. He's looking for people who are hot after His heart. He wants a Church of Davids who are after His own heart (not just His hand). You can seek for His blessing and play with His toys, or you can say, "No, Daddy, I don't just want the blessings; I want You." I want You to come close. I want You to touch my eyes, touch my heart, touch my ears, and change me, Lord. I'm tired of me the way I am. We need to pray for a breakthrough, but we cannot pray for a breakthrough unless we're broken ourselves. Breakthroughs only come to broken people who are not pursuing their own ambition, but who are after the purposes of God.

Don't resist the Holy Spirit when the hand of God tries to mold your heart. The Potter of your soul is simply trying to "soften" you. He wants to bring you to such a place of tenderness that it doesn't take a hurricane-force wind from Heaven for you to even know that He is present. He wants you to be so tender that the gentlest breeze from Heaven, the smallest zephyr from His presence, will set your heart a-dancing, and you'll say, "It's Him!"

_____

_____

_____

_____

_____

_____

_____

Tommy Tenney, *The God Chasers*

*T*he Courage to Risk

"Finally, my brethren, be strong in the Lord, and in the power of his might."
EPHESIANS 6:10

You may not consider yourself to be a person of courage, but you are. If you stop to think about it, you'll see that it requires a great deal of courage just to get out of bed in the morning and face the day. If you were not a person of courage, you'd never be able to ride in a car. After all, cars are involved in 20 percent of all fatal accidents.

You'd never be able to travel by air, rail, or water, because those types of transportation are involved in another 16 percent of fatal accidents. You couldn't cross the street, because 15 percent of all accidents happen on the street. And you certainly couldn't stay home, because 17 percent of all accidents happen there! If you didn't have courage, you couldn't do anything at all. Not even exist! But as David Viscott has written:

> *"If you cannot risk, you cannot grow."*

- If you cannot risk, you cannot grow.
- If you cannot grow, you cannot become your best.
- If you cannot become your best, you cannot be happy.
- If you cannot be happy, what else matters?

Statistically, you are more likely to be kicked to death by a donkey than die in a plane crash. You are eight times more likely to die playing a sport than you are from being involved in a car crash, even if you drive on a daily basis. And you are three times more likely to be struck by lightning than to win the lottery, even though I don't advise anyone to play the lottery.

Why am I talking about death so much? Because most of us think of death as the worst thing that can happen. But death should hold no fear for the Christian. It doesn't even exist. One moment you're here, the next you're in Paradise with the Lord. There is nothing at all to be afraid of. And once we understand that, we can be courageous in the face of lesser threats.

Pat Williams, *American Scandal*

$\mathcal{M}$y Gratitude

Loving what I have—what I am grateful for:

_____

_____

_____

_____

_____

_____

_____

_____

_____

_____

_____

_____

_____

_____

_____

_____

_____

_____

_____

_____

_____

_____

_____

_____

_____

_____

"Give thanks to the Lord, for he is good; his love endures forever."
1 CHRONICLES 16:34-(NIV]

"Trust in the Lord with all thine heart; and lean not unto thine own understanding. In all thy ways acknowledge him, and he shall direct thy paths."

PROVERBS 3: 5, 6 (KJV)

*P*lug Into Your Source

"For it is God which works in you both to will and to do of his good pleasure."
PHILIPPIANS 2:13

Some people believe that God is afraid we're going to take His job. When we start talking about what we're going to do for God or what we're going to dream, some people say, "You'd better not think bigger than God." Well, you can never be bigger than your Source. You can't think or plan or imagine something greater than God, because God is the source of your imagination. He leaked part of His potential into you when He pulled you out of Himself. It's like owning a Sony videocassette recorder with multiple features. It cannot fulfill its purpose or potential until it is plugged into an electrical source. So it is for every man. We must plug into our Source.

> *"If you want to know what the standards for your life are, check God's standards."*

It is imperative, then, that you understand the characteristics and qualities of God, as well as the provisions He has made to enable you to fulfill the purpose for which He created you. Your ability to release your potential is directly related to your knowledge of God and your willingness to stay within the parameters He has established for your relationship with Him.

The quality of a product can also be defined as the characteristic attributes or elements that determine the product's basic nature. Those qualities arise out of the basic nature of the product's source. Or to say it another way, those things that occur naturally in a product also occur naturally in that from which the product was made.

The standards of God are the standards by which your excellence is judged, because you came out of God. Likewise, the characteristics that describe God's basic nature also describe your basic nature. If you want to know what the standards for your life are, check God's standards.

If you want to know what characteristics occur in you naturally, ascertain God's inherent qualities. If God acts by a certain standard or exhibits a certain quality, that standard or quality is part of your life as well.

_____

_____

_____

_____

_____

Myles Munroe, *Releasing Your Potential*

How Do You Say Good-Bye To Shame?

"... and whosoever believes on him shall not be ashamed" ROMANS 9:33

Last night in church, the worship leader read a passage of scripture, and the Lord so rocked my world that I wanted to jump out of my seat, run to the platform, grab a microphone, and share what God showed me. Wisdom kept me seated, so I share this with you.

The passage was Luke 7:36-50. In my Bible it has a subtitle: "A Sinful Woman Is Forgiven." I know this scripture well and used it in the first chapter of my book Lady in Waiting—describing a woman's reckless abandon to Jesus. As I looked more closely at the passage, something new came into focus. This sinful, notorious woman walked into a most condemning situation: the home of Simon the Pharisee. It would be like a prostitute showing up for a covered dish dinner at the pastor's house! This sinful woman did not allow condemning shame to keep her from anointing and kissing the feet of the Holy One of Israel. Now, how did a sinful woman walk past a judgmental, self-righteous man like Simon? This sinner was so focused on Jesus Christ that she was not tripped up by a "shaming Simon"!! This person did something so radical—so passionate. Her single-minded attention on Jesus kept her from being frozen in her steps by shame's chilly finger of condemnation.

> "Focus on the forgiving Savior"

The judgmental "shaming Simons" of this world are daily used by satan (see Rev.12:10-11) to accuse, confuse and trip up God's less-than-perfect children. When a believer focuses on Jesus, the "shaming Simons" of this world wield no power over that believer,

Whenever you get ready to worship Jesus, don't be surprised if "shaming Simon" is in the room—and when this happens, focus on Jesus. Boldly kiss His feet and ignore the groan of a "shaming Simon" in the background!

_____

_____

_____

_____

_____

_____

_____

Jackie Kendall, *Say Goodbye to Shame*

When Change is Mandatory

"For consider him that endured such hostility of sinners against himself, lest you be wearied and discouraged in your minds." HEBREWS 12:3

God loves us just the way we are. but He loves us too much to let us stay the way He found us. That's why there are times when we will not be asked to change. We will be forced to change for the sake of our growth and the benefit of others.

Complications are those painful, difficult things that God allows into your life at those junctures where change is not an option. It is mandatory, not just in its nature, but in its timing as well. Complications happen when God's sovereign plan reaches a "purpose point." The apostle John was exiled to the island of Patmos by an evil Roman emperor who took great joy in persecuting Christians. John was in his nineties at the time, and the imprisonment had to be difficult for him. But it was on that island that the Lord came to him and gave him the word we read today as the Book of Revelation. John could not choose to avoid that major change in his circumstances.

> *"Complications happen when God's sovereign plan reaches a 'purpose point.'"*

God's purpose points must be honored, so He doesn't leave them to us to see that they are. He causes complications to shape and direct our behavior, beliefs, and our biases. When Joseph found out that Mary was pregnant, he tried to make changes by divorcing her privately to spare her name and his shame. But God's plan was to have Joseph and Mary to marry and become the parents of Jesus. So God intervened, and Joseph had to endure all the gossip and embarrassment that surely took place when he took a pregnant woman as his wife.

We have purpose points in our lives too. They are signaled by complications. The important thing to know about complications is that their purpose is not to change our circumstances or our situation. Complications are specifically designed to change us. They are deliberately difficult, purposely painful, and intentionally intense. And we are never the same when we emerge from them.

Dr. Wanda Turner, *Celebrating Change*

November 4

$\mathcal{K}$eeping the Faith

"...because we trust in the living God, who is the Savior of all men, especially of those that believe." I TIMOTHY 4:10

I recently talked to a woman in her late sixties who is going through a health crisis. When we spoke she seemed relaxed and happy in spite of everything. "You don't seem very worried about this," I told her.

She laughed and replied, "I'm not." Then she explained why. "There have been so many times in my life when I had a problem that was too big for me to handle. Every time I said, 'God, I can't do this, so You'll have to take care of it. And every time He did. I've learned that I can trust Him in every situation."

> *"Once you surrender control of your life to God, you learn that you can trust Him in all situations."*

This woman has discovered the reality of what I call "the faith phenomenon." Once you surrender control of your life to God, you learn that you can trust Him in all situations. It's vitally important for us all to remember, especially during these difficult days, that God is still in control of the universe. As the old song says, "He's got the whole world in His hands." Everything is going according to His plan. I love this quote from C. S. Lewis: "I believe in Christianity as I believe in the sunrise; not because I can see it, but because by it I can see everything else."

Faith is to believe what you do not see; the reward for this faith is to see what you believe. —Saint Augustine

America Is Hungry, But the Bread Is Stale

"And Jesus said unto them, "I am the bread of life:" JOHN 6:35A

Why is it that on every corner in America's cities we have little convenience stores that stay open 24 hours a day just to meet the public's demand for their goods? Meanwhile, most of America's churches supposedly satisfy the nation's hunger for God while operating only two hours a week on Sunday morning! Why isn't the Church staying open every night and day? Aren't we supposed to be offering the Bread of Life to the hungry? Something is terribly wrong, and I don't think it is America's hunger for God. They are hungry all right, but they are smart enough to tell the difference between the stale bread of yesterday's religious experience and the fresh bread of God's genuine presence.

> *"The hungry need fresh bread in abundance, not stale crumbs in the carpet from last century's wedding rehearsal dinner."*

Our churches are filled with "career prodigals" who love their Father's things more than their Father. We come to the family dinner table not to ask for more of the Father, but to beg and persuade Him to give us all the things in His house that He promised are rightfully ours. We open the Book and lick our lips and say, "I want all the gifts, I want the best portion, the full blessing; I want all that belongs to me." Ironically, it was the father's blessing that actually "financed" the prodigal son's trip away from the Father's face! And it was the son's new revelation of his poverty of heart that propelled him back into his Father's arms.

Sometimes we use the very blessings that God gives us to finance our journey away from the centrality of Christ. It's very important that we return back to ground zero, to the ultimate eternal goal of abiding with the Father in intimate communion. The hungry need fresh bread in abundance, not stale crumbs in the carpet from last century's wedding rehearsal dinner.

Tommy Tenney, *The God Chasers*

$f$resh Supplies of Power

"And be not conformed to this world: but be you transformed by the renewing of your mind, that you may test what is that good, and acceptable, and perfect, will of God." ROMANS 12:2

Who of us has not at times been conscious of some failure that cut keenly into the very tissue of the heart! And even when no such break may have come there is ever a heart-yearning for more than has yet been experienced. The men who seem to know most of God's power have had great, unspeakable longings at times for a fresh consciousness of that power.

The fresh consciousness of God's presence and power is to one as a fresh act of anointing on His part. Practically it does not matter whether there is actually a fresh act upon the Spirit's part, or a renewed consciousness upon our part of His presence, and a renewed humble spirit depending wholly upon Him. Yet to learn the real truth puts one's relationship to God in the clearer light that prevents periods of doubt and

> *"...the incoming flood expands that into which it comes."*

darkness. Does it not too bring one yet nearer to Him? In this case it certainly suggests a depth and a tenderness of His unparalleled love of which some of us have not even dreamed. So far as the Scriptures seem to suggest there is not a fresh act upon God's part at certain times in one's experience, but His wondrous love is such that there is a continuous act— a continuous flooding in of all the gracious power of His Spirit that the human conditions will admit of. The flood tide is ever being poured out from above, but, as a rule, our gates are not open full width. And so only part can get in, and part which He is giving is restrained by us.

Without doubt, too, the incoming flood expands that into which it comes. And so the capacity increases ever more, and yet more.. . . As the hindrances and limitations of centuries of sin's warping and stupefying are gradually lessened there is a freer better channel for the through-flowing of His power.

Understanding What God Has Given

"Now we have received, not the spirit of the world, but the spirit which is of God; that we might know the things that are freely given to us of God."
1 CORINTHIANS 2:12

God desires for us to know what He has freely given to us. One of the responsibilities of the Holy Spirit is to reveal His plans and purposes to us. They may be hidden for a time, but if we seek Him with our whole heart, we can know what He has given to us.

John the Baptist understood the principle. When asked if he was the Messiah, he replied, "A man can receive nothing, except it be given him from heaven" (John 3:27). John understood his role in the Kingdom of God. He came to pave the way for the Messiah, he was not the Messiah himself. His ministry on earth was very brief, yet Jesus described his life in this way: "'Truly I say unto you, Among those that are born of women there is not a greater prophet than John the Baptist: but he that is least in the kingdom of God is greater than he'" (Matthew 11:11).

> *"...we can know what He has given to us."*

Once we understand what God has given to us, we can walk freely in our calling. However, if we strive to walk in a role that He never gave us, it will result in frustration and failure. God wants to reveal His plan to us by His Spirit. This requires a willingness to seek and accept what He gives us. It may be different from what we though. It may require adjustments to follow His path for our lives. As we learn from the life of John the Baptist, obedience requires death to our own wills.

Ask God to reveal what He has freely given to you. Pray that you receive and embrace only those things He has reserved for you to receive and to accomplish in your life. Then you can be assured of a life full of meaning and purpose, and you can look forward to hearing those all-important words someday, "Well done, My good and faithful servant."

The Lord Our Dwelling Place

"For we know that if our earthly house of this tabernacle were dissolved, we have a building of God, a house not made with hands, eternal in the heavens." 2 CORINTHIANS 5:1

"Lord, thou hast been our dwelling place in all generations." The comfort or discomfort of our outward lives depends more largely upon the dwelling place of our bodies than upon almost any other material thing; and the comfort or discomfort of our inward life depends similarly upon the dwelling place of our souls.

Our dwelling place is the place where we live, and not the place we merely visit. It is our home. All the interests of our earthly lives are bound up in our home; and we do all we can to make them attractive and comfortable. But our souls need a comfortable dwelling place even more than our bodies; inward comfort, as we all know, is of far greater importance than outward; and, where the soul is full of peace and joy, outward surroundings are of comparatively little account.

> *"Where the soul is full of peace and joy, outward surroundings are of comparatively little account."*

It is of vital importance, then, that we should find out definitely where our souls are living. The Lord declares that He has been our dwelling place in all generations, but the question is, Are we living in our dwelling place? The psalmist says of the children of Israel that "they wandered in the wilderness, in a solitary way; they found no city to dwell in. Hungry and thirsty, their soul fainted in them." And yet all the while the dwelling place of God has been standing wide open, inviting them to come in and take up their abode there forever.

The truth is, our souls are made for God. He is our natural home, and we can never be at rest anywhere else. "My soul longeth, yea, even fainteth for the courts of the Lord; my heart and my flesh crieth out for the living God." We always shall hunger and faint for the courts of the Lord, as long as we fail to take up our abode there.

_____

_____

_____

_____

_____

_____

$\mathcal{P}$oor in Spirit, Rich in the Kingdom

"He answered and said, "Whether he be a sinner or not, I know not: one thing I know, that, whereas I was blind, now I see." JOHN 9:25

This extraordinary story of Bartimaeus starts off in such an ordinary way. As Jesus was leaving Jericho, a blind man, Bartimaeus, was sitting by the roadside begging, no doubt quite accustomed to being overlooked, ignored, invisible.

We have all walked past blind people—felt a very real tug on our heartstrings, unable to imagine how it must be to live in darkness. But how well do we really see? Might we be so preoccupied, so narrowly focused on our problems, fears, worries, and burdens that we are blind to the wisdom and truth plainly before us? Or stubbornly denying our hidden weaknesses, prejudices and judgmental attitudes? Does our ego, greed, selfishness or sin stubbornly stare us in the face as we steadfastly try to ignore its presence?

> *"It is easy to let words get in the way of our prayers."*

Bartimaeus began to call out: "Jesus, son of David, have mercy on me". This man cried out because he knew where the answer to his blindness lay. Blessed are the poor in spirit, for theirs is the Kingdom of God. He had that inner confidence of the poor of heart that this man, Jesus, had something he desperately needed—a simple blind man, poor in wealth, yet rich in humble simplicity, faith and trust. His prayer is a classic, the definitive prayer, Jesus, have mercy on me. It is humble, utterly assured, completely yielding.

It is easy to let words get in the way of our prayers. This blind man prayed, not from the mind, but in utter simplicity from deep within his heart, his spirit. Many sternly ordered him to be quiet, but he cried out even more loudly—persistent faithful Bartimaeus.

These two simple concepts, persistence and true faithfulness from deep within, are radically out of place to say nothing of unappreciated in our "gotta have it now, instant gratification" society where conspicuous wealth and power are honored..

Maybe we too need to "sit by the roadside" begging our God for help.

_____

_____

_____

_____

_____

Penelope Black, Holy Trinity Anglican Church, North Saanich, BC Canada

A Bunch of Keys

"And I will give unto you the keys of the kingdom of heaven: and whatsoever you shall bind on earth shall be bound in heaven: and whatsoever you shall loose on earth shall be loosed in heaven." MATTHEW 16:19

To those who would enter these inner sacred recesses here is a small bunch of keys which will unlock the doors. Three keys in this bunch; a key-time, a key-book, and a key-word. The key-time is time alone with God daily. With the door shut. Outside things shut outside, and one's self shut in alone with God. This is the trysting-hour with our Friend. Here He will reveal Himself to us, and reveal our real selves to ourselves. This is going to school to God. It is giving Him a chance to instruct and correct, to strengthen and mellow and sweeten us.

> *"Obedience is the organ of knowledge in the soul."*

The key-book is this marvelous old classic of God's Word. Take this Book with you when you go to keep tryst with your Friend. God speaks in His Word. He will take these words and speak them with His own voice into the ear of your heart. You will be surprised to find how light on every sort of question will come.

He is ever speaking but we will not be quiet enough to hear. One always enjoys listening to his friend. The key-word is obedience: a glad prompt doing of what our Friend desires because He desires it...It aims to learn His will, and then to do it. God's will is revealed in His Word. His particular will for my life He will reveal to me if I will listen, and, if I will obey, so far as I know to obey. If I obey what I know, I will know more. Obedience is the organ of knowledge in the soul.

These are the three keys which will let us into the innermost chambers of friendship with God. And with them goes a key-ring on which these keys must be strung. It is this—implicit trust in God. Trust is the native air of friendship. In its native air it grows strong and beautiful.

Shall we take these keys, and this key-ring and use them faithfully? It will mean intimate friendship with God. And that is the one secret of power, fresh, and ever freshening.

_____

_____

_____

_____

_____

_____

S. D. Gordon, Quiet Talks on Power

God's Wake Up Call

"If you endure disciplining, God deals with you as with sons; for what son is he whom the father does not discipline?" HEBREWS 12:7

Many times, God will allow hardship to befall us that ushers us into change to prevent a greater catastrophe from happening. The scare of sudden chest pains may "encourage" us to be better stewards over our bodies and perhaps a heart attack in the future. It's amazing how many of us don't take the responsibility of living a healthy lifestyle seriously. We expect Jesus to do it all.

We claim the healing power of God and would rather lay hands on somebody in the hospital than tell them to take their hands off that second helping of macaroni and cheese. We want to walk on in Jesus' name, but forget walking on that treadmill you just bought. We want to believe God for lower blood pressure without lowering the amount of time we spend working at the office.

> *"Then God, in His infinite mercy, fires a warning shot."*

Then God, in His infinite mercy, fires a warning shot. A mild heart attack, a stroke, an ulcer, and diabetes are often traceable to the sin of a poorly kept body. The pain and shock of such a diagnosis will usually propel us into change. We'll chew on fresh carrots and celery sticks until the rapture, if necessary. We'll quit that second job and suddenly have time for church, prayer meetings, Bible study, and the usher board.

An alcoholic or a drug addict may find themselves wrecked on the side of the road. That unfaithful husband may come home to changed locks. God has a way of letting you know that He's through letting you slide. By the time He allows trouble to have its way with you, I promise you, He has already asked you to do right. Now He's telling you.

Dr. Wanda Turner, *Celebrating Change*

*T*he Back Bone of Faith

"Now faith is the substance of things hoped for, the evidence of things not seen." HEBREWS 11:1

Faith in God is, by far, the primary means of coming safely through times of struggle and scandal. It is the only thing we can hold onto when the bad guys seem to be winning. Faith gives us the assurance that justice and truth will prevail in the end. It was faith that enabled Martin Luther King Jr. to endure beatings, death threats, and constant verbal abuse to continue his fight for Civil Rights. It was faith that helped Boris Yeltsin stand up against the communist regime that had held the Russian people captive for over seventy years. And ultimately, it will be faith at work in the hearts and lives of the American people that will help us overcome the difficult times we're facing.

> *"It is the only thing we can hold onto when the bad guys seem to be winning."*

Like nearly everything else ... faith can be—and must be—strengthened with practice.

"Faith is like a muscle; it grows with exercise, and the more we know of the trustworthiness and faithfulness of God...His grace, love, power, and wisdom...the more we can trust Him."

-Dr. Bill Bright, founder of Campus Crusade for Christ

Tim Salmon, the elder statesman for the 2002 World Champion California Angels, says this about his faith in Christ: "I'm thankful that I had the opportunity to have my eyes opened and be enlightened as to the joy that is around me and that maybe I take for granted. I've had to persevere in my life, but it was always applied to baseball. For the first time in my life, I had to persevere in something much more important than baseball. That's what this whole spiritual journey is about—growing in our faith and being more Christlike every day." I know exactly what Tim Salmon is talking about, and I hope you do too.

Pat Williams, *American Scandal*

Raise Your Price

"God resists the proud, but gives grace unto the humble." JAMES 4:6B

God does not tolerate spiritual arrogance. James states very clearly that "God resists the proud, but gives grace unto the humble". However, a vast difference lies between self-esteem and being exalted in the flesh.

Humility is not something that debases us and demands that we think of ourselves as something worth less than a copper penny. It is extremely dangerous to believe that this is the definition of meekness. Those who do dare not pursue excellence for fear it will jeopardize their souls. God desires that we strive for greatness as we give Him glory.

> *"It is not God's will for us to go through life feeling that we are worthless and nothing more than a liability to our heavenly Father."*

It is not God's will for us to go through life feeling that we are worthless and nothing more than a liability to our heavenly Father. It is of utmost importance that we place great value on who and what we are. If we do not, it is quite possible that we will sell out for much less than we are worth.

When tempted to sell out, cherish your purity and esteem it highly. If it is worthless, why is satan so desperate for you to relinquish it? If you did surrender at some weak moment in the flesh, make a new consecration with the Lord right now.

Morton Bustard, *The Impassioned Soul*

Use Christ's Strength

"Eye has not seen, nor ear heard, neither have entered into the heart of man, the things which God has prepared for them that love him."
1 CORINTHIANS 2:9B-10

You cannot do all things. You can only do all things through Christ, who gives you the ability. Romans 8:31 gives me great encouragement: "If God be for us, who can be against us?" Now the word for is really the Greek word with. So let's put it this way: "If God is with me, who can be against me?" The implication is that if God has given you something to do and He is with you, nothing or no one is going to stop you from accomplishing what God wants you to do. I don't care who the person is or how much influence he has, if God is with you, it's not important who is coming against you.

> *"I don't care who the person is or how much influence he has, if God is with you, it's not important who is coming against you."*

If you are going to release your potential, you must live each day checking out who's with you instead of who's against you. You may be experiencing political victimization, pressure from your boss or your spouse or your parents, or unfair treatment from your family or your employer, but these influences are not the most important factors in your life. You can spend the rest of your life fighting the many people and circumstances that come against you, or you can focus on God's presence and treat them as a temporary inconvenience. If God is with you, those who accuse or harass you have no power over you.

This week can be a good one because your protection relies not on how much power your accusers have but on how much power Christ has. Jesus promises you peace and victory if you rely on His strength.

_____

_____

_____

_____

_____

_____

_____

_____

Myles Munroe, *Releasing Your Potential*

$\mathcal{F}$aith—the "Fear Buster"

"Above all, taking the shield of faith, with which you shall be able to quench all the fiery darts of the wicked." EPHESIANS 6:16

Fear is like junk mail. We get it. We don't want it. We really don't have any use for it. And we don't have to keep it. We can toss it out with all the other garbage satan sends our way. Faith, my friend, is the "fear-buster" we have in our arsenal of spiritual weapons. Ephesians 6:16 says, "above all, taking the shield of faith, with which you shall be able to quench all the fiery darts of the wicked."

> *"Faith will extinguish every flaming arrow the enemy throws at you, including fear."*

"Above all," it says. That means if you don't take anything else to fight with, take your faith. Faith will extinguish every flaming arrow the enemy throws at you, including fear.

Complacency also can serve as a cover for knowing what's ahead and not liking it. This is pride. We tell God that we don't think He's doing a very good job with us. We refuse to change because we reject the change. But we don't want to tell others that.

This kind of complacency—the refusal to honor the change or the God who called for it—is dangerous. God says He resists the proud (see James 4:6). That means He deliberately sets Himself against the proud. It is the picture of two football players on opposite teams facing each other at the line of scrimmage. You're set, waiting for the snap. And God says that if you think you're big and bad enough to take Him on, come on with it! He will mow you down at the appropriate time. Don't fool yourself into thinking that He will give you a merciful tap, either. The fact that He will flatten you is His greatest act of mercy toward you. Because if He lets you remain standing, somebody else might look at you and think its okay to get up in God's face and try to take Him out.

Dr. Wanda Turner, *Celebrating Change*

Jesus Really Does Love You

"Looking unto Jesus the author and finisher of our faith; who for the joy that was set before him endured the cross, despising the shame ..." HEBREWS 12:2

As just about any seminary student will tell you, Karl Barth was a very deep thinker. Pastor/author Tony Evans remembers that Barth's thought processes were "so deep that we got headaches just trying to work through the course and grasp what he was saying."

Over half a century ago, when the brilliant theologian visited the United States, a young reporter asked him, "What is the greatest thought that has ever come into your mind?"

Without hesitation Karl Barth answered, "Jesus loves me, this I know, for the Bible tells me so." Karl Barth knew that this simple truth was the bottom line of all wisdom and knowledge. No matter how you say it—with small words and simple sentences or with huge words and complex sentences that seem to go on for pages, "Jesus loves me" is what it all comes down to.

> *"His death makes Him our finest counselor when we face our own."*

Jesus loves you and me so much that He was willing to be born into a human body. As the Son of God, Jesus knows everything, but it was only through being clothed in a human body that He came to experience first-hand what it feels like to be hungry, exhausted, cold, hot, ragged, and sweaty.

I like the way Calvin Miller puts it: "Let us remember that the whole idea of the Incarnation was that God became a man because it was the only way God could acquire a nervous system. Had He slipped in and out of the planet without pain, how would He ever have understood ours? His death makes Him our finest counselor when we face our own. Give me as my Savior no Greek god who frolics in indulgence, gluttony, and adultery. Give me, instead, a God who can hang in suffocating pain and tell me, even as He gasps, that life is never pointless."

Pat Williams, *American Scandal*

Keep Those Seeds!

"Now he that supplies seed to the sower both supply bread for your food, and multiply your seed sown, and increase the fruits of your righteousness; being enriched in everything to all bountifulness, which causes through us thanksgiving to God." 2 CORINTHIANS 9:10-11

If in your thoughts you see something beyond where you are, if you see a dream, a goal, or an aspiration that others would think impossible, you may have to hold it. Sometimes you may have to hide it, and most of the time you will have to water it as a farmer waters his crops to sustain the life in them. But always remember they are your fields. You must eat from the garden of your own thoughts, so don't grow anything you don't want to eat. As you ponder and daydream, receive grace for the hard places and healing for the damaged soil. Just know that whenever your children, your friends, or anyone else comes to the table of your wisdom, you can only feed them what you have grown in your own fields. Your wisdom is so flavorful and its texture so rich that it can't be "store bought"; it must be homegrown.

> *"You must eat from the garden of your own thoughts, so don't grow anything you don't want to eat."*

A whispering prayer lies on my lips: I pray that this word God has given me be so powerful and personal, so intimate and applicable, that it leaves behind it a barren mind made pregnant. This seed of greatness will explode in your life and harvest in your children, feeding the generations to come and changing the winds of destiny. . .

In my heart I smell the indescribable smell of an approaching rain. Moisture is in the air and the clouds have gathered. Our fields have been chosen for the next rain and the wind has already started to blow. Run swiftly into the field with your precious seeds and plant them in the soft ground of your fertile mind. Whatever you plant in the evening will be reaped in the morning. My friend, I am so excited for you. I just heard a clap of thunder...in just another moment, there'll be rain!

T. D. Jakes, *365 Days to Healing, Blessings, and Freedom*

Understand Your Function

"The sacrifices of God are a broken spirit; a broke and contrite heart, O God, thou wilt not despise." PSALM 51:17 (KJV)

The God who designed you for eternal life still desires the fellowship with you that He originally intended.

"There is therefore now no condemnation to them which are in Christ Jesus, who walk not after the flesh, but according to the Spirit. For the law of the Spirit of life in Christ Jesus has made me free from the law of sin and death." (Romans 8:1-2)

> *"Only when you recognize that coming to God is for your benefit, not God's, does God's grace make sense."*

God didn't need to save you from sin and death to meet His needs. He was doing fine before you were saved, and He'll continue to do fine no matter what kind of relationship you have with Him in the future. Jesus was touched by your needs. Only when you recognize that coming to God is for your benefit, not God's, does God's grace make sense. Grace is God's reaching out when He didn't need to. Grace is God's caring enough to rework His original plan for the fallen man.

"The Father loves the Son, and has given all things into his hand. He that believes on the Son has everlasting life: and he that does not believe the Son shall not see life; but the wrath of God remains on him." (John 3:36)

Myles Munroe, *Releasing Your Potential*

$\mathcal{A}$ Whole Lot of Shaking

"He that is of God hears God's words: you therefore do not hear them, because you are not of God." JOHN 8:47

When we are complacent due to apathy, we send God an engraved invitation to shake us up. And because we're so satisfied with our lives, we usually don't see it coming. The invitation went out without our knowing it, but God will show up, and He will cause a whole lot of shaking. I want you to know here that there is a very real danger in apathy of inviting a wilderness experience, or worse, of inviting God to ignore you until you choose to bring your prodigal behind home.

> *"When there is a "lack of noise" in our lives, we can sometimes mistake that for peace."*

Is that you? You hear God calling you to change. You know it's Him. But life is too good the way it is. You'd rather sleep in than pray. You'd rather ski, travel, or play than study the Word. That girlfriend or boyfriend is fit, fine, and financially stable, and they're not trying to "tie you down." And all you see is God swinging that ball and chain in your face. "I hear You, Lord. And I love You...but not that much."

When there is a "lack of noise" in our lives, we can sometimes mistake that for peace. But peace is not something that eliminates every sound. Peace is that environment of the spirit that makes God easier to hear. Are you hearing God? If nothing is being said in your spirit, if the Word that is supposed to abide in you is not making itself known within you, you may be in need of a little more one-on-one time with God.

Dr. Wanda Turner, *Celebrating Change*

God Is In Control

"God is greater than our heart, and knows all things." I JOHN 3:20

There's nothing that goes on where God says, "Oops, I missed that one." Every circumstance that happens in life, God has control of.
—Matt Ware

Chances are good that you've never heard of Matt Ware, the young man who is quoted above. Chances are also good that you would have heard of him except for the terrible accident in 1998 that left him paralyzed. Matt was a standout high school basketball player with dreams of further success in the sport. Of course, those dreams died the day Matt was injured.

> *"You don't know what God is up to behind the scenes of your life."*

Matt doesn't understand why this happened to him, but he isn't bitter or angry about it because he knows for certain that his life is in God's hands. He has faith that God always sees the big picture, and he trusts that God is in control of everything. Does that mean God caused Matt Ware to become paralyzed? No! What it does mean is that God knew that it had to happen, and that He allowed it for some greater good that we are not yet able to see from our vantage point.

I know. Sometimes, it's difficult to believe that God is in control of everything that happens. Wherever you are, right now, I want you to stop for a moment and think about the fact that God really is in control of your life and your situation. Let it sink in.

The gifted young pastor and author, Andy Stanley, says, "You don't know what God is up to behind the scenes of your life. You don't know how close you are to a breakthrough. It is no accident you are where you are, and it is not necessarily a problem that you are not where you assume you ought to be. God is very much in control."

$\mathcal{U}$p the Steps of Life

*"Commit thy way unto the Lord; trust also in him; and he shall
bring it to pass."* PSALM 37:5 (KJV)

The obscure side of a struggle is the awesome wrestling match many
people have with success. First success is given only at the end of great
struggle. If it were easy, anybody could do it. Success is success only
because it relates to struggle. How can you have victory without conflict?

> *"The zeal it
> takes to be
> effective at
> accomplishing
> a goal ushers
> you up the
> steps of life."*

To receive something without struggle lessens its
personal value. Success is the reward that God gives
to the diligent who, through perseverance, obtain the
promise. There is no way to receive what God has for
your life without fighting the obstacles and
challenges that block your way to conquest. In fact,
people who procrastinate do so because they are
desperately trying to find a way to reach the goal
without going through the struggle.

When I was a youngster, we kids used to go into the stores and
change the price tags on the items we could not afford. We weren't
stealing, we thought, because we did pay something. It just wasn't nearly
what the vendor wanted us to pay. I guess we thought we would put the
product on sale without the permission of the store manager. I believe
many people are trying to do the same thing today in their spiritual life.
They are attempting to get a discount on the promises of God. That
doesn't work in the Kingdom. Whatever it costs, it costs; there is no
swapping the price tags.

You must pay your own way. Your payment helps you to appreciate
the blessings when they come because you know the expense. You will not
easily jeopardize the welfare of something not easily attained.

The zeal it takes to be effective at accomplishing a goal ushers you up
the steps of life. As you journey up the steps, it becomes increasingly
difficult to be successful without others finding you offensive. Some
people will find your success offensive, whether or not you are arrogant.
They are offended at what God does for you.

T. D. Jakes, *365 Days to Healing, Blessings, and Freedom*

The Body Beautiful

*"Behold, I will do a new thing: now it shall spring forth: shall ye not know it?
I will even make a way in the wilderness, and rivers in the desert."*
ISAIAH 43:19 (KJV)

God intended for your body to live forever. The ability of your finger to heal after you burn it, or of an incision to heal following surgery, attests to the small amount of eternal potential left in your body. God still intends that you will have an eternal body.

In this life, your body is a hindrance. It gets tired, sick, bruised, and discouraged. As it grows older, you have to keep patching it together. That's why our society is so eager to find a fountain of youth. We don't like our aging bodies. We want them to be young again.

I like what Paul says in his second letter to the Corinthians:

> *". . .don't equate your life with your body."*

For which cause we do not lose heart; but though our outward man perishes, yet the inward man is renewed day by day. (2 Corinthians 4:16)

God's making you a new home that will far exceed anything that plastic surgery can do for you. All plastic surgeons can do is patch your old body. God's in the business of giving you a new body. So don't worry if this body isn't all you'd like it to be. Patch it, fix it, do whatever you can to spruce it up. But don't equate your life with your body. God's going to get out of you all that He put in you. He wants you to start releasing your potential with the body you now have and to continue using your eternal capabilities long after this body has decayed. You are much more than your imperfect, deteriorating body.

*T*he Question of Calling

"And Jesus said unto them, "Follow me, and I will make you fishers of men."
And when they had brought their ships to land, they forsook all,
and followed him." MATTHEW 4:19-20

What is His plan for you? The only Person who can answer that question is God. Dietrich Bonhoeffer said that one of the marks of a disciple of Christ is that he's not always sure where he's going. He's just following wherever Christ leads him. In my own life, I've often thought that God was going to take me in a certain direction, only to find out later on that He was actually preparing me for some other step He wanted me to take.

> *"Often He can be found in the routine events of daily life."*

Will God call you to be a missionary to Africa? Perhaps. Will He ask you to go to seminary and prepare for full-time ministry? Maybe. But it's just as likely that He wants you to stay right where you are and keep doing what you've been doing!

Chapter 19 of 1 Kings tells of a time when the great prophet Elijah was waiting for God to appear to him. "Then a great and powerful wind tore the mountains apart and shattered the rocks before the Lord, but the Lord was not in the wind. After the wind, there was an earthquake, but the Lord was not in the earthquake. After the earthquake came a fire, but the Lord was not in the fire. And after the fire came a gentle whisper" (1 Kings 19:11-12 NIV).

It isn't always in the great events and great acts that God can be experienced. Often He can be found in the routine events of daily life, especially when those events are offered up as service to Him by people who are seeking His will for their lives.

Pat Williams, *American Scandal*

*T*he Faith Process

"Through faith we understand that the worlds were framed by the word of God, so that things which are seen were not made of things which do appear."
HEBREWS 11:3

Many of us don't appreciate how faith works. We are so used to living from what we can see, hear, and touch that we have great difficulty moving into the realm of faith. If, for example, someone asks us how we are doing, we usually respond based on the condition of our bodies or our souls. We focus on our illnesses or the depressed thoughts that are weighing us down and neglect to mention the many blessings God has promised us. These promises have a much greater impact on our lives than our physical diseases and our emotional struggles.

> *"Eventually what you say and what you see will match."*

If someone asks you how you are doing, tell them that you're blessed. You might not look like it, but God's blessings are in you somewhere. And each time that you say you are blessed, the blessings within you grow. Eventually what you say and what you see will match.

Faith sees what hasn't been manifested. It deals with what exists but is invisible. The minute you manifest something, it no longer requires faith, because faith is believing, conceiving, and releasing (speaking) until you receive what you desire. "Now faith is the substance of things hoped for, the evidence of things not seen" (Hebrews 11:1).

You were created to live by faith. God established faith as the only system through which men and women can touch His power. Potential demands faith, and faith makes demands on potential.

Myles Munroe, *Releasing Your Potential*

On Being Humble

"Whosoever therefore shall humble himself as this little child, the same is greatest in the kingdom of heaven." MATTHEW 18:4

I love this definition of humility from Andrew Murray: "Humility is perfect quietness of heart. It is to expect nothing, to wonder at nothing that is done to me, to feel nothing done against me. It is to be at rest when nobody praises me, and when I am blamed or despised. It is to have a blessed home in the Lord, where I can go in and shut the door, and kneel to my Father in secret, and am at peace as in a deep sea of calmness, when all around and above is trouble."

> *"Being humble is not the same as being wimpy."*

Rich DeVos is one of the richest men in America. Yet I've noticed that whenever he meets someone for the first time, he always says, "Tell me about you." He doesn't want to talk about himself. That's a humble spirit. Humility is not an absence of strength or self-confidence. Being humble is not the same as being wimpy.

Now, being humble does not mean that you lie about yourself. You're not demonstrating humility if you say, "I can't sing," when you're the first tenor in the Metropolitan Opera. Humble people appreciate their own positive attributes, but they realize that those attributes are, for the most part, gifts. As someone has said, "Humility is not denying the power you have but admitting that the power comes through you and not from you."

People with humility don't think less
of themselves—they just think about themselves less.
—Norman Vincent Peale

The Tragedy of Relinquishing Faith

"But seek first the kingdom of God, and his righteousness; and all these things shall be added unto you." MATTHEW 6:33

Most people who are failures are failures because they were so close to winning. Don't let that happen to you. You don't know how close you are to receiving the promise you have been waiting for. Just because things are getting worse doesn't mean that God has not heard your request. The closer you get to victory, the harder you are going to have to fight. Often when things are the worst, you are close to receiving what you seek.

> *"Often when things are the worst, you are close to receiving what you seek."*

Set your pace and keep on trucking. Look for the positive in life and renew your voice of faith. Believe in God and in yourself. Say, "God, I'm on Your side, and You're on mine. We are going to see this thing through because we are a majority." Trust in the certainty that you can't lose when you and God are in agreement, and bear in mind that God will reward you if you put Him above all else. Finally, commit yourself to believing, conceiving, and releasing (speaking) every day until you receive what you desire. That's how God created you to function.

A life of faith is hard work that at times requires perseverance and patience, but you can't live any other way. Faith is the basis upon which an abundant, satisfying life is built. It is an essential key to releasing all that God put in you to benefit yourself and the world for generations to come. Your potential needs faith to draw it out, because faith is the bucket that draws from the well of potential within you.

Myles Munroe, *Releasing Your Potential*

*I*t Isn't "What," But "Why"

"And whatsoever you do, do it heartily, as to the Lord, and not unto men;"
COLOSSIANS 3:23

Pastor/author A. W. Tozer said, "Let us believe that God is in all our simple deeds and learn to find Him there. Let every man abide in the calling wherein he is called and his work will be as sacred as the work of the ministry." He goes on, "It is not what a man does that determines whether his work is sacred or secular...it is why he does it. Let a man sanctify the Lord God in his heart, and he can therefore do no common act."

> *"It is not what a man does ... it is why he does it."*

If you do everything as "unto the Lord," whatever you do can be woven into the tapestry of God's plan for your life. Everything you experience can be used by Him for your good. Rose Kennedy, the matriarch of the Kennedy clan, suffered through many personal tragedies. Two children were killed in plane crashes, two more were assassinated, and one daughter, Rosemary, was born mentally disabled. At one point, perhaps understandably, Rose Kennedy grew very angry and bitter toward God.

One of the family's maids noticed this and told her, "Mrs. Kennedy, you need to get over this. The only way to do that is to make a manger in your heart and invite Jesus to come in." Such insolence added to Rose's anger, and she fired the maid on the spot.

That night Rose could not sleep. She twisted and tossed in her bed, filled with anguish. Finally, she slipped out bed and got down on her knees. There, she asked God to forgive her and to make "a manger in her heart" for Jesus. From that night on she understood that the Lord was with her in her trials, that He empathized with her in her sorrow, and that He had a plan for her life that would unfold as she walked with Him. She became an example of faith and grace that holds up in every circumstance.

The Spiritual Realm

"What is it then? I will pray with the spirit, and I will pray with the understanding also: I will sing with the spirit, and I will sing with the understanding also." I CORINTHIANS 14:15

How real is the spiritual realm? My lawyer friend from Nigeria tells a personal story of how he was preparing for an important case. He knew that he must be prepared to argue five separate points. He was to appear before his country's supreme court, so it was a very important case.

As he neared the time in which he was to go to court, he began to pray about how he was to argue the case. He spent much time in legal preparation and intercessory prayer. As he went to court, the Spirit spoke to him and said, "Do not argue point one, point two, point three or point four. Only argue point five." Imagine my friend's struggle of faith. If he were reading this wrong, the shame and professional fallout would be devastating.

> *"Seek Him today."*

The time had come to present the case before the judge when my friend said, "Judge, I wish to withdraw points one through four. I wish to argue only point five."

The opposing counsel stood up and objected. "Your honor, he cannot do that!"

"Objection overruled, counsel," said the judge.

My friend went on to present his case around point five only, and then sat down. When the opposing counsel stood to present his case, he stood speechless for 12 minutes. He could not get a word out of his mouth. He finally mumbled a few words and complained to the judge that he was going to have to yield. It seems that the opposing counsel had prepared to argue only points one through four, but failed to prepare for point five. The judge ruled in favor of my friend.

The unseen Lord wants to help us in the physical realm of our work life. We must acknowledge His presence and tap into this incredible resource He has given to each of us. Seek Him today and ask Him to reveal His perfect plan for you this day.

_____

_____

_____

_____

_____

God Inhabits An Old House

"In whom all the building fitly framed together grows unto a holy temple in the Lord: in whom you also are built together for a habitation of God through the Spirit." EPHESIANS 2:21-22

Within our decaying shells, we constantly peel away, by faith, the lusts and jealousies that adorn the walls of our hearts. If the angels were to stroll through the earth with the Creator and ask, "Which house is Yours?" He would pass by all the mansions and cathedrals, all the temples and castles. Unashamedly, He would point at you and me and say, "That house is Mine!" Imagine the shock and disdain of the heavenly host to think that the God whose face they fan with their wings would choose to live in such a shack and shanty! We know where our greatest conflict lies. We who blunder and stumble in our humanity, we who stagger through our frail existence—we continually wrestle with the knowledge that our God has put so much in so little!

> *"Although the tenant is prestigious, the accommodations are still substandard."*

Yes, it is true: Despite all our washing and painting, all our grooming and exercising, this old house is still falling apart! We train it and teach it. We buy books and tapes, and we desperately try to convince it to at least think differently. But like a squeaky hinge on a swollen door, the results of our efforts, at best, come slowly. There is no doubt that we have been saved, and there is no doubt that the house is haunted. The Holy Ghost Himself resides beneath this sagging roof. (Although the tenant is prestigious, the accommodations are still substandard.)

This divine occupation is not an act of a desperate guest who, having no place else to stay, chose this impoverished site as a temporary place to "ride out" the storm of some deplorable situation. No, God Himself has—of His own free will and predetermined purpose—put us in the embarrassing situation of entertaining a Guest whose lofty stature so far exceeds us that we hardly know how to serve Him!

T. D. Jakes, *365 Days to Healing, Blessings, and Freedom*

Believe It To See It

"Now faith is the substance of things hoped for, the evidence of things not seen." HEBREWS 11:1

Faith begins with belief. Actually, faith in someone or something requires unquestioning belief that does not require proof or evidence from the one in whom you have faith. The New Testament word for faith, pistos, means "to believe another's testimony." Thus, faith requires you to function by believing first, instead of seeing or feeling first.

That often creates a problem, because faith requires putting your body under the control of your spirit. Your body says, "I'm not going to believe it until I see it." But God says, "If you're going to operate like Me, you aren't going to see it until you believe it

> *"Many look, few see."*

Living by faith also requires that you put your soul under the control of your spirit. Your soul governs your emotions, your will, and your mind. When you live from your soul, you allow information from your physical body to govern your decisions. Your soul says, "I'm unhappy because the outward circumstances of my life aren't what I'd like." Just because you don't feel what God is saying to you, don't refuse to believe that He knows what He is talking about.

After you believe God's promises, you must begin to see (conceive) them in your life. Seeing and looking are very different. Looking regards the outward appearance, while seeing considers the existence of things that are not yet visible.. God sees, and He requires that you see. He asks you to act as though you already have what you requested.

God is still sending angels to speak things that run contrary to our usual expectations. He says, "You will have a dream and it will come to pass." Then He waits for our words of confirmation: "May it be to me as You have spoken." But what you speak must follow what you believe. Words themselves have no power. Only when words are accompanied by belief can they release God's desires for your life.

_____

_____

_____

_____

_____

_____

Myles Munroe, *Releasing Your Potential*

$\mathcal{M}$y Gratitude

Loving what I have—what I am grateful for:

_____
_____
_____
_____
_____
_____
_____
_____
_____
_____
_____
_____
_____
_____
_____
_____
_____
_____
_____
_____
_____
_____
_____
_____
_____
_____
_____
_____

"I will give thanks to the Lord because of his righteousness and will sing praise to the name of the Lord Most High." PSALMS 7:17-(NIV]

*T*he Confession of Prayer

"Who in the days of his flesh, when he had offered up prayers and supplications with loud crying and tears unto him that was able to save him from death, and was heard in that he feared." HEBREWS 5:7

Now understand, nothing fuels prayer like need. Neither the tranquil mood of a calming organ nor a dimly lit room with hallowed walls can promote the power of prayer like the aching of a heart that says, "I need Thee every hour." The presence of need will produce the power of prayer.

Even the agnostic will make a feeble attempt at prayer in the crisis of a moment. The alcoholic who staggers toward a car he knows he shouldn't drive will, before the night is over, find himself attempting to dial the number of Heaven and sputter in slurred speech a fleeting prayer in the presence of near-mishap and malady.

> *"Prayer is man's confession, 'I do not have it all.'"*

Prayer is man's confession, "I do not have it all." Prayer is man admitting to himself that, in spite of his architectural designs and his scientific accomplishments, he needs a higher power. Prayer is the humbling experience of the most arrogant mind confessing, "There are still some things I cannot resolve."

The presence of prayer is, in itself, the birthplace of praise. Prayer is man acknowledging the sovereign authority of a God "who can!" You ask, "Can what?" God can do whatever He wants to do, whenever He wants to do it. What a subliminal solace to know the sovereignty of God!

Each of us must have the curiosity and the inner thirst to move beyond our images into our realities. It is difficult, sometimes even painful, to face the truth about our circumstances and then possess the courage to ask for God's best for our lives. If prayer is to be meaningful, it cannot be fictitious. It must be born out of the pantings of a heart that can admit its need. If we refrain from airing our particular dilemmas with anyone else, at least we must be honest enough to come before God with an open heart and a willing mind to receive the "whatsoevers" that He promised to the "whosoevers" in His Word!

_____
_____
_____
_____
_____
_____

T. D. Jakes, *365 Days to Healing, Blessings, and Freedom*

The Plans of Tomorrow

"It is even a vapor, that appears for a little time, and then vanishes away."
JAMES 4:14B

A group of businesspeople meet at my office every week for fellowship, study, and prayer. One man attended our group for several years. Jim was well liked and in good health. One Thursday he showed up as usual. The next morning I received a call, "Jim is dead! He died in his easy chair last night!" Jim had no prior problems and there was no indication he was about to go be with the Lord. Naturally, it came as a shock to us all.

Whenever things like this happen close to home, it brings us face to face with our mortality. A friend of mine said he was challenged by someone to do an experiment. He challenged him to live his life for one year as if it were the last year he would live. He responded to the challenge and did as proposed. It changed his life forever. He began to focus on different priorities and people when he viewed life in these terms.

> *"Life is fragile."*

James 4:13-15 gives us a perspective on viewing tomorrow.

Listen now, you that say, "Today or tomorrow we will go into such a city, and continue there a year, and buy and sell, and get gain": whereas you know not what shall be tomorrow. For what is your life? It is even a vapor, that appears for a little time, and then vanishes away. For you ought to say, 'If the Lord is willing, we shall live, and do this, or that'"

Life is fragile. Consider where you are investing your time and energies. Someone once said they had never heard anyone on his deathbed say that he wished he had made more money in his lifetime or he wished he had made a certain deal. Usually it is something like, "I wish I had spent more time with my kids." Ask the Lord to give you His priorities for your life.

Abandonment

"So likewise, whosoever he be of you that forsakes not all that he has, he cannot be my disciple." LUKE 14:33

There must enter into your heart whole new attitudes toward your entire life. If you are to branch out beyond just a time of prayer each day, other parts of your life—and even your whole viewpoint of life—will have to be altered. This new attitude must come for a very special reason—so that you may go on deeper, still deeper, into another level with your Lord.

"It is required that you begin to abandon your whole existence, giving it up to God."

To do this, you must have a fresh attitude toward yourself as well as toward the Lord; it is an attitude that must go much deeper than any you have known previously.

To do this, I introduce a new word to you. The word is abandonment. To penetrate deeper in the experience of Jesus Christ, it is required that you begin to abandon your whole existence, giving it up to God. Let us take the daily occurrences of life as an illustration. You must utterly believe that the circumstances of your life, that is, every minute of your life, as well as the whole course of your life—anything, yes, everything that happens—have all come to you by His will and by His permission. You must utterly believe that everything that has happened to you is from God and is exactly what you need.

Such an outlook towards your circumstances and such a look of faith towards your Lord will make you content with everything. Once you believe this, you will then begin to take everything that comes into your life as being from the hand of God, not from the hand of man. –Jeanne Guyon

Sharing Maximizes Potential

"...for you have created all things, and for your pleasure they are and were created." REVELATION 4:11B

This blending and support is also the way potential is meant to be used. Even as the beauty of a symphony is minimized when each instrument's part is played in isolation, so the wealth of our potential is minimized when we do not share it with others. Potential is maximized and fulfilled only when it is shared. This sharing of potential is God's way of bringing to pass His plans and purposes for men and women.

> *"Your purpose is equal to your potential, and your potential is equal to your purpose."*

God's nature is built around sharing and giving. Before the world was created, everything existed in Him. All that we have seen, now see, and yet will see comes from Him. God could have kept all this stuff inside Him, but it wouldn't have benefited Him there. He had to release it through creativity before the beauty and power of His potential could be revealed.

Everything God called into being He gave a purpose that meshes with the larger purpose of the world. Your gifts, talents, and abilities are your share of the endowment God gives to mankind to bless all creation. In essence, you show forth God's nature and reveal His potency when you fulfill your potential. Your purpose is equal to your potential, and your potential is equal to your purpose. The more you understand your purpose, the more you will discover what you can do.

Myles Munroe, *Maximizing Your Potential*

The Trusting Place

"But you, when you pray, enter into your inner room, and when you have shut your door, pray to your Father which is in secret; and your Father which sees in secret shall reward you openly." MATTHEW 6::6

We need time for prayer, unhurried time, daily time, time enough to forget about how much time it is. I do not mean now: rising in the morning at the very last moment, and dressing. It may be hurriedly, and then kneeling a few moments so as to feel easier in mind; not that. I do not mean the last thing at night when you are jaded and fagged, and almost between the sheets, and then remember and look up a verse and kneel a few moments; not that. I am not criticizing that. Better sweeten and sandwich the day with all of that sort you can get in. But just now I mean this: taking time when the mind is fresh and keen, and the spirit sensitive, to thoughtfully pray. We haven't time. Life is so crowded. It must be taken from something else something important, but still less important that this.

> *"One must get alone to find out that he never is alone."*

Sacrifice is the continued law of life. The important thing must be sacrificed to the more important. One needs to cultivate a mature judgment, or his strength will be frizzed away in the less important details, and the greater thing go undone, or be done poorly with the stragglings of strength. If we would become skilled intercessors and know how to pray simply enough, we must take quiet time daily to get off alone.

The Master said: "Enter into your inner chamber, and when you have shut your door" the door is important. It shuts out and it shuts in. "Pray to thy Father who is in secret." God is here in this shut-in spot. One must get alone to find out that he never is alone. The more alone we are as far as men are concerned the least alone we are so far as God is concerned.

S. D. Gordon, *Quiet Talks on Prayer*

God-Inspired Delays

"When he had heard therefore that [Lazarus] was sick, he stayed two days still in the same place where he was." JOHN 11:6

Delays in our life are not always easy to handle or to reconcile in our minds. Often, when God does not answer our prayers in the time that we feel He should, we appoint all sorts of characteristics to God's nature that imply He does not care. Such was the case with Lazarus' sisters when

> *"My friend, don't take the delays lightly"*

Lazarus became ill and died. Jesus was a close friend to Lazarus and his two sisters, Mary and Martha (Mary, you may recall, was the woman who came and poured perfume on Jesus' feet.) when Jesus arrived two days later, Martha shamed Him by saying, "If You had come he would not have died." She implied that He didn't care enough to come when sent for. It was a matter of priorities for Jesus, not lack of love.

God often has to delay his work in us in order to accomplish something for His purposes that can be achieved only in the delay. Jesus had to let Lazarus die in order for the miracle that was about to take place to have its full effect. If Jesus had simply healed a sick man, the impact of the miracle would not have been as newsworthy as resurrecting a man who had been dead for four days. This is Jesus' greatest "public relations act" of His whole ministry. What many do not realize is that the key to the whole story is in the next chapter. *"For this cause the people also met him, because they heard that he had done this miracle . . ."* (John 12:18 - KJV)

If Jesus had not raised Lazarus from the dead, there would have been no crowds to cheer the Lord when He came into Jerusalem riding on a donkey.

God often sets the stage so that His glory is revealed through the events that He orchestrates. My friend, don't take the delays lightly. Do not faint as God places you in what seems to be a holding pattern. God is at work. God knows the purposes for His delays. Don't give up, for they are for His greater glory; so we need to remain faithful.

Os Hillman, *Today God is First*

*E*yes of Faith

"For our sakes, no doubt, this is written: that he that plows should plow in hope; and that he that threshes in hope should be partaker of his hope."
1 CORINTHIANS 9:10

Ruth certainly must have considered the probability of remaining single if she went with Naomi. Even though it promised no prospects of a husband, she chose to follow Naomi and her God back to Bethlehem. Ruth chose to trust God with her future. She looked not with sensual sight, but through "eyes of faith." Even though Ruth was young in her faith in the God of Israel, she chose to trust with her heart for the future her eyes could not yet see. Your hope cannot be put in some dreamed-up future. It must be in the God who knows your past, present, and future, and loves you enough to give you the best.

> *"Your hope cannot be put in some dreamed-up future."*

Don't put your own devices to work. You can only see the outward man from today's perspective. God sees men's hearts from the perspective of eternity. With His perspective, He can see much better what you need. Trust Him and let Him show you His dependable love for you.

To develop security, give your heart and emotions to the Lord. You are very special to God—so special that He has plans for you. God knows when your heart aches for these precious things. But He also knows that these earthly things will not make you secure.

The Holy Spirit Connection

"Now we have received, not the spirit of the world, but the spirit which is of God; that we might know the things that are freely given to us of God."
1 CORINTHIANS 2:12

There are things about you, concerning who you can be, that you haven't discovered yet—holy things that only the Holy Ghost can explain. God reveals His deep things to you through the Holy Spirit because He knows you would not believe them if they were simply told to you through your mind. Your mind cannot possibly comprehend all that God has prepared for you to be.

> *"You'll never be fulfilled without God, because you are looking for what God has."*

Forget what others have told you about who you can be. That's a joke. Don't even consider it. That is not all you can be, because the deepest things you can know about yourself are not in your mind or your emotions or even in your body. They are in your spirit. The deepest things you can know about yourself are what you get from your spirit.

When you hunger for the deep things of God, a hunger that God Himself puts within you, you will not be satisfied until the Holy Spirit reveals God's secret wisdom to you. Your spirit yearns for the deep things of God that He has within Him about you. There is a deep in you crying out to the deep things in God. You will never be satisfied, even after you are saved, because there is something inside you that continually calls out for more. And the thing you are calling for is locked up in God—the wisdom of God concerning you. You will never be fulfilled until you get filled with what God has that is supposed to be in you. That's why you have to come to God. You'll never be fulfilled without God, because you are looking for what God has.

Myles Munroe, *Understanding Your Potential*

The Curse of Comparison

"For all that is in the world, the lust of the flesh, and the lust of the eyes, and the pride of life, is not of the Father, but is of the world." 1 JOHN 2:16

A few years ago I was invited to speak at a series of seminars in Germany for a period of three months. Among the many wonderful memories I still carry is a lesson I learned about the principle of maximization. It occurred during my first personal experience with Germany's world-famous autobahn (expressway).

> *"I quickly began to understand the curse of comparison."*

The autobahn is a network of roads, without speed restrictions, that crisscross Germany and many other neighboring countries. One day as we were traveling from a city in northern Germany to the south, my host asked if I would like to experience driving without speed limitation. This felt like a dream come true. At first I was excited, thrilled, and anxious as I felt adrenaline rush through my entire body. The feeling of having the responsibility for power without externally imposed limits also brought other mixed emotions, including temporary confusion.

Now, here I was with an open invitation to maximize the ability of the car. As other cars raced passed me with the ease of a low flying jet, I watched as my speed gauge tilted past 80 mph. My host smiled and asked, "What are you afraid of? We're still standing still."

Not wanting to feel intimidated by this opportunity, I further depressed the pedal and felt the thrill of a car traveling at 115 mph. This feeling of supremacy was further enhanced ever time I passed another vehicle. In fact, I heard myself saying every time we passed another car, "Why don't they pull over, park, and let a real driver through?"

Suddenly, a Mercedes Benz cruised past me at 150 mph, seemingly coming out of nowhere. Instantly I felt like I was standing still. My host turned to me and said with a chuckle, "So you see, you are not traveling as fast as you can, but only as fast as you will."

As his words lodged in my mind, I quickly began to understand the curse of comparison and the limitations of self-pride.

Myles Munroe, *Maximizing Your Potential*

Rivers of Living Water

"If any man thirsts, let him come unto me, and drink. He that believes on me, as the scripture has said, out of his heart shall flow rivers of living water."
JOHN 7:37B-38

The heart of the sentence is in the last word—"water." Water is an essential of life. Absence of water means suffering and sickness, dearth and death. All the history of the world clusters about the water courses. Study the history of the rivers, the seashores, and lake edges, and you know the history of the earth. Now plainly Jesus is talking of something that may, through us, exert as decided an influence upon the lives of those we touch as water has exerted, and still exerts, on the history of the earth.

> *"There must be a flooding inside before there can be a flowing out."*

Now mark that little, but very significant, phrase—"Out of"—not into, but "out of." All the difference in the lives of men lies in the difference between these two expressions. "Into" is the world's preposition. Every stream turns in; and that means a dead sea. Many a man's life is simply the coast line of a dead sea. "Out of" is the Master's word. His thought is of others. The stream must flow in, and must flow through, if it is to flow out, but it is judged by its direction, and Jesus would turn it outward. There must be good connections upward, and a clear channel inward, but the objective point is outward toward a parched earth. But before it can flow out it must fill up. And outflow in this case means an overflow. There must be a flooding inside before there can be a flowing out. And let the fact be carefully marked that it is only the overflow from the fullness within our own lives that brings refreshing to anyone else.

When there was a flood in the river, there was a harvest in the land. Has there been a harvest in your life?

_____

_____

_____

_____

_____

_____

_____

S. D. Gordon, *Quiet Talks on Power*

Conquering the Enemy Within

"And if any man thinks that he knows anything, he knows nothing yet as he ought to know. But if any man loves God, the same is known of him."
1 CORINTHIANS 8:2-3

You need to allow new meditations to dwell in your heart by faith, for your life will ultimately take on the direction of your thinking.

My mouth shall speak of wisdom; and the meditation of my heart shall be of understanding. (Psalm 49:3 - KJV)

Let the words of my mouth, and the meditation of my heart, be acceptable in thy sight, O LORD, my strength, and my redeemer. (Psalm 19:14 – KJV)

> *"We have to begin with the thoughts we think."*

O how love I thy law! it is my meditation all the day. (Psalm 119:97 - KJV)

Many weaknesses, such as procrastination and laziness, are just draperies that cover up poor self-esteem and a lack of motivation. They are often symptoms of the subconscious avoiding the risk of failure. Remember that "nothing shall be impossible unto you" if you will only believe! (See Matthew 17:20).

We have to begin with the thoughts we think. I pray that somehow the Spirit will reveal the areas where you need Him to heal your thinking so you can possess what God wants you to have. Then you will be able to fully enjoy what He has given you. Many people have the blessing and still don't enjoy it because they conquered every foe except the enemy within!

T. D. Jakes, *365 Days to Healing, Blessings, and Freedom*

$\mathcal{A}$ Wrong Environment

"Now I pray to God that you do no evil; not that we should appear approved, but that you should do that which is right, though we be as reprobates."
2 CORINTHIANS 13:7

Nutritious vegetables cannot grow in poor soil and healthy fish cannot thrive in polluted waters. Neither can we maximize our potential in a wrong environment. The apostle Paul speaks to this principle when he says, "Bad company corrupts good character." (1 Corinthians 15:33 NIV) That means, no matter how good our intentions may be, if we get in with bad company, we will eventually think and act as they do. We will not change them, they will change us.

> *"Many dreams die because they are shared with the wrong people."*

Many dreams die because they are shared with the wrong people. Joseph learned that lesson the hard way. Indeed, he landed in a pit and was sold into slavery because his brothers were jealous of their father's favoritism toward him and they were offended by his dreams that placed him in authority over them. This is really not so surprising because older brothers rarely enjoy being dominated by younger ones. Had Joseph kept his dreams to himself, his brothers' resentment may not have developed into a plan to murder him.

Remember, others do not see what you see. They cannot completely understand the vision God has given you. Protect your potential by choosing carefully those with whom you share your dreams and aspirations, and by maintaining an environment in which your potential can be fulfilled. To maximize your life you must manage your environment and the quality of the people and resources that influence you. Your greatest responsibility is to yourself, not others.

Myles Munroe, *Maximizing Your Potential*

$\mathcal{T}$he Birthplace of Faith

"Father, I thank you that you have heard me. And I knew that you hear me always: but because of the people which stand by I said it, that they may believe that you have sent me." JOHN 11: 41B-42

Prayer must be in faith. But please note that faith here is not believing that God can, but that He will. It is kneeling and making the prayer, and then saying "Father I thank Thee for this; that it will be so, I thank Thee." Going again and again, and repeating the prayer with thanks...because prayer is the deciding factor in a spirit conflict and each prayer is like a fresh blow between the eyes of the enemy, a fresh broadside from your fleet upon the fort.

> *"The faith that believes that God will do what you ask is not born in a hurry; it is not born in the dust of the street, and the noise of the crowd."*

There should be no unnatural mechanical insistence that you do believe. Some earnest people make a mistake there...and I can easily tell you why. The faith that believes that God will do what you ask is not born in a hurry; it is not born in the dust of the street, and the noise of the crowd.

There is a fine word much used in the Psalms, and in Isaiah for this sort of thing—waiting. Over and over again that is the word used for that contact with God which reveals to us His will, and imparts to us anew His desires. It is a word full of richest and deepest meaning. Waiting is not an occasional nor a hurried thing. It means steadfastness, that is holding on; patience, that is holding back; expectancy, that is holding the face up to see; obedience, that is holding one's self to go or do; it means listening, that is holding quiet and still so as to hear.

S. D. Gordon, *Quiet Talks on Prayer*

Your Choice: To Seek or Brood

"For all seek their own, not the things which are Jesus Christ's."
PHILIPPIANS 2:21

Unfortunately, it generally takes devastation on a business level to make most men commit more of their interest in relationships. Job probably could have reached out to his children for comfort, but he had lost them too. His marriage had deteriorated to the degree that Job said his wife abhorred his breath (see Job 19:17). Then he also became ill. Have you ever gone through a time in your life when you felt you had been jinxed? Everything that could go wrong, did! Frustration turns into alienation. So now what? Will you use this moment to seek God or to brood over your misfortune? With the right answer, you could turn the jail into a church!

> *"Have you ever gone through a time in your life when you felt you had been jinxed?"*

Job said, "Behold, I go forward, but He is not there" (Job 23:8a · KJV). It is terrifying when you see no change coming in the future. Comfort comes when you know that the present adversity will soon be over. But what comfort can be found when it seems the problem will never cease? Job said, "I see no help, no sign of God, in the future." It actually is satan's trick to make you think help is not coming. That hopelessness then produces anxiety. On the other hand, sometimes the feeling that you eventually will come to a point of transition can give you the tenacity to persevere the current challenge. But there often seems to be no slackening in distress. Like a rainstorm that will not cease, the waters of discouragement begin to fill the tossing ship with water. Suddenly you experience a sinking feeling. However, there is no way to sink a ship when you do not allow the waters from the outside to get on the inside! If the storms keep coming, the lightning continues to flash, and the thunder thumps on through the night, what matters is keeping the waters out of the inside. Keep that stuff out of your spirit!

Potential Is Never Given for Itself

"And the multitude of them that believed were of one heart and of one soul: neither said any of them that any of the things which he possessed was his own; but they had all things common." ACTS 4:32

Even as a solitary instrument cannot produce the majestic music of a symphonic orchestra, so human beings cannot glorify their Creator in isolation. I need your potential to maximize mine and you need my potential to maximize yours. All we have been given is meant to be shared. Potential is never given for itself. Whatever God gives to you, He gives for others.

After man had finished naming all the animals and no suitable helper for him was found among them, God performed another significant act of creation. Why? "It is not good for man to be alone." (Genesis 2:18-KJV) God did not make woman because man asked for a wife, nor because a helper for man was a good idea. Man needed a companion because he could not realize his potential without sharing it with someone. His solitary existence was not good.

> *"Potential is never given for itself."*

To be solitary or alone is not the same as being single. To be alone is to be isolated and cut off from others. Communication is impossible because you have no one like yourself to share with. This is what God says is not good.

To be single is to be unmarried. Marriage is not a requirement or a prerequisite for the fulfillment of your potential. You do not necessarily need a husband or a wife. What you do need, however, is someone with whom you can share your potential. This is true because your personal satisfaction is connected to your fulfilling God's purpose for your life, and your purpose cannot be achieved in isolation. You need those people who will call forth your potential and into whom you can pour your life. You may be wired to be single, but you are not designed to live isolated and alone.

God is Not An Option

"As the branch cannot bear fruit of itself, except it remains in the vine; no more can you, except you abide in me." JOHN 15:4

If you cut yourself off from God, your potential is aborted. No matter how hard you try to plant yourself in other organizations and activities, God says, "You are dead." Even if you plant yourself in religion, you are dead unless you know God and draw your nutrients from Him.

Our need for God is not an alternative or an option. Like the plants and the animals, which cannot be maintained without the soil, and the fish, which cannot live outside the water, we cannot flourish and bear fruit apart from God.

> *"Our need for God is not an alternative or an option."*

When Jesus says in John 14:6, "I am the way, the truth, and the life: …" He isn't trying to convince us that He's the best way. He didn't use that word. Life rooted in God is a necessity. There is no option. Although you can say to a plant, "You can either stay in the soil or get out of the pot and sit on the windowsill," the plant doesn't really have a choice.

If the plant chooses the windowsill, it will die. There is no alternative to the soil for the plant to meet its basic needs. So it is with human beings and God. If you stay within God's Word, His Word takes root in your heart and becomes established. His power is released as you stay alive with His Word. If, however, you pull yourself out of God, you shut down your productivity and forfeit the blessings God wants to give you. You become as limited as the books, people, education, etc. that are feeding your thought patterns.

Do you want joy? Go to God. Do you need peace? Set your roots firmly in the Word and power of God. Do you need help to control your temper? Spend time with God. Jesus promises: "…with God all things are possible" (Matthew 19:26). God is the soil you unconditionally need.

$\mathcal{P}$rerequisite for Potential

"I am the vine, you are the branches. He who abides in me, and I in him, the same brings forth much fruit; for without me you can do nothing." JOHN 15:5

Living a victorious life does not depend on us. It depends on who we are hooked up to. There are many individuals who I expected to be successful in life—their lives showed tremendous potential—but they lost their relationship with their Source. Jesus says, "If you abide in Me, you will be fruitful. But you cannot do it on your own." No branch can live by itself; it must remain attached to the vine. Neither can it bear fruit apart from the vine. Jesus is the true vine. You are a branch. If you remain in Christ and Christ in you, you will bear abundant fruit.

> If you remain in me and my words remain in you, ask whatever you wish and it will be given you.
> John 15:7 NIV)

"He wants to fulfill your potential"

Jesus' words are almost frightening—whatever you wish. God will give you whatever you ask for so long as you remain in Him. What a promise! When you open your life completely to God, the Holy Spirit's crowbar firmly resists satan's attempt to recap your well. The wealth of your potential becomes limitless and free. Whatever you imagine will be done, because God won't allow you to think it unless you can do it.

Thus the secret to a happy, productive life is remaining attached to your Divine Source. If you abide in Christ, His word will abide in you. You can ask whatever you wish and it will be given to you. God will provide from the depths of His grace-freely, abundantly, victoriously. You don't have to hustle. You don't have to plead. God is always waiting to help you live a full, fruitful, complete life. From His storehouse of riches, God will supply all you can imagine, and more because He wants you to fulfill your potential.

Myles Munroe, *Understanding Your Potential*

How High Can You Jump?

"And Peter answered him and said, 'Lord, if it be you, tell me to come unto you on the water.'" MATTHEW 14:28

The people who are blessings to humanity are usually men and women who decide there is more to them than what other people have said. People who bless the world are people who believe there is an ability inside them to accomplish something that has never been done. Though they may not know exactly what they can do, they try because they believe they can accomplish something.

> *"You aren't doing more because no one has challenged you"*

I remember the day I found out that I can jump really high—about eight feet high. Now, I can't jump that high intentionally, but I did it once when I was a little boy.

There was a lady who lived behind our house from whose fruit trees we would occasionally feast and help ourselves. When we were little kids, we would crawl under the fence. One day while I was on her side of the fence, her very vicious dog suddenly appeared. I had just touched down after climbing the fruit tree. As I carefully considered the distance between the fence, the dog and myself, I knew I had to make a run for it. I ran toward the fence with the dog close behind me. As the fence came closer and closer, all I could say was "O God, I'm dead." All I could think was "jump." As I left the ground, my heart was pounding and my chest felt like an arcade full of shouting people. I was so afraid! When I landed, I was safely on the other side of the fence.

When I turned around and looked at the dog, he was barking angrily because he couldn't get over the fence. I just thought, "Yea, good for you." Suddenly I became very proud because I had gotten away from him. But when I started to realize what I had done, I looked at the fence and thought, "How did I do that?"

I thank God for that dog. He was a blessing in my life. I never jumped that high before, and I never have since, but at least I know that I did it. I discovered that day there is a lot more potential in me than I realized was there.

Winning the Prize Requires Running the Race

"Do you not know that they which run in a race all run, but one receives the prize? So run, that you may obtain." 1 CORINTHIANS 9:24

Potential is like soil. It must be worked and fed to produce fruit. King Solomon referred to this process of releasing the fruitfulness of man when he said, "The purposes of a man's heart are deep waters, but a man of understanding draws them out" (Proverbs 20:5 · NIV). Notice, the drawing out of man's potential requires effort. Like the fisherman who brings forth the treasures of the sea by hard work and the farmer who harvests the fruit of the ground by the sweat of his brow, so man must labor to tap even a portion of god's potential within him.

> *"Potential is like soil. It must be worked and fed to produce fruit."*

Through wisdom is an house builded; and by understanding it is established: And by knowledge shall the chambers be filled with all precious and pleasant riches (Proverbs 24:3-4 · KJV).

Understanding and wisdom are the keys to the success of man's mission. His race to maximize everything God has given him begins with knowing what God requires of him and how. He expects him to reach the finish line. The primary principle in cultivating one's life for maximum living is to destroy ignorance by the pursuit of knowledge, wisdom, and understanding. The search for knowledge requires effort. You must seek it like a treasure that is precious to you. You cannot touch God's knowledge, however, without diligence and exertion.

Knowledge must always precede action or much time and effort will be wasted through misguided efforts and dead-end directions. God, who planned your life and granted you the potential to fulfill His plans, works for and with you when you seek to know Him and to understand and follow His ways.

Myles Munroe, *Maximizing Your Potential*

The Whisper of God

"Do you see this woman? I entered into your house, you gave me no water for my feet: but she has washed my feet with tears, and wiped them with the hairs of her head." LUKE 7: 44

Have you ever wondered how certain people seem to have a certain attachment to God? For some reason, God just seems to be near them all the time. I can tell you that it isn't because they preach so well, or because they are such stellar singers. No, they know how to dismantle their egos and glory. They lay it all aside just to worship at His feet in brokenness and humility. And it is for these precious few that God Himself will stop His ascent to Heaven just to whisper His secrets into their waiting hearts.

> *"God cannot pass by a broken and contrite heart."*

Did you notice that God didn't break Mary's alabaster box? Mary had to break it. If you want to have that kind of encounter with God, then you will have to "break" yourself. The highest level of worship comes from brokenness, and there are no shortcuts or formulas to help you "reach the top." No one can do it for you; that is something only you can do. But if you do, God will stop just to spend time with you.

If He hears that cracking tinkle when you break your alabaster box of personal treasures; if He notices the rustling sound as you bow to dismantle your own glory; you are going to stop Him in the middle of whatever He's doing, because God cannot pass by a broken and contrite heart. He is going to move Heaven and earth just to come visit with you.

If you want to know why some churches have revival, or why some people have intimacy when multitudes do not; the answer is that these are people of brokenness. The breaking of your heart arrests the ears and eyes of God, and it begins when your love for Him supersedes your fear of what others may think. You can't seek His face and save your "face." The "end" of your glory, the dismantling, if you please, is the beginning of His glory.

Dismantle Your Glory

"This people draws near unto me with their mouth, and honors me with their lips; but their heart is far from me." MATTHEW 15:8

We have lost the art of adoring the Lord. Our worship gets so cluttered with endless strings of shallow and insincere words that all we do most of the time is "take up space" or "put in prayer time" with a passionless monologue that even God must ignore. Some of us come to Him clinging to such heavy burdens that we are too frustrated and distracted to see the Father or understand how much He loves us. We need to return to the simplicity of our childhood. Every night that I'm home, I rock my six-year-old daughter to sleep because I love her. Usually she will lay back in my arms, and just before she drifts off to sleep she will remember the problems of the day and say something like, "Daddy, this little boy was mean to me on the playground at school". To her these seem like giant problems. I always try to reassure her that everything will be all right in those moments because she is resting in my arms and because I love her. It doesn't matter what anyone said on the playground, and none of her little failures have any power to hurt her because she is in my arms.

> *"You cannot back your way into the door of eternity; you have to walk into it."*

Too often we come to Him at the end of our day and "worship" Him with premanufactured mechanics and memorized words. Then, since we are almost totally absorbed with our "playground" offenses and the temporal problems of the day, we lay back in His presence just long enough to say our string of words and deliver our wish list.

What He wants us to do is just look at Him. He has set before you an open door, but you will have to "face" Him. You cannot back your way into the door of eternity; you have to walk into it. You will have to stop looking at and listening to other things. He is beckoning to you to "come up hither," and He'll show you the "hereafter" (see Rev. 4:1.).

Tommy Tenney, *The God Chasers*

Mercy In Spite of Our Mess

"Neither is there any creature that is not manifest in his sight: but all things are naked and opened unto the eyes of him with whom we have to give account." HEBREWS 4:13

Forgive me for condemning and judging anybody else. I know that if it were not for Your mercy, I would be guilty of the very things for which I have disdained others. Help me not to be hypocritical.

This kind of prayer and confession enhances your relationship with God as you begin to realize that you were saved by grace; you are saved by grace; and you will be saved by grace! Knowing this, how can you not be grateful? You know that He loves you so much that He stays in the house you haven't fully cleaned. He hates the acts; He despises the thoughts; but He loves the thinker. Neither is there any creature that is not manifest in his sight: but all things are naked and opened unto the eyes of him with whom we have to give account.

> *"God knows all our business and that all our thoughts parade around naked before His scrutinizing eyes."*

Seeing then that we have a great high priest, that is passed into the heavens, Jesus the Son of God, let us hold fast our profession. For we have not a high priest which cannot be touched with the feeling of our weaknesses; but was in all points tempted like as we are, yet without sin. (Hebrews 4:14-15)

Immediately after the writer of the Book of Hebrews tells us that God knows all our business and that all our thoughts parade around naked before His scrutinizing eyes, he mentions the high priest that we have in Christ. He knows we are going to need a high priest for all the garbage and information that the Holy Spirit is privy to, yet others would never know. What greater compassion can be displayed than when the writer goes on to say that God, through Christ, can be touched by how I feel. No wonder Jeremiah said His mercies are "new every morning"! (See Lamentations 3:22-23.)

_____

_____

_____

_____

_____

_____

T. D. Jakes, *365 Days to Healing, Blessings, and Freedom*

$\mathcal{F}$eeling Drained?

"... ever learning, and never able to come to the knowledge of the truth."
2 TIMOTHY 3:7

One secret to living a continuously empowered life is to guard yourself against the things that can disconnect you from the power source.

We cannot remain connected to God if we are weighted down by our busyness. We can spend so much time doing things for God that we neglect our relationship with Him.

Are you feeling drained? Do the activities that were once life-giving now seem empty and meaningless to you? Does your heart cry out because you know that there is more available than what you are currently tapping into? We know that our physical bodies require constant replenishment. If we fail to eat, drink, or sleep, we will suffer for it. Similarly, our spiritual bodies also need recharging.

> *"The way up is down; to lay hold you must let go."*

I've never met a "God chaser" who didn't occasionally grow weary in the chase. The only difference between a "God chaser" and a "pew warmer" is his/her determination to be plugged in. One secret to living a continuously empowered life is to guard yourself against the things that can disconnect you from the power source. Obviously, sin will do that—but so will weariness.

We cannot remain connected to God if we are weighted down by our busyness. Bitterness and unforgiveness are also power drains; they steal our energy—physically, emotionally, and spiritually. Failure to forgive also can disconnect us from the power source. We cannot be fully committed to furthering God's Kingdom while we have set up and are still defending the borders of our personal kingdoms. The way up is down; to lay hold you must let go; to be filled you must become empty. It isn't the easy way...but if you want a power that doesn't rise and fall with circumstance and whim, it is the only way!

Tommy Tenney, The Daily Chase

Υou Can Receive Whatever You Ask

"If you abide in me, and my words abide in you, you shall ask what you will, and it shall be done unto you." JOHN 15:7

Man's tremendous potential also includes the capacity to influence both physical and spiritual things. This capacity is a colossal power that we seldom use. Jesus pointed to this power when He told Peter (after Peter had confessed, "You are the Christ, the Son of the living God" (Matthew 16:16):

> *"If you are dealing with just the physical aspects of your life, you are missing the real thing."*

"Blessed are you, Simon Bar-Jonah: for flesh and blood has not revealed it unto you, but my Father which is in heaven. And I say also unto you, That you are Peter, and upon this rock I will build my church; and the gates of Hades shall not prevail against it. And I will give unto you the keys of the kingdom of heaven: and whatsoever you shall bind on earth shall be bound in heaven: and whatsoever you shall loose on earth shall be loosed in heaven." (Matthew 16:17-19)

Jesus is encouraging us to look beyond the physical circumstances of our lives to the spiritual dimension. If you are dealing with just the physical aspects of your life, you are missing the real thing. Look beyond the problems in your job or with your spouse or in your church to the spiritual realities that underlie them. Say in the natural what you want to happen in the spiritual. The power to affect both realms is yours.

During His time on earth, Jesus gave His disciples a blank check. He promised them that they could receive whatever they requested.

Therefore I say unto you, Whatsoever things you desire, when you pray, believe that you receive them, and you shall have them." (Mark 11:24)

That's God's promise concerning your potential. He's waiting to give you whatever you request, so long as you sink your roots deep into His Word and allow His words to influence and direct your entire life.

_____

_____

_____

_____

Myles Munroe, *Releasing Your Potential*

Of No Reputation

"But made himself of no reputation, and took upon him the form of a servant, and was made in the likeness of men:" PHILIPPIANS 2:7

And the angel said unto her, Fear not, Mary: for thou hast found favour with God. And, behold, thou shalt conceive in thy womb, and bring forth a son, and shalt call his name Jesus (Luke 1:30-31)

Mary, the mother of Jesus, had the baby, but the angel was sent from the Father to give the name. She couldn't name Him because she didn't fully understand His destiny. Don't allow people who don't understand your destiny to name you. They also probably whispered that Jesus was the illegitimate child of Joseph. Maybe there has been some nasty little rumor out on you too. Rumors smear the reputation and defame the character of many innocent people. However, none lived with any better moral character than Jesus—and they still assaulted His reputation. Just be sure the rumors are false or in the past and keep on living. I often say, "You can't help where you've been, but you can help where you're going."

> *"You can't help where you've been, but you can help where you're going."*

And it came to pass in those days, that Jesus came from Nazareth of Galilee, and was baptized of John in Jordan. And straightway coming up out of the water, he saw the heavens opened, and the Spirit like a dove descending upon him: And there came a voice from heaven, saying, Thou art my beloved Son, in whom I am well pleased (Mark 1:9-11).

In the chilly river of Jordan, with mud between His toes, it was the voice of the Father that declared the identity of Christ. And he can declare yours too.

Do You Want To Be Healed? Well Do You?

"The paralyzed man answered him, 'Sir, I have no man, when the water is stirred, to put me into the pool: but while I am coming, another steps down before me.'" JOHN 5:7

John 5:2-9 tells the story of a man who waited at the pool of Bethesda to be healed from an infirmity. He had been going to the pools for 38 years, but there was no one there who would put him into the healing water when the right time came. Scripture says Jesus saw him and knew that he had been sick for a long time and asked him, "Wilt thou be made whole?" In other words, "Do you want to be healed?"

> *"Our faith can move mountains and quench the arrows of wickedness. And yet we still struggle with celebrating change."*

That seems like such an obvious question, when you think about it. The man is sick. He waits by the healing pools. Obviously he wants to be healed, or he wouldn't be there. We go to church Sunday in and Sunday out. The church is a place where we're supposed to get healed. Obviously we want to be free of our sin, or we wouldn't be there, right? Right?

We don't have to be slaves to sin, discontentment, and complacency. We have the power of the Holy Spirit, which is the Spirit of Truth. We have in us the same power that raised Jesus from the dead. Our faith can move mountains and quench the arrows of wickedness. And yet we still struggle with celebrating change. We struggle with peace, joy, and contentment. We struggle with conceiving, believing, and receiving the love of God. We're weak and impotent. We do all the things that make it look like we want to be holy, fired-up saints. Then Jesus, the Truth, walks up and asks us, "Do you want to be healed?" Well, do you?

Dr. Wanda Turner, *Celebrating Change*

Take the Necessary Risks

"Greet Priscilla and Aquila my helpers in Christ Jesus: who have for my life risked their own necks: unto whom not only I give thanks, but also all the churches of the Gentiles." ROMANS 16:3-4

You can't do much of anything without taking a risk. For instance, as someone has written,

To laugh is to risk appearing the fool.
To weep is to risk appearing sentimental.
To reach out to another is to risk involvement.
To express feelings is to risk exposing your true self.
To place your ideas, your dreams, before the crowd is to risk their loss.
To love is to risk not being loved in return.
To live is to risk dying; to hope is to risk despair.
To try is to risk failure, but risks must be taken;
Because the greatest hazard in life is to risk nothing.

> *"Only a person who risks is free."*

The person who risks nothing, does nothing, has nothing, and is nothing. Only a person who risks is free.

Eric Jensen says, "Sometimes the thing that will help you become a winner is not something you dread doing or don't want to do, but rather, something you are dying to do yet don't have the courage to try. Successful people are those who are willing, at some critical point, to take a risk."

Let me close by taking you back to August 1964, as Winston Churchill lay dying in London's King Edward VIII Hospital. Former President Dwight Eisenhower, who partnered with Churchill to end Nazi aggression during World War II, sat by his bedside, holding his hand.

No words were spoken. After about ten minutes, Churchill let go of Eisenhower's hand and slowly, painstakingly formed his famous "V" for victory sign. Eisenhower, fighting back tears, pulled his chair back, stood up, saluted, turned, and walked out of the room. Outside in the hall he told his aide: "I just said goodbye to Winston, but you never say farewell to courage."

Pat Williams, *American Scandal*

Look Into His Face and Let Him Lavish

"Except you be converted, and become as little children, you shall not enter into the kingdom of heaven." MATTHEW 18:3

We're God's children, and as His kids we have access to His favor in much the same way that my kids have access to mine. His Fatherly love for us is unconditional—but our childlike faith and love for Him isn't always where it should be. Sometimes we'll pout and refuse to receive His love when we don't get our way. And even when we do get our way, our love for Him can be shallow.

> *"Too often we run from blessing to blessing, pleading with God to dispense His gifts."*

Too often we run from blessing to blessing, pleading with God to dispense His gifts...and almost as soon as we have them, we turn our attention from Him and look longingly at the next "thing" that catches our eye, rubbing our hands together in presumptive anticipation of the next blessing. And to some extent God will overlook our immaturity—if we've proven that our love for Him is deeper than our love for His "things." impostors!

There's an irony in the way God operates. When we're grabbing for the gifts from His hands, He seems to dispense them slowly. But when we get our eyes off of the "toys" and onto His face—when we want Him, regardless of the blessings and regardless of the cost—that is when He lavishes His gifts upon us.

Tommy Tenney, *The Daily Chase*

Desire Is Kindled In the Furnace of Need

"Whatsoever things you desire, when you pray, believe that you receive them, and you shall have them." MARK 11:24

How strong is your desire for accomplishment in your life? It takes more than a mere whimsical musing over a speculative end. It takes floor-walking, devil-stomping, anointed tenacity to overcome the limitations that are always surrounding what you want to do for your God, yourself, and your family! Desire is kindled in the furnace of need—an unfulfilled need. It is a need that refuses to be placated and a need that will not be silent. Any man will tell you that where there is no desire, there is no passion. Where there is no passion, there is no potency. Without desire, you are basically impotent!

> *"Desire is kindled in the furnace of need."*

Desire gives you the drive you need to produce. Even natural reproduction is an impossibility to a person who is devoid of passion and desire. Many people who set out to accomplish goals are so easily discouraged or intimidated by their own anxieties that they relinquish their right to fight for their dreams. However, if there is a tenacious burning desire in the pit of your stomach, you become very difficult to discourage. How many cold nights I have warmed my cold feet by the fires of my innermost desire to complete a goal for my life. No one knows how hot the embers glow beneath the ashes of adversity.

Having pastored in the coal fields of West Virginia, I know about wood and coal stoves. You can bank the fire by placing ashes all around it. Then it will not burn out as rapidly and will last through the night. In the frosty chill of the morning you do not need to rebuild the fire, for beneath the ashes lay crimson embers waiting to be stirred. These embers explode into fire when they are stirred correctly. Many people have gone through situations that banked their fire. The fire isn't dead, but its burning is not as brilliant as it once was. If you have an inner desire to survive or succeed, then you only need a stirring for the embers of passion to ignite in your life.

_____

_____

_____

_____

_____

_____

T. D. Jakes, *365 Days to Healing, Blessings, and Freedom*

$\mathcal{A}$ Prayer of Faith

"But godliness with contentment is great gain." I TIMOTHY 6:6

The goal of a trial is to prove you, so contentment in a trial is found only in faith. No matter how difficult your struggle is, a good, solid dose of faith is necessary for you to make it through the challenge and come out celebrating change.

Today I make a quality, Godly decision to crucify the lusts of my flesh. I make a conscious, deliberate decision to put away wrath and evil thoughts or deeds. I decide for Christ. I decide with Christ. I decide in Christ.

> *"I may not know where my steps lead, but I know whose path I walk."*

I'm on the brink of a miracle. That which I cannot do myself, change, or edit, I can trust the almighty God to make the difference. I choose to love, I choose to commit, I choose the will of God, for He that hath begun a good work in me, shall perform it to the day of Christ. I trust God. I lean on God. I am in a spiritual labor room, awaiting, in pain, for the birth of something new, exciting, and supernatural. I won't faint.

I won't give up. I shall not be moved, for I am like a tree planted by the water (Word) and I shall not be moved. God has not given me the spirit of fear, but of love, power, and a sound mind. I don't fear man. I fear God who made man. I may not know where my steps lead, but I know whose path I walk. Victory is my destiny. Success is my destiny. I am strongest at my weakest. Why me? For God's glory! He said every time you go through, God has something for you. Our place of power is reached by our experience of pain, for on the other side of pain is power! Allow yourself the pleasure of failure. God gives a test for a testimony.

We have to believe that He will not leave us confounded or without hope. We have to know that all things, even the things that torture us at the moment, work together for our good, because we love Him and are called by Him.

And there appeared an angel unto him from heaven, strengthening him. (Luke 22:43 - KJV)

Dr. Wanda Turner, *Celebrating Change*

Challenge Tradition

"And it shall come to pass in the last days, says God, I will pour out of my Spirit upon all flesh: and your sons and your daughters shall prophesy, and your young men shall see visions, and your old men shall dream dreams:"
ACTS 2:17

Traditions are powerful enemies of potential because they are full of security. We don't have to think when we do something the way we've always done it. Neither do we receive the incentive to grow and be creative because our new ideas may interfere with the conventional way of doing things.

The tragedy is that the tradition, which probably served its purpose well when it was started, prevents the accomplishment of the purpose for which it was established. Remember, no matter how good the present system is, there's always a better way. Don't be imprisoned by the comfort of the known. Be an explorer, not just a passenger. Don't allow yourself to become trapped by tradition or you will do and become nothing. Use your imagination. Dream big and find new ways to respond to present situations and responsibilities. Then you

> *"Don't allow yourself to become trapped by tradition or you will do and become nothing."*

will uncover never-ending possibilities that inspire you to reach for continually higher achievements. We are sons of the "Creator," who created us to be creative. Nowhere in Scripture did God repeat an identical act.

Refrain from accepting or believing, "We've never done it that way before." Now is the time to try something different. The release of your full potential demands that you move beyond the present traditions of home, family, job, and church—in essence, throughout your life. To maximize your new life you must be willing to release the old.

_____

_____

_____

_____

_____

_____

_____

_____

Myles Munroe, *Maximizing Your Potential*

$\mathcal{M}$y Gratitude

Loving what I have—what I am grateful for:

_____
_____
_____
_____
_____
_____
_____
_____
_____
_____
_____
_____
_____
_____
_____
_____
_____
_____
_____
_____
_____
_____
_____
_____

"God is my strength and power: and he maketh my way perfect."
II SAMUEL 22:33 (KJV)

In Conclusion . . .

*T*he road ahead

"There is a path which no fowl knoweth, and which the vulture's eye hath not seen." **JOB 28:7 (KJV)**

As you map a course for the New Year, it's not necessary to know the precise destination or the exact road you should take to get there, just pick the path that seems nearest right under the circumstances and head that direction

A wise woman once said: "When you drive at night, you may only be able to see only a block ahead with your headlights, but you can make the whole trip that way!"

Lean on God and let go of fear. Fear is not what governs us. God governs us, and God is Love, so the result is always good. You can trust this goodness in all situations and bask in the warmth of His love.

Know that you always "abide under the shadow of the Almighty, and that "He is my refuge and my fortress: my God: in him will I trust" (Psalm 91:1&2)

If the way gets dark and turbulent, just follow your head lights and watch for signs from God; and you'll find your way—one block at a time.

$\mathcal{M}$y Self Promise. . .

Seeing my perfect self—aiming for a better me in the year ahead

_____
_____
_____
_____
_____
_____
_____
_____
_____
_____
_____
_____
_____
_____
_____
_____
_____
_____
_____
_____
_____
_____
_____

"For the Lord God is a sun and shield: the Lord will give grace and glory: no good thing will he withhold from them that walk uprightly."
PSALM 8:11

Index of Authors

The inspirational devotions appearing in this book are extracted from the following writings.

Penelope Black, Sermons, Canon, Anglican Church of Canada
Morton Bustard, *The Impassioned Soul*
Gene Edwards, *100 days in the Secret Place*
S.D. Gordon, *Quiet Talks on Power*
S.D. Gordon, *Quiet Talks About Jesus*
S.D. Gordon, *Quiet Talks On Prayer*
Os Hillman, *Today God is First*
T.D. Jakes, *365 Days to Healing, Blessings, and Freedom*
Debby Jones & Jackie Kendall, *Lady In Waiting–Developing Your Love Relationships*
Debby Jones & Jackie Kendall, *Lady in Waiting–Meditations of The Heart*
Jackie Kendall, *Say Goodbye to Shame*
Myles Munroe, *Maximizing Your Potential*
Myles Munroe, *Releasing Your Potential*
Myles Munroe, *Understanding Your Potential*
Oral Roberts, *Still Doing the Impossible*
Tommy Tenney, *The God Chasers*
Tommy Tenney, *The Daily Chase*
Dr. Wanda Turner, *Celebrating Change*
Pat Williams, *American Scandal*

Index of Readings

February 11	You See What You Believe	Dr. Wanda Turner
February 12	Green Light	T.D. Jakes
February 13	Multiplied Rewards	Oral Roberts
February 14	From the Bottom Up	T.D. Jakes
February 15	Don't Rob Yourself of Forgiveness	Tommy Tenney
February 16	Consistently Inconsistent	Dr. Wanda Turner
February 17	Heaven Hears	Morton Bustard
February 18	Open Communication	T.D. Jakes
February 19	Understand Your Potential	Myles Munroe
February 20	What Are You Hungry For?	Tommy Tenney
February 21	God Works for Your Good	T.D. Jakes
February 22	Can You Take the Heat?	Dr. Wanda Turner
February 23	God's Heroes	Tommy Tenney
February 24	Five Essentials	S.D. Gordon
February 25	Release and Resolve	T.D. Jakes
February 26	God's System: Faith	Myles Munroe
February 27	The Power to Run the Race	Tommy Tenney
February 28	Pain Is Not Forever	Morton Bustard
February 29	How Does God Operate?	Myles Munroe
March 1	Just Tell Me—Is That Him?	Tommy Tenney
March 2	Water In the Desert	Morton Bustard
March 3	Knock the Limits off Your Life	Myles Munroe
March 4	The Personal Power Test	S.D. Gordon
March 5	Forgive Yourself!	Tommy Tenney
March 6	No Place Like Home	Morton Bustard
March 7	On the Anvil of the Knees	S.D. Gordon
March 8	Thank God for Small Things	T.D. Jakes
March 9	You Are Not Junk	Myles Munroe
March 10	Relinquish What You Don't Understand	Tommy Tenney
March 11	Making It Through The Night	Morton Bustard
March 12	Nurturing to Endure Trials	T.D. Jakes
March 13	You Have Part of God	Myles Munroe
March 14	The Testing Ground	Dr. Wanda Turner
March 15	Ask What You Will	S.D. Gordon
March 16	We Need Feelings	T.D. Jakes
March 17	Life Is Seasonal	Morton Bustard
March 18	There's No Retirement In The Bible	Myles Munroe
March 19	No One Hears Like the Lord	T.D. Jakes
March 20	Challenge Tradition	Myles Munroe
March 21	We Can Do It!	T.D. Jakes
March 22	You Must Cooperate	Myles Munroe
March 23	The Gift of Goodness	Pat Williams
March 24	Belief or Unbelief	Os Hillman
March 25	Expressing The Hidden You	Myles Munroe
March 26	The Job of Unloading is Yours	Tommy Tenney
March 27	Beauty for Ashes	Dr. Wanda Turner
March 28	Hard Work—and Then Some	Pat Williams

May 9	The Buck Stops Here	Pat Williams
May 10	Delayed Results	S.D. Gordon
May 11	A Second Chance to Find Who You Are	T.D. Jakes
May 12	The Step Ladder of Success	Myles Munroe
May 13	The Habit of Peace	Pat Williams
May 14	Following Only the Father's Commands	Os Hillman
May 15	He's Looking In Your Direction	T.D. Jakes
May 16	The Yardstick of Success	Myles Munroe
May 17	Change Starts With You	Pat Williams
May 18	Dissatisfaction With a Fraction	Myles Munroe
May 19	Don't Lose Your Fire	T.D. Jakes
May 20	Claiming Joy!	Pat Williams
May 21	From Thought to Action	Myles Munroe
May 22	"Milk Babies" in Padded Pews	Tommy Tenney
May 23	Pray No Matter the Season	Morton Bustard
May 24	Finish What You Start	Pat Williams
May 25	God Has A Plan	Pat Williams
May 26	Dividends From a High Price	Debbie Jones & Jackie Kendall
May 27	Supernatural, Not Spectacular	Morton Bustard
May 28	Live Day by Day	Gene Edwards
May 29	Ruin Everything That Isn't God	Tommy Tenney
May 30	Do The Pigeon Walk	Debbie Jones & Jackie Kendall
May 31	I Am Come In My Father's Name	T.D. Jakes
June 1	Releasing Your Potential	Myles Munroe
June 2	Instant Faith, Instant Healing	Oral Roberts
June 3	You Could Never Repay Me, but You Are Forgiven	Tommy Tenney
June 4	Singleness of Heart	Dr. Wanda Turner
June 5	Rush Hour Character	Pat Williams
June 6	The Entrance Key	Morton Bustard
June 7	We Don't Have a Lock on God	Tommy Tenney
June 8	His Script	Debbie Jones & Jackie Kendall
June 9	Don'tBury Your Potential	Myles Munroe
June 10	Delayed Blessing	Oral Roberts
June 11	Sit in the Lap of the Blesser	Tommy Tenney
June 12	Yesterday is Gone	Dr. Wanda Turner
June 13	Getting Up and Doing it Again	Pat Williams
June 14	What is Wisdom?	Myles Munroe
June 15	Virtue Is Irresistible	Debbie Jones & Jackie Kendall
June 16	Live Effectively	Myles Munroe
June 17	True Riches	Oral Roberts
June 18	Can God Interrupt Your Schedule?	Tommy Tenney
June 19	Wisdom by the Buckets	Dr. Wanda Turner
June 20	God Encounters Of the First Kind	Tommy Tenney